Communications in Computer and Information Science 1186

Commenced Publication in 2007
Founding and Former Series Editors:
Phoebe Chen, Alfredo Cuzzocrea, Xiaoyong Du, Orhun Kara, Ting Liu,
Krishna M. Sivalingam, Dominik Ślęzak, Takashi Washio, Xiaokang Yang,
and Junsong Yuan

More information about this series at http://www.springer.com/series/7899

Sanjay K. Sahay · Nihita Goel ·
Vishwas Patil · Murtuza Jadliwala (Eds.)

Secure Knowledge Management In Artificial Intelligence Era

8th International Conference, SKM 2019
Goa, India, December 21–22, 2019
Proceedings

Springer

Editors
Sanjay K. Sahay
Birla Institute of Technology and Science
Goa, India

Vishwas Patil
Indian Institute of Technology Bombay
Mumbai, India

Nihita Goel
Information Systems Development Group,
TIFR
Mumbai, India

Murtuza Jadliwala
The University of Texas at San Antonio
San Antonio, TX, USA

ISSN 1865-0929   ISSN 1865-0937   (electronic)
Communications in Computer and Information Science
ISBN 978-981-15-3816-2   ISBN 978-981-15-3817-9   (eBook)
https://doi.org/10.1007/978-981-15-3817-9

This Springer imprint is published by the registered company Springer Nature Singapore Pte Ltd.
The registered company address is: 152 Beach Road, #21-01/04 Gateway East, Singapore 189721, Singapore

Preface

The International Conference on Secure Knowledge Management (SKM) in Artificial Intelligence Era (SKM 2019), a multidisciplinary conference, was jointly organized by the Department of Computer Science and Information System, BITS Pilani, K. K. Birla Goa Campus India, with the University of Texas at San Antonio, USA, and the University at Buffalo, USA, held during December 21–22, 2019, to bring together researchers and practitioners from academia, industry, and government on a global scale. SKM is an important research area that deals with methodologies for systematically gathering, organizing, and securely disseminating knowledge and information. The first SKM conference was organized in 2004 at the University at Buffalo, USA, and over the years it has been held every two years in SUNY Albany, SUNY Stonybrook, UT Dallas, Rutgers, Dubai, Tampa, etc. 2019 was the first time that SKM was held in India. Also, in conjunction with SKM, a workshop on Digital Payment Systems was organized. SKM 2019 focused on revolutionary technologies such as artificial intelligence, machine learning, cloud computing, big data, and IoT. In the conference, delegates presented and discussed the most recent innovations, trends, and concerns, including theoretical and practical challenges encountered with an emphasis on artificial intelligence.

Prof. G. Raghurama, Director at BITS Pilani, K. K. Birla Goa Campus, inaugurated the conference and addressed the participants. The conference dignitaries Prof. H. R. Rao (Steering Committee member), Prof. Sanjay K. Sahay (General Chair), BITS Pilani K. K. Birla Goa Campus, Prof. Ram Krishnan, General Co-Chair, UTSA and Dr. Nihita Goel, Program Committee chair, TIFR, Mumbai also welcomed and addressed the participants. The conference started with a keynote talk by Dr. Shriram Revankar, Vice President of Adobe. He addressed the issue of trust and loyalty in artificial intelligence. His talk positioned trust and loyalty as computable entities that can play a significant role in today's human-machine collaborative societies. Prof. Sandeep Shukla, Chair Professor, IIT Kanpur delivered a talk on cyber security of critical infrastructures. Mr. Anil Nair, MD at Cisco, and Mr. K. P. M. Das, Director, Cyber Security and Trust, Cisco discussed the digital transformation in India. They pointed out that India has what is commonly known as the two-third:one-third problem, which is that two-thirds of the population resides in rural areas while they have access to only a third of the country's resources. The government recognizes this, and citizens are realizing too, that India can alleviate the situation rapidly with smart digital interventions. Prof R. K. Shyamsundar, IIT Bombay, India addressed the challenges of ownership and privacy in medical data sharing and how medical data has become vital for society. In addition, an invited talk was delivered by Srihari Muralidhar, Aarhus University, Denmark on "Digital payments adoption by low-income population in Bengaluru: Lessons from the road." Dr. Vishnu Pendyala, Cisco and San Jose State University, USA spoke on security trust in online social networks. Also, a tutorial on "Blockchain for Enterprise" was delivered by Dr. Mani Madhukar, IBM, India.

SKM 2019 received many high-quality submissions. Authors comprised a mix from India, US, Canada, and Italy. A total of 34 research papers were received by the Technical Program Committee (TPC). The TPC of SKM 2019 comprised of researchers and industry practitioners from all corners of the world. Each of the submitted papers received at least two reviewers. The review process was double-blind, and after the careful review process, the top 12 papers were selected for publication in this proceedings volume, with an acceptance rate of 35%. The conference was organized over two days with a very compact schedule. Beyond the technical program of the research papers, the conference was enriched by many other items. For young researchers, a five-minute innovation challenge was organized in which students presented their idea in five minutes. The winner and runner-up were awarded cash prizes.

We are very much thankful to the delegates, speakers, and the authors for their active participation in SKM 2019, especially with regards to the sharing of innovative ideas and view. We are also thankful to Ms. Kamiya Khatter (Associate Editor at Springer Nature), for providing continuous guidance and support. Also, we extend our heartfelt gratitude to the reviewers and TPC members for their efforts in the review process. We are indeed thankful to everyone who was directly or indirectly associated with the organizing team of the conference leading to a successful event. We also gratefully acknowledge Indo-U.S. Science and Technology Forum for partially funding the workshop and the conference via grant No. IUSSTF/AUG/WS/162/2019. We hope the proceedings will inspire more research in Secure Knowledge Management, Digital Payments, and the application of artificial intelligence.

December 2019

Sanjay K. Sahay
Nihita Goel
Vishwas Patil
Murtuza Jadliwala

Organization

Chief Patron

Raghurama G.   BITS Pilani, Goa Campus, India

General Chair

Sahay Sanjay K.   BITS Pilani, Goa Campus, India

General Co-Chair

Krishnan Ram   University of Texas at San Antonio, USA

Program Committee Chairs

Goel Nihita   Tata Institute of Fundamental Research, Mumbai, India
Jadliwala Murtuza   University of Texas at San Antonio, USA
Patil Vishwas   IIT Bombay, India

Steering Committee

Kwiat Kevin   Air Force Research Laboratory, USA
Memon Nasir   New York University, USA
Rao Raghav   University of Texas at San Antonio, USA
Thuraisingham Bhavani   University of Texas at Dallas, USA
Upadhyaya Shambhu   University at Buffalo, The State University
                                of New York, USA

Program Committee

Agarwal Swati   BITS Pilani, Goa Campus, India
Agrawal Manish   University of South Florida, USA
Bano Wajeeda   Mangalore University, India
Bedi Punam   Delhi University, India
Chakraborty Tanmoy   IIIT Delhi, India
Cheng Yuan   California State University, USA
Chowdhury Dipanwita   IIT Kharagpur, India
Das Debasis   IIT Jodhpur, India
Dhal Subhasish   IIIT Guwahati, India
Geethakumari G.   BITS Pilani, Hyderabad Campus, India
Halder Raju   IIT Patna, India
Husain Mohammad   California State Polytechnic University, USA
Jain Shweta   John Jay College of Criminal Justice, USA

Jaiswal Raj	BITS Pilani, Goa Campus, India
Krishnan Ram	University of Texas at San Antonio, USA
Kumar Kuldeep	NIT Jalandhar, India
Maiti Anindya	University of Texas at San Antonio, USA
Maity Soumyadev	IIIT Allahabad, India
Masoumzadeh Amirreza	University at Albany, NY, USA
Medrano Carlos	Arizona State University, USA
Narang Pratik	BITS Pilani, Pilani Campus, India
Narendra Kumar	IDRBT, Hyderabad, India
Ninglekhu Jiwan	University of Texas at San Antonio, USA
Niyogi Rajdeep	IIT Roorkee, India
Pal Abhipsa	IIM Bangalore, India
Park Jaehong	University of Alabama in Huntsville, USA
Paul Souradyuti	IIT Bhilai, India
Raghu	Arizona State University, USA
Ramanujam R.	IMSc Chennai, India
Rana Nripendra	Swansea University, USA
Rao Raghav	University of Texas at San Antonio, USA
Rathore Heena	Hiller Measurements, USA
Rathore Hemant	BITS Pilani, Goa Campus, India
Sahay Sanjay K.	BITS Pilani, Goa Campus, India
Samtani Sagar	University of South Florida, USA
Shan J.	Miami University, USA
Sharma Ashu	Mindtree, Hyderabad, India
Shekhar	Mangalore University, India
Shetty Rathnakara	Mangalore University, India
Shukla Sandeep	IIT Kanpur, India
Shyamasundar R. K.	IIT Bombay, India
Srinathan Kannan	IIIT Hyderabad, India
Subramanyan Pramod	IIT Kanpur, India
Thakur Rahul	IIT Roorkee, India
Upadhyay Nitin	Goa Institute of Management, India
Upadhyaya Shambhu	University at Buffalo, The State University of New York, USA
Vaish Abhishek	IIIT Allahabad, India
Valecha Rohit	University of Texas at San Antonio, USA
Wang J.	University of Texas at Arlington, USA

External Reviewers

Dutta Hridoy	IIIT Delhi, India
N. Naren	IIT Kanpur, India
Samant Abhay	University of Texas at Austin, USA
Santanam Raghu	Arizona State University, USA
Sureshkanth Nisha	University of Texas at San Antonio, USA
Wijewickrama Raveen	University of Texas at San Antonio, USA
Xu Liwei	University of South Florida, USA

Abstracts

Challenges of Ownership and Privacy in Medical Data Sharing

R. K. Shyamasundar

Department of Computer Science and Engineering,
Indian Institute of Technology Bombay, India
rkss@cse.iitb.ac.in

Sharing of medical data has become vital for the society. Three common usage patterns are:

1. Information sharing among the medical community is immensely important both from the perspective of growth of medical science and patient treatment. Medical wisdom is realized through a large number of experiments by multiple parties. In the creation of such datasets, privacy, provenance, and ownership play a vital role. Privacy is very important as the medical information of individual patient needs to be kept private, while the data is used for purposes of individual treatment and also warnings to the community. Provenance and ownership play a vital role in constructing intermediate results or new experiments from intermediate ones across groups of researchers or laboratories.

2. Medical information is being standardized in the form of Electronic Health Record (EHR). EHR systems enable easier and faster sharing of medical information among different health care providers serving the same patients. It is also expected to eliminate duplicate medical tests, like pathology tests, X-rays, EEG, etc., that are often repeated by different health-care providers. EHR systems are provided as a service by health care providers. Currently, EHR systems are fragmented and are incompatible with one another. Thus, collaboration among different health care providers becomes a challenge if the same patient seeks care from different providers. Privacy is an important concern when multiple providers share health information of any patient. It must be ensured that the patient consents before her data is shared and owns the data for sharing. Of course, the patient has the right to selectively share information with the provider of her choice; this has to be guaranteed by the service provider. Currently, health care providers are responsible for storing and managing the data and need to be trusted for first sharing the information with the patient and no one else without the consent of the patient.

3. Medical databases like Hippocratic databases accept responsibility for the security and privacy of information they manage without impeding legitimate use and disclosure. Sharing and privacy is usually realized through restricted views of the database in these systems.

We shall discuss various security architectures that promote sharing of medical data satisfying the various requirements without a centralized trust and enables interoperability, based on information flow security models, blockchain technology, and various cryptographic encryption techniques.

Cyber Security of Critical Infrastructures:
A C3I Perspective

Rohit Negi and Sandeep K. Shukla

National Interdisciplinary Center for Cyber Security and Cyber Defense
of Critical Infrastructures, Indian Institute of Technology Kanpur,
Uttar Pradesh, India
{rohit,sandeeps}@cse.iitk.ac.in

Critical Infrastructures are infrastructures such as power grids, water/sewage systems, industrial manufacturing, air-traffic control, and railway signaling systems – which if compromised, could harm a nation's economic security as well as the health and lives of people. Most critical infrastructures are cyber-physical systems which have physical dynamics controlled by centralized or distributed software-based controllers – that are aided by sensors carrying information on the current physical state of such systems, and by actuators to effect changes in the physical dynamics of the systems. The sensors, actuators, the information flow through communication network, and the controllers themselves are the cyber components of critical infrastructures. In recent years, an increasing trend of making these components targets of cyber attacks have necessitated research and development of cyber-security methods, tools, and manpower training.

Starting with the Maroochy Sewage treatment plant attack in early 2000, there has been a steady increase in cyber attacks, for example with the most recent attacks on the Ukraine power grid and an attack on a Nuclear plant in India – thus one can find many examples of cyber attacks on critical infrastructures. In most cases, these attacks are attributed to nation state sponsored actors – who have deep financial and technology access, making sophisticated attacks plausible.

In response to the Stuxnet attack on the Nuclear facilities in Iran, there was a presidential executive order in the US in 2013, and a corresponding enactment of a legislation in 2014 – leading to the development of a cyber-security framework for adoption by utilities of various critical infrastructure sectors. Even though it is voluntary to implement such a framework – it provides a very succinct description of basic structures, processes, and measures for risk-assessment based cyber-security strategy and implementation.

The basic functions prescribed in this framework by NIST are identify-protect-detect-respond-recover. The identification of cyber assets and the risk analysis of their exposure, as well as strong cryptographic authentication for both equipment and human actors are the goals of the 'identify' function. The 'protect' function includes various protection mechanisms starting from perimeter defense, zone division, authenticated communication, access control, etc. The 'detect' function entails intrusion detection, malware detection, vulnerability assessment, and penetration testing. The 'respond' function is activated when an attack is detected – followed by containment, localization, and possibly islanding to reduce the extent of damage. The 'recovery' function entails recovering from an attack by bringing back the system to its full functionality – and better implementation of a recovery plan should minimize the downtime due to an attack.

Depending on how well these functions are implemented and well strategized – an organization (e.g., utility), is placed in various tiers of cyber readiness (partial, risk-informed, repeatable, and adaptive). An organization has to profile itself – accordingly, and a better profile is to be targeted with a measurable pathway to achieve a better tier and profile in terms of cyber readiness.

With this framework in mind, the national interdisciplinary center for cyber security and cyber defense of critical infrastructure (aka C3I center at IIT Kanpur) has a research program that enables the development of various tools, methods, and information required by utilities to implement the NIST framework, and also become better positioned for cyber attacks. In a recent survey by Siemens and Ponemon Institute – it was found that in 2019, only about 42% of respondents involved in utilities claim that they have good readiness for cyber security. 54% of the respondents believe that there will be a major cyber attack on their installation within the next 12 months. This shows the urgency and immediacy for such developments.

C3I has developed various industry scale test beds that are the – first of their kind in India, for example – power distribution, power generation and synchronization of renewables with the grid, power transmission, multi-stage water treatment plants, and industrial manufacturing plants with discrete control testbeds on which cyber-security research is being carried out. These test-beds are controlled by multiple PLCs, various industrial protocols, as well as SCADA supervision and control. There are industrial automation products from all well-known manufacturers. This allows the center to do vulnerability assessment and penetration testing experiments (VAPT) – leading to the disclosure of over 15 critical to high vulnerabilities in industry products such as PLC, SCADA, RTU, etc. 8 of these disclosed vulnerabilities are already in the NVD database or ICSA database. More vulnerabilities are being discovered at the center. The penetration testing techniques being used are being automated into tools so that engineers can easily repeat such processes on their own industrial set up.

C3I also developed intrusion detection tools – both model driven – implemented on the PLC itself for detecting false data injection attacks – and data-driven – using machine learning models detecting anomalies in the physical signals of the plant dynamics themselves.

Malware analysis especially for zero-day malware has to be taken seriously. C3I has developed a multitarget malware analysis tool leveraging memory forensics, static and dynamic information of the executables, and network activity monitoring – which would allow all new executables to be first pass through malware detection/classification tool before being put into any equipment such as PLC/RTU or SCADA workstations. This malware analysis tool along with intrusion detection tools form the backbone of a 'detect' function.

Threat intelligence collection from open source feeds, and local honeypots, has provided us with a protect functionality – whereas a cyber-asset registration, management, and patching tool developed at C3I gives us part of the identify functional capability.

A http traffic monitoring and payload classification tool developed at C3I provides basic protection from manipulation of web services – noting the fact that web services form the basis of today's automation tools for remote configuration and monitoring.

In summary, the C3I center is aiming to develop comprehensive solutions with novel technological innovations so tools and methods are made available to implement the entire NIST framework. This talk will provide a glimpse of the research and development of translatable technologies at the C3I center.

Trust and Loyalty in AI

Shriram Revankar

Adobe Systems, Bengaluru, India
shriram.revankar@gmail.com

Trust and loyalty are common topics of social discourse and have been of great interest throughout the recorded history of our civilization. Although trust and loyalty have been explored well before the information technology era, they are often seen as extensions of each other and sometimes intertwined with faith and morality. The intent of this talk is to position them as computable entities that can continue to play as significant a role in today's human-machine collaborative societies as they played in human only environments. The importance of exploring computational mapping of trust and loyalty has increased owing to pervasive adoption of artificial intelligence (AI) in our social and work environment.

Trust plays a pervasive role in removing friction from a wide variety of social transactions. Without trust, the simplest of our day-to-day activities such as driving on roads or buying groceries become cumbersome activities. Early initiatives in establishing trust in a digital environment were based on assumptions of an adversarial world. Perimeter and network security, encryption, authentication, authorization, and access control were extensively used as means to establish trust and trusted environments. However, the prior art is sparse on computational mapping of loyalty. Stephen Marsh provides a formalism to trust as a computational concept. One may argue that this formalism incorrectly mixes aspects of loyalty with trust. In this talk, I explore both trust and loyalty as separable computational constructs in the context of AI.

Trust is defined as "willingness to be vulnerable under conditions of risk and interdependence." Although, there is no universal agreement on this definition of trust, the concept of 'risk and interdependence' provides us effective means to understand the state of the art in computational adaptation of trust. Trust in information technology has become important because people and societies extensively rely on IT for many day-to-day transactions.

I argue that the essential nature of risk and interdependence changes drastically with ubiquity of AI. Hence, much of the traditional trust mechanisms need to be explored anew. I propose that trust building mechanisms need to be integral to design of AI systems. An AI system should make the 'risk of dependence' learnable and explicit for humans to trust it. The trust building mechanism should assist a human to build an introspectable model of the AI system. The model in turn will enable humans to assess the risk of dependence and hence help establish the appropriate level of trust. I will illustrate this through examples and use cases.

Loyalty, on the other hand, has been either ignored or often confused as an extension of trust. Loyalty is defined as never mere emotion, but practical action for a cause. Hence loyalty comes into play when there is an action taken by an AI system on our behalf. The action may yield a positive or a negative payoff. A loyal AI system therefore is expected to always achieve a positive payoff. While we may not usually ask if a piece of software is loyal to us, we should do so in the case of an AI system. Our dependence on AI systems is bidirectional, and an AI agent may proxy for us in making decisions. Kate Crawford described some of the negative payoffs (e.g. allocation harm and representational harm) an AI system may impart. There have been several studies that have exposed negative impacts of biases in AI systems.

The Simple assertion that AI systems should be loyal to whoever owns it or pays for it is not very useful for implementation and explicit evaluation of loyalty. Practical implications of a system being loyal and to who, and the problems loyalty poses are many. I will illustrate this through some practical examples and then argue for a game theory based computational realization for loyalty. I will also briefly talk about other efforts involved in minimizing the discriminatory negative payoffs from AI systems.

Igniting Digital Transformation

Anil Nair[1] and K P M Das[2]

[1] Cisco Systems, Mumbai, India
[2] Cisco Systems, Bengaluru, India
{nairanil,kpmdas}@cisco.com

Digital transformation: As the second fastest digitizing nation in the world, India has what can is commonly known as the two-third:one-third problem, which is that two thirds of the population resides in rural areas while they have access to only a third of the country's resources. The government recognizes this, and citizens are realizing too that India can alleviate the situation rapidly with smart digital interventions. Cisco too believes that digitization is implicit in the transformation of India and has invested substantially to advocate this in an initiative: CDA (Country Digital Acceleration). This is a part of a global program in 31 countries touching half the population of the globe. Under this program in India, Cisco invests in POCs (proof of concepts) that are aligned with the national agenda and include several projects under Digital India, Skill India, Start-up India, as well as Defence and Cyber Security. These POCs showcase digital possibilities to address the rapid/explosive/exponential and inclusive growth that India needs for accelerated growth. Some of the key themes in Cisco's CDA program are Education, Transportation, Agriculture, Rural Connectivity, Telemedicine, Smart Cities, Innovation Labs, Cyber Security, and Government. For each of the digital themes mentioned above, the foundation rests on an end-to-end Secure Knowledge Management architecture framework. Five key security architecture considerations to ponder are:

1. Is the architecture designed to stop threats at the perimeter of the knowledge system?
2. Can architecture protect knowledge workers and users wherever they are? (work and home environments are merging)
3. Can the architecture control who has access to the components of the knowledge system?
4. Is the architecture simple and integrated – not too fragmented?
5. Can security issues be discovered quickly and contained effectively?

Design of the secure knowledge management framework will rest on a few principles. These principles include, but are not limited to, the following:

- Zero Trust
- Never Trust – Always Verify
- Threats Pervasive, Persistent
- Default Least Privilege Access
- Dynamic Policies

The digital transformation of India has begun and our POCs under the CDA (Country Digital Acceleration) program showcase digital possibilities. Cisco is fully invested in this journey and aspires to spearhead the agenda not only to digitize India but secure it as it leapfrogs to a new level of prosperity as a Smart Nation.

Digital Payments Adoption by Low-Income Populations in Bangalore: Lessons from the Road

Srihari Hulikal Muralidhar[1] and Jacki O'Neill[2]

[1] Department of Digital Design and Information Studies, Aarhus University,
Aarhus, Denmark
srihari@cc.au.dk
[2] Microsoft Research India, Bengaluru, India
jaoneil@microsoft.com

Digital payments, in recent years, have increasingly been promoted as a key driver of financial inclusion by various interests such as governments, philanthropic foundations, banks, and private players. Mobile money, it is argued, reduces transaction costs associated with physical banking and enables real-time transactions such as P2P transfers, bill payments, and so on. However, the actual successes of mobile money deployments at scale are limited. M-PESA in Kenya, which has been claimed to be the biggest success to date, has itself come under critique in recent times for various reasons. Nonetheless, the belief that "cashless technologies are the way to achieve an inclusive economy" has been guiding the Indian government as well and was, in fact, argued to be one of the main motivations for undertaking the controversial 'demonetization exercise'. On the one hand, we have macro-level data showing a steady increase in the use of UPI-based payments over the last three years. On the other, we are also confronted with data that shows we have not become less-cash, let alone 'cashless'. What are the ground realities on the adoption and use of digital payments in the country, especially among the low-income populations? What do we even mean by 'financial inclusion'? How can digital payments help achieve it? In this talk, we aim to shed light on some of these issues from our work with auto-rickshaw drivers in Karnataka, India. Our experiences have taught us that auto-rickshaw drivers, as low- and semi-literate, low-income, first-time smartphone, and digital money users, can tell us a lot about poverty, exclusion, and technology-use, and we aim to share some of them. We argue that the dominant understanding of 'financial inclusion' needs rethinking, a shift in emphasis towards 'why' or 'what for' from 'how'. The means by which we achieve financial inclusion should not make us lose sight of what we want to ultimately achieve with/by financial inclusion. It is also our contention that structural problems such as poverty and marginalization should not be reduced to a problem of 'lack of access' to bank accounts or technology. Digital payments, therefore, do not represent a 'magic bullet' that will help us achieve financial inclusion.

Contents

Social Networks

Cyber Security

UnderTracker: Binary Hardening Through Execution Flow Verification

Rajesh Shrivastava[1($\boxtimes$)], Chittaranjan Hota[1], Govind Mittal[2], and Zahid Akhtar[3]

[1] Birla Institute of Technology and Science, Pilani, Hyderabad Campus, Hyderabad, India
{p2015005,hota}@hyderabad.bits-pilani.ac.in
[2] Birla Institute of Technology and Science, Pilani, India
gmittal649@gmail.com
[3] University of Memphis, Memphis, USA
zahid.eltc@gmail.com

Abstract. Programs are developed in a manner so that they execute and fulfill their intended purpose. In doing so, programmers trust the language to help them achieve their goals. Binary hardening is one such concept, which prevents program behavior deviation and conveys the intention of the programmer. Therefore, to maintain the integrity of the program, measures need to be taken to prevent code-tampering. The proposed approach enforces code verification from instruction-to-instruction by using the programmer's intended control flow. *UnderTracker* enforces execution flow at the instruction cache by utilizing the read-only data-cache available in the program. The key idea is to place a control transfer code in data-cache and to call it from instruction cache via labels. *UnderTracker* injects labels into the binary without affecting the semantics of the program. After the code execution starts, it verifies every control point's legality before passing the control to the next instruction, by passively monitoring the execution flow. This paper proposes an efficient technique, called *UnderTracker*, to strengthen the binary integrity of an I/O intensive running program, with the nominal overhead of only 5–6% on top of the normal execution.

Keywords: Superblock · Execution flow verification · Systems security

1 Introduction

One of the most lucrative attack vectors present in a binary is the code reuse attack, and therefore it becomes paramount to protect it. Existing protection methods such as stack canaries [1], Data Execution Prevention (DEP) and Address Space Layout Randomization (ASLR) [2] are not sufficient to mitigate code reuse attacks [3]. Stack canaries guard the binary against overwriting of the stack by inserting a random set of bytes before the return addresses. The presence of DEP does not allow a page in the default heap or stack to be executed. ASLR only randomizes the base address of a program.

© Springer Nature Singapore Pte Ltd. 2020
S. K. Sahay et al. (Eds.): SKM 2019, CCIS 1186, pp. 3–20, 2020.
https://doi.org/10.1007/978-981-15-3817-9_1

The majority of the existing approaches [4–7] used control flow information to protect code tampering. Most existing code protection solutions implement security by computing check-sum or hash in the code segment and verify these protection mechanisms within the code segments. All of these methods provide a good solution for code tamper-proofing, but various code-reuse attacks [3,8,9] have shown that all such methods are vulnerable against Return Oriented Programming (ROP) attacks [10]. ROP attack exploits the code through the data segment, which is separate from the code segment in modern processors. Wurster et al. [11] deployed a kernel-level patch which allows an adversary to tamper the processor's instruction cache, without modifying the data cache. Memory leak vulnerability such as buffer overflow also makes a system vulnerable against runtime attacks such as stack smashing and code-reuse. Control-Flow Integrity (CFI) [4] is the most promising technique to prevent various control flow hijacking and code-reuse attacks. This method ensures that the running program follows the predefined flow of execution. Earlier CFI solutions for Commercial Off-the-Shelf (COTS) binaries [6, 12–15] checked the validity of execution path by adding validation checks in control flow. These CFI methods generated control flow graphs (CFGs) and presented no solution as to how to select the minimum number of control points which will cover the whole binary. The available solutions came up with invalid edges, which make the solution practically infeasible.

This paper proposes a framework named as *UnderTracker* for code self-verification with the assisted discovery of a set of super-blocks identification and low-overhead software security hardening. A super-block is a dominator of basic blocks, which covers the entry points of all successive basic blocks. If one can verify a super-block then it automatically covers all other basic blocks in the same superblock [16]. In a super-block, there is only one entry point and multiple exit points. If one needs to execute one specific basic block inside a super-block then the complete super-block needs to be executed.

UnderTracker divides the whole process into two phases. The first phase computes superblocks from the Control Flow Graph (CFG) of a binary. This step greatly reduces the number of control points that need security monitoring. The entry point of each superblock is stored in the read-only data section, and they are called using jump labels. The second phase executes the super-block through a specific jump label present in the read-only data section ".rodata". A jump call that is protected by random verifier fetches injected code from data segment to code segment. At the time of execution, runtime labels (control points) protect the execution sequence. The visited labels are then verified passively by a monitor program, running locally or remotely. Thus, passive verification of labels and control points is performed with negligible overhead. Our contributions in this work are as follows:

- In contrast to earlier methods, this paper uses jump-oriented programming, which utilizes the read-only data segment of the program's binary. Therefore, it is immune to attacks that are based on the instruction cache. All the information of a super-block is available in the read-only data section in the form of a label.

- The execution flow is tied up with a protected data cache, which enforces each return statement to match the corresponding function call. This provides for an important check while the program traverses its corresponding execution flow graph.
- Verification of super-blocks is done passively which is independent of running the program. Therefore, the verification process verifies binary without intervening the running program.

As a proof of concept, this paper was tested with a prototype implementation of our technique in the x86 platform. It inserts the protective labels directly into the disassembled binary. The starting instruction of the super-block along with the verification code is appended to the ".rodata" segment. Our proof also offers the passive monitoring of verification code by another program, which was running remotely.

The rest of the paper is organized as follows. Section 2 discusses related work, and Sect. 3 proposes a security framework to prevent execution flow from runtime attacks. Section 4 discusses the analyses of security measures and attack resistance of the UnderTracker. Section 5 discusses the solution presented in this paper. Section 6 concludes our results and discusses future work.

2 Related Work

Abadi et al. [4] used a labeling system on execution flow and verified these labels at runtime. They only ensured that the program follows the paths allowed by the CFG. They inserted a label that was determined by the CFG, just before the target address of an indirect transfer, and corresponding code to check the label of the target at each indirect transfer. The program aborted if there was a label mismatch. This method prevented code modification but failed to prevent an attack from the data cache such as an ROP based attack [10]. They also restricted indirect call and shadow stack [17] to maintain the state of the return call. Zhang et al. [6] proposed compact control flow integrity and randomization. In their work, they found all legal targets of indirect control transfer instructions and then limited the control flow through indirect transfers to flow only through them. But protection of all indirect jumps or legal statements generated high overhead and made the solution infeasible. Ding et al. [18] implemented a path-sensitive variation of CFI. The authors performed runtime point-to-point analysis to compute the legal control transfer targets. In that, they verified control transfer points during runtime using memory handlers. Carlini et al. [19] discussed the effectiveness of CFI and present a static stateless policy without a shadow stack for CFI protection. The authors compared various works done earlier in CFI and also presented counter attacks for each protection mechanism. But they targeted only the CFG based protection mechanism used by the instruction cache. According to them, CFI cannot be protected only from the instruction cache. If both the data and the instruction cache are involved in CFI protection then only it could provide effective protection. Qiang et al. [7] presented a fully context-sensitive CFI to prevent control hijacking. In their work, the authors developed a fully context-sensitive CFI method by calculating the hash of each valid control flow path and validate these hash values by processor traces. In this work, they separated the checking code from protected programs to increase the transparency and to decrease the runtime overhead. Das et al. [20] developed a method to prevent CFI against memory attacks during execution. In this work, they used the starting of each basic block as a control point. Information about basic blocks and their addresses were stored in different locations. During execution, with the help of Intel's Process Trace (Intel PT), they identified the address of the basic block and verified it against the stored information. Controlling entry of every basic block corresponds to huge overhead. Wurster et al. [11] already showed any protection on the instruction level are vulnerable against a data cache attack.

Andriesse et al. [21] proposed a different approach to protect code integrity using ROP. Authors used ROP as a defense mechanism and used ROP gadgets to protect code integrity. They also verified the existence of these gadgets in memory to avoid overhead. They implemented a prototype model and tested it on a small binary. They proposed several heuristics to find vulnerable points in the binary and inserted ROP gadgets chain across them. They used the RC4 encryption scheme to encrypt them. During execution, the verification function of the ROP chain called loader function for every gadget to check for integrity. Encryption schemes increased the overhead of execution and heuristics made the process mostly manual. Shrivastava et al. [22] demonstrated a method to protect binaries using ROP gadgets. In this work, they injected the complete function address into a ROP chain. Then the corresponding ROP chain equipped with random gadgets will protect the binary from a tampering attempt. The ROP chain fetches the address of functions from the data cache, which is intermixed with gadgets. They have not used any monitoring method, therefore without any monitoring, security framework will not work effectively. Hota et al. [23] proposed a ROP based protection method that employed genetic algorithms. In this work, the genetic algorithm was used to identify the set of best gadgets, to reduce the performance overhead. They also identified authentication points to protect from any tampering attempt. They also used the ROP chain method to protect binary, by inserting the ROP chain into memory through a buffer overflow. In this paper, they concluded that the length of a ROP chain is directly proportional to the strength of security. Shrivastava et al. [24] secured a complex event processing system by passive monitoring using a side-channel attack technique named flush and reload. The author uses deduplication to spy on a running binary and continuously flush and reload to check whether the binary available in memory or not. This monitoring method calculates the hit ratio to figure out the cache miss. As, the authors used flush and reload, therefore the overhead of the program increased significantly. Also, if there is a cache miss, then it results in a high number of false positives.

3 Security Framework

3.1 Threat Model

This paper makes the following assumptions about the host environment:

– An adversary can debug a binary present in the system [11].
– An adversary might exploit stack or heap overflow vulnerability.
– An adversary might investigate that the system level defenses like DEP and ASLR may be present.
– An adversary can bypass these protections by using code reuse attacks or by finding some other memory vulnerability.
– An adversary can take advantage of each security weakness, which one can find.
– If an adversary can find any potential bug then one can also execute arbitrary code or invoke arbitrary system calls with runtime attacks.

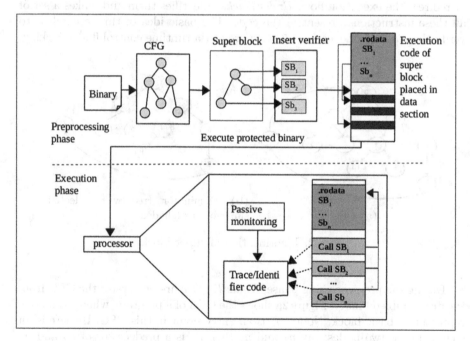

Fig. 1. Overview of proposed approach

3.2 Proposed Model

Figure 1 explains the overview of the security framework proposed in this work. This framework is divided into two Phases. Phase I consists of the pre-processing phase which includes the binary hardening step and metadata collection. Phase II monitors and verifies the execution of the binary.

Phase I: Pre-processing. This step involves patching of the source file with labels and preparing metadata for the use of the monitor program. The reduction of the number of control points to verify during execution is the primary task of this phase. For this purpose, our method generates a CFG. After generating the CFG, the superblock of the graph is computed. This greatly reduces the number of points in the binary that need to be protected and covers the whole binary. Superblocks satisfy the following two properties:

1. All basic blocks must belong to one and only one of the super-blocks.
2. If a verification test covers a super-block, then it automatically covers all of its basic blocks.

UnderTracker ensures execution flow and prevents code-reuse attacks. In assembly code, various instructions are used to transfer control from memory location to another memory location. Such instructions use operations like *call*, *ret*, and *jmp*. An adversary generally tries to exploit these controlled instructions to hijack or redirect the execution flow. *UnderTracker* identifies them and makes a set of all these instructions present in the code. The basic idea of this research is to verify these points of execution flow to prevent a runtime control flow hijacking.

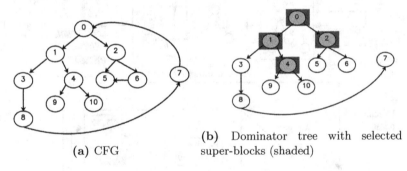

(a) CFG

(b) Dominator tree with selected super-blocks (shaded)

Fig. 2. Identification of super block

During the pre-processing phase, *UnderTracker* first generates the CFG from the disassembled binary. Figure 2a shows the CFG of a program, where each node represents a basic block. Node "0" is an entry point in this CFG. If there is an edge between two nodes, say n_1 and n_2 then n_1 is a predecessor of n_2 and n_2 is the target of a branch or jump at the end of n_1. *UnderTracker* generates super blocks from the CFG, as shown in Fig. 2b by using the method suggested by Christensen et al. [25]. Super blocks minimize at least half of the control points, which help to minimize the performance overhead. These super blocks are recorded and then used for the labeling step. At runtime, the *UnderTracker* verifies the execution flow based on these super-block labels.

Algorithm 1 is based on an algorithm [25,26]. This algorithm starts with the definition of super-block, where every node dominates itself. If a node n_j dominates all pred(n_i), then n_j *dom* n_i.

Algorithm 1. Computation of super-block using dominator tree

Input:
- M: CFG matrix.
- n: number of nodes.
- $entry$: root node of CFG.
- $pred(k)$: list of all predecessors of node k.

Output:
$D[n]$: list of all the nodes that dominate n.

Initialisation:
$D[entry] \leftarrow entry$;
$i \leftarrow 0$;
$flag \leftarrow true$;
foreach *(i < n)* **do**
    if *(i ≠ entry)* **then**
        | $D[n] = allnodes$;
    end
    $i \leftarrow i + 1$;
end
$i \leftarrow 0$;
while *flag* **do**
    $flag = false$;
    foreach *(i < n)* **do**
        if *(i ≠ entry)* **then**
            $D'[n] = n \cup (\cap D[p])$;
            // $p \in pred(n)$.
            if *(D'[n] ≠ D[n])* **then**
                $flag = true$;
                $D[n] = D'[n]$;
            end
        end
        $i \leftarrow i + 1$;
    end
end
return D[n];

Algorithm 1 starts with the initialization of $D[entry] = \{entry\}$ i.e. the start point of CFG. After this step, other than the *"entry node"*, initialize the list of dominator of each node to contain all other nodes. Then use a flag to identify the dominating nodes. Here, the following equation is used.

$$D'[n] = \bigcap_{p \in pred(n)} D[p] \cup \{n\}. \tag{1}$$

where p must belong to the predecessor of n. The Algorithm 1 iterates over all the nodes of the graph until no changes are made to D for any n. Algorithm 1 concludes with the list $D[n]$ containing all the nodes that dominate n.

Figure 2b contains the resultant dominator graph of a sample CFG. The super-block verification test covers all legal execution flow paths.

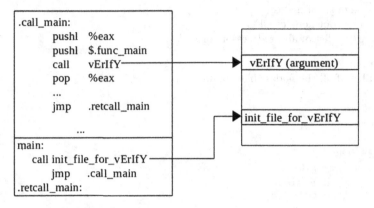

Fig. 3. Patching of a sample assembly code.

- Injection of verification code
  After identification of super blocks, *UnderTracker* injects verification codes into the disassembled file as presented in Fig. 3. The program snippet initializes a file pointer and opens a file that will be polled by the monitor. The code is appended with a unique program to output the labels, which simply takes in a label name as input and writes it to a unique file managed by the monitor.
- Protective labeling
  Algorithm 2 uses assembly code (generated with the *"gcc -S"* option), the list of controlled points of the program and list of user-defined functions as input. In assembly code, *UnderTracker* searches for vulnerable code points to be controlled (super-blocks) as described in Section IV. After an exploitable instruction is found, the algorithm traverses back and finds the *".text"* section. Then it inserts the label template as given in Algorithm 2 with the corresponding super block details. This algorithm returns a modified assembly code, which is ready to be compiled.
  Figure 4 shows the effect of the patching step in the pre-processing step. In this step, labels are injected into the *".rodata"* section of the assembly code. This method pushes all executable codes of super-block into the data cache and a program can call these labels using basic *jmp* instruction. In the first subfigure of Fig. 4, for the foo() function to call bar() function, first jumps to label *".call_bar_fea0"*. The program pushes *"call_bar_fea0"* on the stack. Then, the verification function is called to write the string onto the file being monitored. After the verifier function, the bar() function is called to achieve the actual intent of the program. Later, the control is passed back to the

---

Algorithm 2. Security labels insertion

Input:
- S: list of points to be secured.
- asm: assembly code file.
- $func$: list of user-defined functions.

Output: Secured assembly file.

Initialization:
$asm \leftarrow list(asm)$;
// convert whole assembly file into a list of instructions.
$current\_func \leftarrow \phi$;
$regex = regular\_expression(func\_call, jump\_stmt, return\_stmt)$;
foreach $instruction \in asm$ **do**
    $match = search(instruction, regex)$;
    // Search for valid matching regular expression which can be a function call, jump statement, or a return statement.
    if *(match==func_call)* $\vee$ *(match==jump_stmt)* $\vee$ *(match==return_stmt)* **then**
        $current\_func = match$;
        find .text section;
        Insert .rodata before .text section;
        Insert following template in .rodata section;
        .label_x:
            .string "call_super-block"
        .call_super-block:
            pushl .label_x
            call verify_code
        // insert instruction specific code.
        if $match == function\_call$ **then**
            pushl param1
            pushl param2
            pushl . . .
            call function
            jmp .retcall_super-block
        end
        else if $match == jump\_stmt$ **then**
            Insert following template in current_func;
            test_condition:
                je .label_jump_if_zero
        end
        else if $match == return\_stmt$ **then**
            // do-nothing.
        end
        Insert following template in current_func;
            jmp .call_super-block
            .retcall_super-block:
    end
    else
        append the instruction into the secured binary;
    end
end
return secured binary.

```
.section .rodata          .section .rodata          .section .rodata
.str_fea0:                .str_ba1c:                .funcname_foo:
      .string                  .string "jump_"           .string  "ret_foo"
"call_bar_fea0"           jump_L2_ba1c:             .ret_foo:
.call_bar_fea0:               pushl %eax                 pushl %eax
      pushl %eax              pushl $.str_ba1c           pushl
      pushl $.str_fea0        call    vErIfY       $.funcname_foo
      call    vErIfY         pop        %eax            call    vErIfY
      pop   %eax             pop        %eax            pop   %eax
      pop   %eax             test   %eax, %eax          pop   %eax
      call  bar              je           .L2           jmp   .end_foo
      jmp                    jmp                         ...
.retcall_bar_fea0         .retjump_L2_ba1c
                                    ...                          ...

        ...               foo:  ...               foo:
                             Jmp .jump_L2_ba1c          ...
foo:  ...                    .retjump_L2_ba1c           jmp   .ret_foo
      jmp   .call_bar_fea0       ...               .end_foo:
.retcall_bar_fea0:       .L2:                            ...
      ...                       ...                       ...
```

1. Protection for a function   2. Protection for a jump   3. Protection for a return
call to bar() from function   statement which jumps to   statement of function foo()
foo()   label .L2 if EAX is zero

Fig. 4. Label template

function callee by using the *jmp .retcall_bar_fea()* instruction. The foo() functions contain the "jmp" call to the label and a return label, for the program control to resume from the next instruction.

In the second and third subfigures of Fig. 4, similar steps are taken. The label *"jump_L2_ba1c"* contains the condition that it tests also so that the condition is completely protected. The label *"funcname_foo"* contains only a call to the verification function, to tell the program is returning, so the monitor can use it to pop the call stack. Therefore, *UnderTracker* takes care of all user-defined function calls, conditional, unconditional and return statements.

Phase II: Execution. The second phase of the security framework is to execute the program binary in an intended way. When this secure binary executes in memory, each transfer of control from a control point jumps to a specific injected label. The program then first passes a string unique to the label and writes the string to a file and continues. The monitor program continuously verifies this file remotely.

Each super-block writes the verification information into a file. This file is used by another program, which already knows the intended execution flows for the particular binary. This secondary program continuously monitors the visited labels. It keeps track of all the control points that were missed by the running program. It then treats any unexpected or deviated execution flow accordingly.

As illustrated in Fig. 5, a finite automaton model is used to perform passive monitoring on a running executable. This monitoring can be either done locally or remotely and it would not affect the functioning of *UnderTracker*. Our passive monitoring system continuously tracks control points by dividing its functioning into the following four states:

1. *Start State (S1):* All control points are matched with their labels, which are visited as in their actual intended execution flow graph.
2. *Acceptable State (S2):* This state verifies security labels. A small number of control points were missed and skipped verification may be due to memory write operation. The acceptable number of misses can be chosen by the administrator.
3. *Suspicious State (S3):* A larger number of labels were missed, and there is a significant amount of deviation from the actual execution flow graph. This could be an indication that an adversary has tried to replace or tamper control points.
4. *Compromise State (S4):* The system is compromised and the majority or even all control points are not getting executed according to the CFG.

To estimate the execution flow integrity, *UnderTracker* uses information stored in log files recorded by the passive monitoring system. The transition from one state to another is discovered by monitoring the execution traces for a certain period of time. The estimates[1] used by our simulation is listed as below:

1. If no control point is mismatched per iteration then the system is in the S1 state.
2. If no more than one control point is mismatched in each iteration due to the memory management policy of the operating system, then the system is in the S2 state.
3. If there is more than one mismatched control point in an iteration or more than three consecutively mismatched control points, then the system is in the S3 state.
4. For worse situations, which contain more mismatches than the aforementioned ones, then the system is in the S4 state.

All four states are further grouped into two regions, the first two states come under "no attack - no action" zone. The monitoring program continuously toggles between S1 (start) and S2 (acceptable) state. Once the automaton moves to "under attack/action required" zone, it never goes back to the former safe zone. After the automaton states go to *S3 (suspicious)* state, the administrator is notified but the program would still be executing. The administrator can check for the cause of this, and may or may not allow the program to continue. After *S3* state, if there are still label mismatches that are detectable by the monitor then the monitor raises an interrupt and transitions to the *S4 (compromised)* state. After the monitor is in the *S4* state, the program is halted.

---

[1] The estimates used above were chosen are as an example. They can be changed depending upon the use-case.

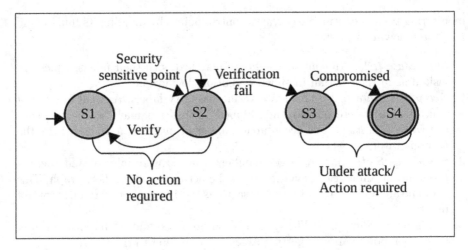

Fig. 5. Monitoring model

4   Result Analyses

We simulated *UnderTracker* on Intel Xeon 3.70 GHz with Intel x86_64 architecture equipped with a 16 GB RAM. The GCC version used was 5.4.0 on Linux Ubuntu 16.04 operating system. *UnderTracker* enforces a strict execution policy for executed code, resulting in the following assurance:

– *UnderTracker* always maintains control of the execution-flow.
– Only valid, legitimate instructions are executed.
– Function returns cannot be redirected, mitigating ROP and JOP attacks.
– Jump instructions can target only valid instructions.
– Call instructions can target only valid functions after verification of labels.
– All system calls go through a defined policy check.

Our method is based on both self-verification as well as passive monitoring of the execution flow so that evading the existing order of label becomes challenging. As the program execution continues, it hits the corresponding labels and prints them to a file. This file is continuously polled by the monitor, which tries to match the order of the labels with the set of allowed execution patterns. This method hardens the security because if the attacker was able to feed the exact visited labels along with the correct order to the monitor, then the program would already have been running in one of the intended ways. Since the label deployed in the binary are for purely for obfuscation purposes and do not perform control flow modifications, therefore to hijack the execution flow, at least one of the labels needs to be changed. This change will be immediately detected by the monitor, which can take an appropriate action later on.

As a result, the implementation of the label involves the predictable execution of the CFG specific to the program, when it is in a non-tampered state. This paper uses this property, to implement a monitoring scheme for the augmented code using self-verification code information. *UnderTracker* provides reliability by operating at the higher granularity and ensuring that every label in the binary is being executed as expected. An associated alarm is raised upon the detection of a considerable number of correct label misses. In this way, even if the attacker was to leave some of the labels in place, the failure of anyone label would be counted as a tampering attempt. The labels prevent the direct manipulation of the code section while the monitoring scheme verifies the integrity of the label order itself.

4.1 Attack Resistance

RIPE [27] benchmark is used to test attack resistance. RIPE consists of various code reuse attacks that can bypass ASLR, DEP, and stack canaries. We evaluated test cases by disabling system security such as ASLR and DEP. In that case, RIPE was successfully attacked in our system and our defense framework *UnderTracker* reacted on 80% of attacks. These 80% attacks tried to tamper either *"call"* or *"ret"* instructions.

The security framework provided by *UnderTracker* works against all the common attacks, who attempt to deviate from the intended execution flow. A code tampering attack which deviates from execution flow is based on bypassing the indirect jump instruction or hijacking of the return address.

A code reuse attack executed by RIPE, which needs indirect jump instructions. As these instructions are mostly inside the super-block, *UnderTracker* allows execution control to transfer only to the super-block address. Therefore, it can easily thwart these attacks and make it harder in turn for an attacker to avoid this. Other than RIPE, We also test the proposed method with the following attack models:

1. Condition check bypass:

$$set * (unsigned\,char*)\,Address = 0x90 \tag{2}$$

Equation 2 is a representational form of a system command which can be easily executed while the binary is being debugged. This command can replace a given address with *0x90* i.e. NOP (no operation) instruction. With the help of this instruction, an adversary can bypass the controlled code, as it can simply overwrite the actual instructions with a NOP slide. Although the instruction might change because of NOP, the addresses of these commands still do not change. When control reaches to the overwritten instructions, the program will do nothing, but will simply increment the instruction pointer. The goal of this attack is to avoid some conditional checks and modify the execution flow according to the attacker's will.

Analysis: This attack does not change the address of any instruction. It simply replaces specific "jmp" instructions with NOP, which will only increment the instruction pointer by one instruction. Our framework evades this reverse engineering attack attempt very effectively. Since all controlled points along with their verifier functions are placed in the read-only data section therefore, they are immutable. Hence, if an attacker wishes to bypass the jmp instruction then he would necessarily have to go to the corresponding label present in the *.rodata* section. This will in turn force the "jmp" instruction to be verified by the monitor. If the attacker can evade the security by any means, then he/she would have to output the correct order of labels. If he/she does that, then the binary is already running in the correct order and no action is needed.

2. Code reuse attack:
   UnderTracker was tested against customized code reuse attacks like ROP. These attack programs used buffer overflow vulnerability to launch an attack. We simulated these attacks with our security framework and *UnderTracker* was able to successfully detect all the attacks.
   Analysis: ROP-based attacks need either a memory vulnerability or a code injection step. Memory vulnerabilities allow an attacker to upload a malicious payload and bypass at least one of the control points. Code injection works by injecting a patch to bypass authentication or important check points. Our approach will cover all control points. If an adversary can bypass any or all control sequences then a passive monitoring system will detect it immediately.

4.2 Performance Overhead

Since control labels are stored in the *".rodata"* section and during execution it will continuously output the label name to a file, therefore it adds a certain amount of overhead when compared to an unprotected program. In an I/O intensive program, the overhead produced by *UnderTracker* is minimal, since the overhead produced by the continuous input and/or output from the program will eventually far exceed the overhead produced by *UnderTracker* verifier function.

Figure 6 shows an analysis of the effective performance overhead of *Under-Tracker*. We used the *Linux perf* utility to estimate the execution time. The X-axis represents a number of iterations of the program were run. Y-axis shows the excess time in percentage that the program took when protected by the *Under-Tracker* approach. As the number of runs increased, the overhead decreased. As, wireless network servers and IoT environments run constantly, therefore this approach is well suited for them as well as any system that performs continuous memory operations.

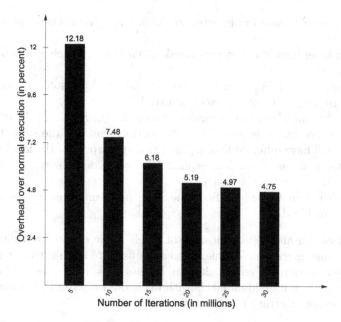

Fig. 6. Performance overhead

5 Discussion

Table 1 shows a comparison between existing solutions and proposed approach. The proposed approach works effectively and provide security against code tampering attack. *UnderTracker* addresses the execution flow verification problem by utilizing binary hardening using label monitoring. Our proposed approach consists of the following steps:

- Patching step: This step involves patching the disassembled code with appropriate labels.
  1. The controlled points in the code are identified by computing the dominator tree of the CFG.
  2. The controlled code points that intersect with the dominator tree nodes are shifted to the read-only data section into a pair of unique labels, along with the verification method call.

Table 1. Comparison of related work

Author	Method	Overhead	Memory monitoring
Abadi et al. [4]	Static checks	5%	No
Andriesse et al. [21]	ROP gadgets	4%	Yes
Das et al. [20]	Hardware based checks	6%	Yes
Ding et al. [18]	Path tracking	8%	No
Proposed	In-memory CFI verification	5%	Yes

    3. Jump instructions are inserted at the address from where the code was shifted.

    4. Each label location is incorporated into a graph, which is a subgraph of the CFG.

- Monitoring step: The graph produced in the patching step is used by the monitor to keep track of the execution trail.
- Each label name is generated randomly to distinguish it from the other similar labels. For example, two different functions can call the same function, but they will have different labels. The primary purpose of the label augmentation step is to use a random explicit label so that the execution sequence is obfuscated from the adversary.
- These labels can be self-verified when the program control uses the code contained inside them.

As obfuscation and self-verification of labels alone cannot provide a viable solution because given ample time, one can substitute or inject their labels to bypass all verifications. If an attacker can bypass these labels, he can hijack the system by replacing individual labels with malicious ones from the same binary, therein achieving arbitrary functionality.

6   Conclusion and Future Scope

This paper presents an execution flow protection scheme named *UnderTracker* to harden the security framework of a binary code. It is divided into active and passive protection approaches. Active protection involves inserting labels at the control points, while passive protection involves monitoring the visited labels to match the intended execution flow of the binary. These labels are stored in the "*.rodata*" section (read-only) of binary. At runtime, an adversary is not allowed to modify this section. A control transfer from one branch or one instruction to another is allowed if and only if this transfer is already present in the CFG computed during the pre-processing step. Each label uses a random verification code which is generated at compile time of the source file. The visited labels are then verified by a passively running monitor while the compiled binary is executing on a system. Each label points to a call to the verifier function and the protected control transfer instruction. Every time the verifier function is called the label is passed to the monitor so as to get verified. Then the program proceeds forward with its normal execution.

One of the important features of this paper is its approach to minimize the number of controlled points. After computing the dominator tree of the CFG, it is ensured that the number of controlled points is at most half of the maximum possible points. Another feature is that it uses basic jump labels for verification and protection to ensure execution flow integrity. Therefore, the overhead over a prolonged time for an I/O intensive binary drops down to only 5–6%.

This is an open problem to protect IoT devices from code tampering attempts. In the future, variants for ARM, MIPS architecture can be developed. Also, a similar solution can be developed for the Android operating system. There is scope to reduce performance overhead with a lower overhead self-verification method, without using the passive monitor as used in this work.

Acknowledgement. This work is supported by the Ministry of Electronics and Information Technology (MeitY), Govt. of India and the Netherlands Organization for Scientific research (NWO), Netherlands.

References

1. Marco-Gisbert, H., Ripoll, I.: Preventing brute force attacks against stack canary protection on networking servers. In: 2013 12th IEEE International Symposium on Network Computing and Applications (NCA), pp. 243–250. IEEE (2013)
2. Wei, T., Wang, T., Duan, L., Luo, J.: Secure dynamic code generation against spraying. In: Proceedings of the 17th ACM Conference on Computer and Communications Security, pp. 738–740. ACM (2010)
3. Checkoway, S., Davi, L., Dmitrienko, A., Sadeghi, A.-R., Shacham, H., Winandy, M.: Return-oriented programming without returns. In: Proceedings of the 17th ACM Conference on Computer and Communications Security, pp. 559–572. ACM (2010)
4. Abadi, M., Budiu, M., Erlingsson, Ú., Ligatti, J.: Control-flow integrity principles, implementations, and applications. ACM Trans. Inf. Syst. Secur. (TISSEC) **13**(1), 4 (2009)
5. Burow, N., et al.: Control-flow integrity: precision, security, and performance. ACM Comput. Surv. (CSUR) **50**(1), 16 (2017)
6. Zhang, C., et al.: Practical control flow integrity and randomization for binary executables. In: 2013 IEEE Symposium on Security and Privacy (SP), pp. 559–573. IEEE (2013)
7. Qiang, W., Huang, Y., Zou, D., Jin, H., Wang, S., Sun, G.: Fully context-sensitive CFI for COTS binaries. In: Pieprzyk, J., Suriadi, S. (eds.) ACISP 2017. LNCS, vol. 10343, pp. 435–442. Springer, Cham (2017). https://doi.org/10.1007/978-3-319-59870-3_28
8. Buchanan, E., Roemer, R., Shacham, H., Savage, S.: When good instructions go bad: generalizing return-oriented programming to RISC. In: Proceedings of the 15th ACM Conference on Computer and Communications Security, pp. 27–38. ACM (2008)
9. Prandini, M., Ramilli, M.: Return-oriented programming. IEEE Secur. Priv. **10**(6), 84–87 (2012)
10. Bittau, A., Belay, A., Mashtizadeh, A., Mazières, D., Boneh, D.: Hacking blind. In: 2014 IEEE Symposium on Security and Privacy, pp. 227–242. IEEE (2014)
11. Wurster, G., Van Oorschot, P.C., Somayaji, A.: A generic attack on checksumming-based software tamper resistance. In: IEEE Symposium on Security and Privacy, 2005, pp. 127–138. IEEE (2005)
12. Pappas, V., Polychronakis, M., Keromytis, A.D.: Transparent ROP exploit mitigation using indirect branch tracing. In: USENIX Security Symposium, pp. 447–462 (2013)

13. Wang, M., Yin, H., Bhaskar, A.V., Su, P., Feng, D.: Binary code continent: finer-grained control flow integrity for stripped binaries. In: Proceedings of the 31st Annual Computer Security Applications Conference, pp. 331–340. ACM (2015)

14. Xia, Y., Liu, Y., Chen, H., Zang, B.: CFIMon: detecting violation of control flow integrity using performance counters. In: 2012 42nd Annual IEEE/IFIP International Conference on Dependable Systems and Networks (DSN), pp. 1–12. IEEE (2012)

15. Zhang, M., Sekar, R.: Control flow and code integrity for COTS binaries: an effective defense against real-world ROP attacks. In: Proceedings of the 31st Annual Computer Security Applications Conference, pp. 91–100. ACM (2015)

16. Agrawal, H., et al.: Detecting hidden logic bombs in critical infrastructure software. In: International Conference on Cyber Warfare and Security. Academic Conferences International Limited (2012). Page 1

17. Dang, T.H.Y., Maniatis, P., Wagner, D.: The performance cost of shadow stacks and stack canaries. In: Proceedings of the 10th ACM Symposium on Information, Computer and Communications Security, pp. 555–566. ACM (2015)

18. Ding, R., Qian, C., Song, C., Harris, B., Kim, T., Lee, W.: Efficient protection of path-sensitive control security. In: 26th USENIX Security Symposium (USENIX Security 2017), Vancouver, BC, pp. 131–148. USENIX Association (2017)

19. Carlini, N., Barresi, A., Payer, M., Wagner, D., Gross, T.R.: Control-flow bending: on the effectiveness of control-flow integrity. In: USENIX Security Symposium, pp. 161–176 (2015)

20. Das, S., Zhang, W., Liu, Y.: A fine-grained control flow integrity approach against runtime memory attacks for embedded systems. IEEE Trans. Very Large Scale Integr. VLSI Syst. **24**(11), 3193–3207 (2016)

21. Andriesse, D., Bos, H., Slowinska, A.: Parallax: implicit code integrity verification using return-oriented programming. In: 2015 45th Annual IEEE/IFIP International Conference on Dependable Systems and Networks (DSN), pp. 125–135. IEEE (2015)

22. Shrivastava, R., Hota, C., Shrivastava, P.: Protection against code exploitation using ROP and check-summing in IoT environment. In: 2017 5th International Conference on Information and Communication Technology (ICoICT 2017), Melaka, Malaysia, May 2017

23. Hota, C., Shrivastava, R.K., Shipra, S.: Tamper-resistant code using optimal ROP gadgets for IoT devices. In: 2017 13th International Wireless Communications and Mobile Computing Conference (IWCMC), pp. 570–575. IEEE (2017)

24. Shrivastava, R.K., Mishra, S., Barua, S., Hota, C.: Resilient complex event processing in IoT using side-channel information. In: Proceedings of the 10th International Conference on Security of Information and Networks, pp. 80–87. ACM (2017)

25. Christensen, H.K., Brodal, G.S.: Algorithms for finding dominators in directed graphs. Ph.D. thesis, Aarhus Universitet, Datalogisk Institut (2016)

26. Lengauer, T., Tarjan, R.E.: A fast algorithm for finding dominators in a flowgraph. ACM Trans. Program. Lang. Syst. (TOPLAS) **1**(1), 121–141 (1979)

27. Wilander, J., Nikiforakis, N., Younan, Y., Kamkar, M., Joosen, W.: RIPE: runtime intrusion prevention evaluator. In: Proceedings of the 27th Annual Computer Security Applications Conference, pp. 41–50. ACM (2011)

Toward Relationship Based Access Control for Secure Sharing of Structured Cyber Threat Intelligence

Md. Farhan Haque[✉] and Ram Krishnan

Electrical and Computer Engineering,
University of Texas at San Antonio, San Antonio, USA
{md.farhan.haque,ram.krishnan}@utsa.edu

Abstract. Cyber Threat Intelligence (CTI) represents cyber threat information which are critical to an organization. Structured Threat Information Expression (STIX) and Trusted Automated Exchange of Intelligence Information (TAXII) provide a standard to represent and share CTI in an efficient, structured and machine readable manner. In this paper, we provide a CTI sharing scenario in an organizational context and develop a Relationship Based Access Control (ReBAC) implementation to securely share CTI structured in STIX. We further discuss an organization's scope for future analyses and actions on shared CTI.

Keywords: Cyber Threat Intelligence (CTI) · Structured Threat Information Expression (STIX) · Trusted Automated Exchange of Intelligence Information (TAXII) · Relationship Based Access Control (ReBAC)

1 Introduction and Motivation

Cyber Threat Intelligence (CTI) is a type of cyber threat information which goes through certain cyber security standards through the scrutiny of cyber security experts and are collected from reliable sources. CTI provide essential cyber threat information which can be critical to maintain safety and protect integrity of an organization in cyber space. These CTI can also provide valuable insights about cyber attacks and a significant amount of research material to counter against future cyber attacks. In today's data driven world, there is a high demand for CTI sharing in a large quantity. An efficient CTI sharing can boost Cyber Threat Intelligence of an individual organization. Haass, Ahn and Grimmelmann [17] presented the importance of CTI sharing to develop a fast and efficient threat response system.

CTI generally contain detailed information related to a cyber attack. For example - a simple Phishing [20] email attack can have several key features such as attacker information, attack techniques used, target of attack, tools and software used to launch the attack. A well agreed standard is required in order to

© Springer Nature Singapore Pte Ltd. 2020
S. K. Sahay et al. (Eds.): SKM 2019, CCIS 1186, pp. 21–37, 2020.
https://doi.org/10.1007/978-981-15-3817-9_2

clearly express and share several key features of an attack process in an efficient and machine readable manner.

Structured Threat Information Expression (STIX™) [4] is a language and serialization format used to exchange CTI maintained by OASIS [2]. STIX enables organizations to share CTI in machine readable manner, allowing other organizations and security communities to better understand an attack and take preventive measures.

Organizations can benefit from sharing these CTI in a controlled manner. For example - Three organizations A, B and C where A trusts B more than C. The level of sharing between A and B might be significantly different than that of between A and C due to Information leakage [8], Privacy [22] concerns etc. Haass et al. [17] raised concerns over irresponsible sharing of classified CTI from government organizations into private sectors.

Organizations require some Access control [27] over CTI sharing based on the different sharing requirements. There are various forms of access control models such as Mandatory Access Control (MAC), Discretionary Access Control (DAC), Role Based Access Control (RBAC) and Relationship Based Access Control (ReBAC) etc. It is not well understood the effectiveness of all these access control models for CTI sharing. In our work, we investigate the applicability of ReBAC for CTI sharing. ReBAC seems a natural fit as organizations are able to facilitate different levels of sharing based on the sharing relationships established among them.

Gates [16] coined the term Relationship Based Access Control (ReBAC) which is a access control model based on the relationship between accessor and owner/controller of a resource. We adopt a variant of Cheng, Park and Sandhu's [9] regular expression based User-to-User Relationship-Based Access Control (UURAC) model to control CTI sharing. The advantages of this model are discussed in Sect. 5. We focus on sharing CTI in a structured manner and adopt STIX [4] standards in our implementation. We also provide further insights on the analysis of CTI to improve organizational cyber defense system.

To summarize, our contributions in this paper are as follows

1. We demonstrate the applicability of ReBAC for effective sharing of CTI by presenting an example CTI sharing scenario.
2. We develop a prototype implementation of a CTI sharing ecosystem named as CTI System and instantiate the system for an example sharing scenario and demonstrate the system's operations.

2   Background

In this section, we discuss few key concepts involving our work.

2.1   Structured Threat Information Expression

Structured Threat Information Expression or STIX [4] is a standard to express CTI in a structured way. STIX standards has two key components - STIX Domain Objects (SDO) and STIX Relationship Objects (SRO).

STIX Domain Objects or SDOs are individual information blocks to express certain CTI categorically. Each block communicates a high level CTI concept and builtin properties inside each block explain the specific details about that concept. For example - Threat Actor SDO represents individuals, groups or organizations which may have malicious intent and more likely pose cyber security threats to other individuals or organizations. Threat Actor SDO has few properties such as name, goals and motivation of the threat actor. We can also specify skill level of the threat actor (beginer, intermediate, expert etc.) in the properties. SDO properties consist of a well combination of pre-established vocabularies and open ended descriptions and provide the flexibility to capture a wide range of CTI. These kind of structured representation makes easier for industries to understand and share CTI with minimum human intervention. There are twelve SDOs in STIX which involve crucial CTI related to vulnerabilities, attack pattern, course of action etc.

STIX Relationship Objects connect two SDOs and demonstrate inter SDO relationships. The Malware SDO represents CTI related to malicious codes or programs to compromise a system. We can link Threat Actor SDO and Malware SDO by using a "Uses" relationship - Threat Actor (SDO) Uses (SRO) Malware (SDO). We can use multiple SDOs, SROs together to represent complicated CTI in a very structured manner.

2.2   Trusted Automated Exchange of Intelligence Information

Trusted Automated Exchange of Intelligence Information or TAXII [11] is a suggested application protocol to exchange CTI over the network. CTI in STIX format can also be transported with other communication protocols. TAXII supports two sharing models - Collection and Channel.

1. **Collection:** Collection operates on a request-response model where CTI data can be hosted on a TAXII server and consumer can get CTI data by request. We adopt this model of CTI sharing in our work and applied Access control [27] to prevent any leakage of unauthorized sensitive CTI data.
2. **Channel:** Channel sharing operates on publish-subscribe model. CTI producers publish the CTI data on TAXII server and consumers need to be subscribed to get the CTI data.

2.3   Relationship Based Access Control

Access control is a known mechanism to control access to resources in computer based systems. There are several forms of access control models such as Mandatory Access Control (MAC), Discretionary Access Control (DAC) and Role Based Access Control (RBAC) [27] etc. There is a more recent form of access control model named as Relationship Based Access Control (ReBAC) [16]. For example, please see [9,12–14]. ReBAC operates based on the relationship between two entities and access to a resource is determined based on the relationship types between those entities. ReBAC is popular in online social networks [15] scenario because of its intuitive relationship based structure. We use ReBAC in our implementation because organizations may not be related or may be loosely related and only come together to share different levels of CTI. This kind of sharing requirement can easily be facilitated with the establishment of sharing relationships among different organizations.

3 Related Work

Johnson et al. [21] defined cyber threat information is as any information that can help an organization identify, assess, monitor, and respond to cyber threats. The authors put emphasize on the importance of CTI sharing and provided few use cases for cyber threat information sharing such as nation-state attacks against a specific industry sector, distributed denial of service attack against another industry sector, financial conference phishing attack etc. Haass et al. [17] demonstrated a case study for information sharing challenges within a public/private not-for-profit partnership organization called ACTRA - Arizona Cyber Threat Response Alliance, Inc. STIX [4] is a language to represent CTI in a structured way for organizations to consume CTI in an automated and machine readable manner. STIX is maintained by OASIS [2] and well accepted standard to represent structured CTI.

Gates [16] introduced Relationship Based Access Control (ReBAC) where access to a resource depends on the relationship between owner and accessor. Over the years, several numbers of ReBAC models have been proposed in the literature. Fong [13] proposed a modal logic based relationship based access control policy in a social network context. Crampton and Sellwood [12] provided a relationship based access control policy based on path conditions which are similar to regular expression. Cheng et al. [9] provided a regular expression policy based relationship based access control model for online social networks. Cheng et al.'s model makes an authorization decision based on multiple policies which is beneficial for our organizational CTI sharing scenario in a non social network context.

There are plenty of opportunities to perform analysis on STIX structured CTI to extract meaningful information and apply them to better organizational cyber security. Iannacone et al. [19] provided an ontology to develop for cyber security knowledge graph similar to Google's knowledge graph which incorporates information from both structured and unstructured information sources. Syed, Padia, Finin, Mathews and Joshi [28] proposed Unified Cybersecurity Ontology (UCO) which integrates and incorporates data from various cyber security standards and also mapped with archived STIX 1.0 [6]. We plan to design a CTI Knowledge base compatible with STIX 2.0 to extract useful information and integrate into organizational cyber defense system.

4   Cyber Threat Intelligence Sharing Scenario

4.1   Sharing Requirements

In this section, we discuss about different sharing requirements based on geographical location (Intracity, Nationwide), intra organization system (Intrasystem), inter organization system (Nationwide) and collaboration with law enforcement agencies (Lawenforcement).

4.1.1   Sharing Requirement 1 - Intracity

Imagine there is a surge of Ransomware [23] attacks directed towards critical organizations in San Antonio, Texas such as banks, airports, hospitals etc. These attacks are circulated through Email spoofing [26] and Social engineering [29] tactics. Three health institutions Sacred Lake, Ace Health and Church Hospital in San Antonio understand these cyber threats against the city and can agree share CTI related to threat-actor (attacker information) and malware CTI.

4.1.2   Sharing Requirement 2 - Intrasystem

Institutions under Ace Health system want to boost their cyber defense system and protect privacy of valuable patient data. These organizations can agree to share system vulnerability CTI since they trust each other.

4.1.3   Sharing Requirement 3 - Lawenforcement

Cyber criminals [7] can launch plenty of cyber attacks; some of which may have serious consequences in real world and pose serious security risks towards infrastructures and employees of an organization. These cyber crimes may need to be reported to law enforcement agencies and share CTI related to attacker's identity. Organizations can agree to share threat-actor (attacker information) CTI with law enforcement agencies.

4.1.4   Sharing Requirement 4 - Nationwide

Health organizations across different cities understand the risk of attack with similar high level attack techniques such as phishing emails of online deals from a suspicious organization. These organizations can agree to share attack-pattern (attack technique) CTI.

4.2   CTI Categorization in STIX

The above section shows the need for categorization of CTI based on different sharing requirements. STIX provides an standard to structure and categorize CTI aligned with the above sharing needs. Figure 1 shows the high level view of STIX generation process of an organization named as Ace Health SA.

Threat Detection System is a representation of a system which monitors different system parameters and is able detect varieties of cyber threat components

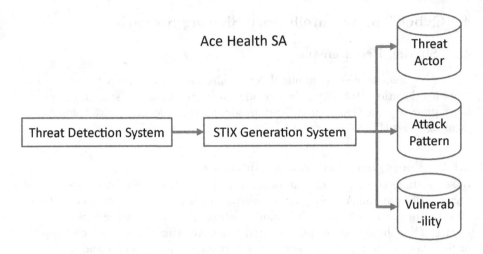

Fig. 1. Organizational STIX Generation

such as attacker identity, vulnerability, attack technique etc. The STIX Generation System receives the cyber threat components from Threat Detection System and generates STIX documents of different predefined STIX categories such as Threat Actor, Attack Pattern, Vulnerability etc.

STIX standard is open ended specification to structure CTI and provides the flexibility of STIX design at the discretion of security engineers. We take advantage of this feature of STIX and develop the STIX structures for predefined STIX categories. For example - a Threat Actor type STIX is required to have a threat-actor SDO, may or may not have malware SDO and must have a relationship between threat-actor and malware SDOs if malware SDO is present. Figure 2 demonstrates Threat Actor type STIX when malware SDO is present. We also specify the property requirements for threat-actor SDO. Figure 3 shows the required builtin properties that should be present in threat-actor SDO of Threat Actor type STIX.

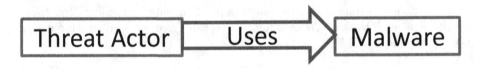

Fig. 2. Threat Actor STIX Structure

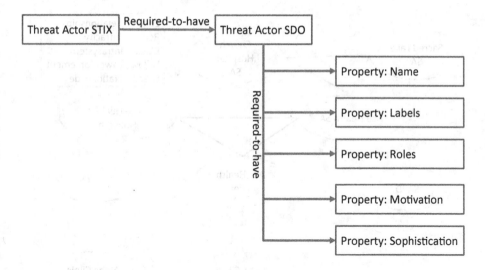

Fig. 3. Threat-Actor SDO properties Structure

5   Relationship Based Access Control Policies for Cyber Threat Intelligence Sharing

We explore the applicability major forms of access control models such as Mandatory Access Control (MAC), Discretionary Access Control (DAC) and Role Based Access Control (RBAC) model for our CTI sharing scenario.

Access Control List (ACL) [27] is one of the DAC approaches where we have to maintain a list of subject's access rights for each object. In our scenario, each individual STIX type would be objects and organizations would be subjects. Then we have to maintain access control list for each STIX type for each organization. For example - we keep a list of organizations allowed to read Threat Actor type STIX of Ace Health SA. We can also do the same for other STIX types. This kind of approach is cumbersome work for an individual organization and consumes huge amount of system and human resources.

RBAC [27] is a popular form of access control in enterprise scenario where access to a resource is granted based on the role. But RBAC may be ineffective in organizational CTI sharing scenario because organizations may only want to share CTI when there is an active sharing need between them. Fong et al. [13] demonstrated few advantages of ReBAC with respect to RBAC model.

5.1   ReBAC in CTI Sharing Scenario

We now present a relationship based organizational CTI sharing scenario in Fig. 4. Organizations have established different types of sharing relationships among themselves to facilitate various levels of CTI sharing. We consider four sharing relationships - Intracity, Intrasystem, Lawenforcement and Nationwide

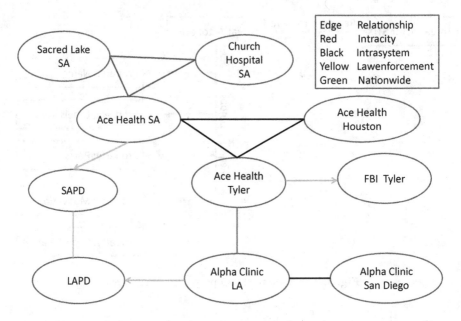

Fig. 4. Organizational CTI sharing scenario (Color figure online)

in accordance with our sharing requirements. Each type of sharing relationship is represented in a different color. For example - Intracity is represented in red, Intrasystem is in black, Lawenforcement is in yellow and Nationwide is in green. We can state ReBAC policies which align with our sharing requirements in Sect. 4.

1. **Intracity:** Intracity relationship will give access to threat-actor and malware type STIX CTI.
2. **Intrasystem:** Intrasystem relationship will give access to vulnerability type STIX CTI.
3. **Lawenforcement:** Lawenforcement relationship will give access to only threat-actor type STIX CTI.
4. **Nationwide:** Nationwide relationship will give access to attack pattern type STIX CTI.

There are many ReBAC models available in the literature and discussed in the previous sections. Cheng et al.'s ReBAC model utilizes multiple access control policies to make proper authorization decisions and provides more finer grained control over the sharing of resources. We adopt this ReBAC model into our implementation due to this feature. The model defines both user and resource as potential target for an authorization decision in online social networks [15] context. A typical example of user as target is when an user performs an action on another user such as poking in a social network like Facebook.

In our sharing scenario, users are organizational employees and we do not consider them as actionable targets. We rather focus on CTI resources owned by an organization as targets. Thus allows us to consider three policies from Cheng et al.'s access control policy taxonomy. They are system specified policy (SP) for a resource, outgoing action policy for users denoted as Accessing User Policy (AUP) and incoming action policy for a resource named as Target Resource Policy (TRP).

1. **System Specified Policy:** System specified policy (SP) determines the access or denial of a system wide Access Request [9] from a requesting/accessing user or employee of an organization to access a CTI resource owned by another organization under same CTI sharing ecosystem. An instantiation of SP for our ReBAC based CTI sharing scenario - (read, Threat Actor, (Requesting Organization, (Lawenforcement, 5))).
2. **Accessing User Policy:** Each organization's system admin sets up an Accessing User Policy (AUP) to control all the outgoing requests from the employees and prevents any unsolicited outgoing request from that organization. An instantiation of AUP for our ReBAC based CTI sharing scenario - (read, (Ace Health SA, (Intracity-Lawenforcment, 3))).
3. **Target Resource Policy:** System admin of an organization also sets up Target Resource Policy (TRP) for each resource of that organization to control the access of their own CTI resources. This policy provides organizations more control over their own CTI as organizations do not have any control over joining or leaving organizations in the CTI sharing ecosystem.
   In Fig. 4, Ace Health SA trusts SAPD with Lawenforcement relationship and wants to share Threat Actor (attacker information) CTI. CTI sharing ecosystem also denoted as CTI System which maintains System specified Policies (SP) that may allow the sharing of Threat Actor CTI with any two organizations having direct or indirect Lawenforcement relationship between them. Later when SAPD establishes another Lawenforcement relationship with LAPD, LAPD will then gain the access to Ace Health SA's Threat Actor CTI according to System specified Policy (SP) for Threat Actor type CTI. But if Ace Health SA is unwilling to share it with LAPD, they can control LAPD's access to their Threat Actor CTI through the enforcement of their own Target Resource Policy (TRP) for Threat Actor type CTI. An instantiation of TRP for our ReBAC based CTI sharing scenario - (read-inverse, Threat Actor, (Ace Health SA, (Lawenforcment-Intrasystem, 4))).

6 Implementation

In this section, we discuss about our implementation for the development of a sample CTI sharing ecosystem involving all the organizations showed in Fig. 4 with the application of ReBAC as an access control model. We divide our implementation into two parts - implementation framework and secure communication protocols. Implementation framework provides the necessary features to initialize the CTI System and update the system for later use. Secure communication protocols demonstrate the CTI System's operating procedure after system has been properly setup through implementation framework components.

6.1   Implementation Framework

Our implementation framework has three key components which are demonstrated in Fig. 5.

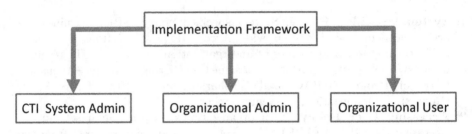

Fig. 5. Implementation framework

6.1.1   CTI System Admin

CTI System Admin is responsible for managing CTI sharing ecosystem which involves maintenance of various access control policies and sharing ecosystem graph. The admin also maintains a white list of suggested organizations allowed to join the sharing ecosystem. The admin also keeps a list of allowable relationship types that can be established among these suggested organizations.

The CTI System admin manages System specified Policies (SP) integral to the implementation of Cheng et al.'s access control model. System specified policy (SP) is a per action per resource type policy. Some typical actions for our implementation are read, write, copy etc. Resource types are defined from Report Label Vocabulary [3] of STIX literature. A few examples of resource types are attack-pattern, threat-actor (attacker information), tool, vulnerability etc. There is also a graphical user interface available to monitor the CTI sharing ecosystem represented in a Graph Data Structure where organizations are denoted as nodes and sharing relationships among the organizations are denoted as edges. The graph is implemented in popular graph database Neo4j [25].

6.1.2   Organizational Admin

Each organization may have one or more dedicated admins who perform two major operations. First operation is to maintain two organizational policies: Accessing User Policy (AUP) and Target Resource Policy (TRP). AUP is per action policy and puts control over all the employee's outgoing requests in the organization. TRP is per action per resource policy and provides control over organization's own CTI resources. Second operation is to send a sharing relationship add or delete request to another organization. We have implemented the add request feature and plan to incrementally implement deletion request in future.

6.1.3   Organizational User

Organizational employees are authorized to request CTI resource types such as attack-pattern, threat-actor (attacker information), tool, vulnerability etc. from another organization. The decision on request to access a CTI resource type is determined through the evaluation of three policies - Accessing User Policy (AUP) of requesting organization, Target Resource Policy (TRP) of requested resource type from owner organization and System specified Policy (SP) for the same resource type from CTI sharing ecosystem. The implementation is also applicable for employees requesting CTI resources from their own organization but that does not present an interesting implementation scenario.

6.2   Secure Communication Protocols

In this section, we demonstrate two protocols for secure processing of communication requests between organizations. The first protocol is sharing relationship addition request protocol which demonstrates the back and forth communication among two organizations and CTI System to securely establish a sharing relationship between organizations. The second protocol is resource request protocol which demonstrates the secure processing of a resource request from an employee of an organization to the resource owner organization.

These protocols are machine to machine or server to server communication protocols between organizations and CTI System and are built on top of known communication protocols such as Needham-Schroeder [24]. These protocols are an approach which demonstrate the handling of a request initiated from an organization in CTI sharing ecosystem. Organizational admins are authorized to initiate sharing relationship addition request protocol and organizational users are only authorized to initiate resource request protocol for an organization. CTI System processes the requests and makes decisions to allow or deny requests based on access control policies and identities of organizations. We plan to implement a sharing relationship deletion request protocol in future.

Both the protocols have two implementation prerequisites in order to establish a secure communication. First prerequisite is to implement Needham-Schroeder [24] public key protocol to mutually authenticate two participating organizations and CTI System. Second prerequisite is to share a session key between those two organizations for further communication in a secure manner after Needham-Schroeder protocol has been implemented.

6.2.1   Prerequisite 1 - Needham-Schroeder Public Key Protocol

The Needham–Schroeder protocol is an authentication protocol between two entities. The protocol has two variations - symmetric key and public key. We adopt public key protocol with the assumption that each organization and CTI System have their respective RSA public-private key pairs. We implement the modified version of the protocol free from man-in-the-middle attack. An instantiation of Needham-Schroeder public key exchange among Sacred Lake SA, CTI System and Ace Health SA is shown in Fig. 6.

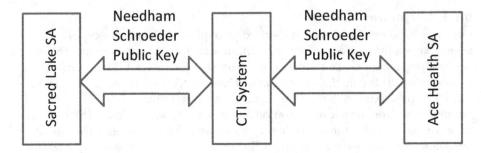

Fig. 6. Needham-Schroeder public key protocol

6.2.2   Prerequisite 2 - Session Key Share

Needham-Schroeder public key protocol in Fig. 6 provides a three way mutual authentication among Sacred Lake SA, Ace Health SA and CTI System. Since Needham-Schroeder pubic key protocol does not establish a shared session key; Sacred Lake SA and Ace Health SA need to share a session key for secure communication and data exchange after Needham schroeder authentication. Figure 7 shows secure sharing of session key between Sacred Lake SA and Ace Health SA after Needham-Schroeder public key protocol has been implemented. These two prerequisites are mandatory process before both protocol 1 and 2 are implemented.

6.2.3   Protocol 1 - Relationship Addition Request Protocol

Needham-Schroeder implementation ensures the identities of both Sacred Lake SA and Ace Health SA. CTI System is the central body which processes any request from any of the organizations and updates sharing ecosystem graph or makes access authorization decisions. To establish an Intracity sharing relationship with Ace Health SA, Sacred Lake SA sends an encrypted and Integrity [1] protected request to Ace Health SA. Ace Health SA verifies the integrity of the request and forwards the request to CTI System along with their own signed approved request. After successful verification of signed requests from

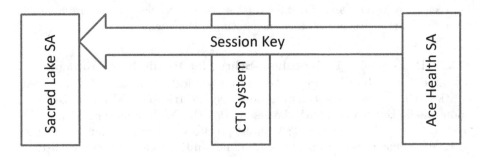

Fig. 7. Session key share

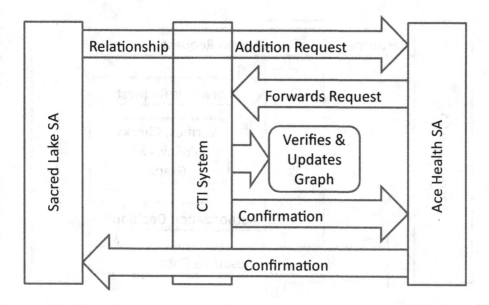

Fig. 8. Relationship request protocol

both Sacred Lake SA and Ace Health SA, CTI System establishes the requested sharing relationship between them and updates the sharing ecosystem graph. The brief communication protocol is shown in Fig. 8.

6.2.4   Protocol 2 - Resource Request Protocol
The protocol operates almost similar way as protocol 1. Sacred Lake SA wants to read Threat Actor [5] type CTI which typically contains attacker information owned by Ace Health SA and sends an encrypted and integrity (signed) protected request to Ace Health SA after both prerequisite 1 and 2 have been completed. Ace Health SA verifies the request and forwards the request to CTI System along with their own approved signed request. After successful verification of signed requests from both Sacred Lake SA and Ace Health SA, CTI System makes an authorization decision by verifying the Accessing User Policy (AUP) of Sacred Lake SA, Target Resource Policy (TRP) for Threat Actor type CTI of Ace Health SA and System specified Policy (SP) for Threat Actor type CTI of CTI System with respect to sharing ecosystem graph. CTI System then sends the authorization decision to Ace Health SA. Based on the authorization decision; Ace Health SA may or may not pull Threat Actor type CTI from their TAXII [11] server and send towards Sacred Lake SA. The brief resource request protocol is shown in Fig. 9.

Figures 6, 7, 8 and 9 show the generalized and brief overview of exchanges among Sacred Lake SA, Ace Health SA and CTI System. A more detailed description of these exchanges and the complete implementation project can be found at github [18].

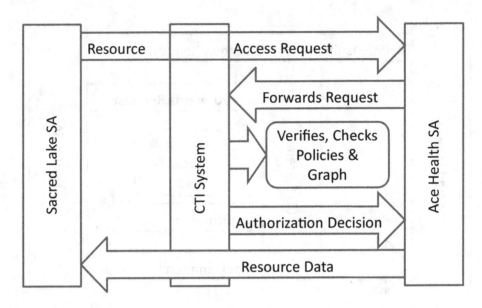

Fig. 9. Resource (CTI) request protocol

7   Relationship Based Access Control Authorization Decision Process

The request to access a CTI resource is processed by CTI System. In order make an authorization decision, the CTI System takes account of three policies. They are - Accessing User Policy (AUP) of accessing/requesting organization, Target Resource Policy (TRP) of owner organization for the requested resource type and overall System specified Policy (SP) of CTI System for the same resource type. These three policies are verified against the CTI System sharing ecosystem graph. Each policy evaluation result is represented by a boolean result of true or false. If the requesting organization and resource owner organization are matched with relationship type and are within the maximum allowable distance or hop count limit specified in the policy, the policy yields in a true result. The specific details about these policies and their structures are elaborated in Cheng et al.'s UURAC [9] model.

These three type of policies may yield in different boolean results individually and can cause a decision conflict. In case of a decision conflict, Cheng et al. propose disjunctive, conjunctive or prioritized approach to resolve the conflict. We incorporate and enforce conjunctive approach in our implementation which interprets as the access to a resource is granted only if all the three policies into consideration yield in a boolean true result individually.

8 Future Work

In this paper, we present a practical approach to share structured CTI in a secure and automated manner through the application of ReBAC. Our work lays the foundation for an elaborate analyses of these shared CTI resources in future. We now propose some of the scopes of those analyses-

1. **Attack Reconstruction:** There may be a need for an organization to reconstruct/extrapolate the complete attack scenario from a received CTI of a particular type. For example- a CTI of Threat Actor [5] type focuses on attacker information. But the receiving organization may need to know further high level attack related information which involves that attacker in order to understand the attack and attacker's method of operations at a detail level. One possible approach could be to apply a machine learning algorithms to predict attack related information such as attack techniques, attack tools used etc. based on the Properties [5] received as a content of Threat Actor type CTI.

2. **Course of Action:** Organizations can establish their own security defense mechanisms to counter different cyber attacks. For example - a mass email could be sent to all the employees within the organization in case of sighting of a phishing attack to warn about the suspicious email. Organizations could use machine learning algorithms discussed in previous point to construct the full attack from received CTI containing partial attack features and map those attacks to appropriate Course of Actions [10].

3. **Cyber Threat Intelligence Knowledge Graph:** The knowledge graph is a knowledge base used by Google and it's services to enhance search engine's results with information gathered from a variety of sources. A machine learning based approach could be applied to develop a similar type of knowledge graph for structured CTI. The graph could provide useful relevant information to a CTI receiving organization such as attacks of similar nature, previous course of actions taken for similar type of attacks etc.

9 Conclusion

To summarize, we present the necessities to share CTI in an organizational scenario and provide a framework implementation to share structured CTI in a secure and machine readable manner. We also use Trusted Automated Exchange of Intelligence Information (TAXII) protocol to host CTI resources on organizational servers and exchange those CTI within organizations in a Request-response model. Our adoption of Cheng et al.'s [9] relationship based access control model demonstrates the applicability of this form of access control outside social network context. We further analyze STIX [4] framework and propose few directions in Future Work section to extract valuable insights from shared CTI. These insights could be incorporated into an organization's cyber defense system in order to develop a more secure and responsive cyber security infrastructure at an organizational level.

Acknowledgment. This work is partially supported by DoD ARO Grant W911NF-15-1-0518, NSF CREST Grant HRD-1736209 and NSF CAREER Grant CNS-1553696.

References

1. Confidentiality, Integrity, Availability: The three components of the CIA Triad. https://security.blogoverflow.com/2012/08/confidentiality-integrity-availability-the-three-components-of-the-cia-triad/. Accessed 13 Aug 2019
2. Oasis Cyber Threat Intelligence (CTI) TC. https://www.oasis-open.org/committees/tc_home.php?wg_abbrev=cti. Accessed 09 July 2019
3. Report Label. http://docs.oasis-open.org/cti/stix/v2.0/cs01/part1-stix-core/stix-v2.0-cs01-part1-stix-core.html#_Toc496709303. Accessed 02 July 2019
4. STIX: A structured language for cyber threat intelligence. https://oasis-open.github.io/cti-documentation/. Accessed 01 July 2019
5. Threat Actor. https://oasis-open.github.io/cti-documentation/stix/intro. Accessed 04 July 2019
6. Barnum, S.: Standardizing cyber threat intelligence information with the structured threat information expression (STIX). Mitre Corp. **11**, 1–22 (2012)
7. Burden, K., Palmer, C.: Internet crime: cyber crime-a new breed of criminal? Comput. Law Secur. Rev. **19**(3), 222–227 (2003)
8. Chaabane, A., Acs, G., Kaafar, M.A., et al.: You are what you like! Information leakage through users' interests. In: Proceedings of the 19th Annual Network & Distributed System Security Symposium (NDSS). Citeseer (2012)
9. Cheng, Y., Park, J., Sandhu, R.: A user-to-user relationship-based access control model for online social networks. In: Cuppens-Boulahia, N., Cuppens, F., Garcia-Alfaro, J. (eds.) DBSec 2012. LNCS, vol. 7371, pp. 8–24. Springer, Heidelberg (2012). https://doi.org/10.1007/978-3-642-31540-4_2
10. Course of Action. https://oasis-open.github.io/cti-documentation/stix/intro. Accessed 08 July 2019
11. Connolly, J., Davidson, M., Schmidt, C.: The trusted automated exchange of indicator information (TAXII). The MITRE Corporation, pp. 1–20 (2014)
12. Crampton, J., Sellwood, J.: Path conditions and principal matching: a new approach to access control. In: Proceedings of the 19th ACM symposium on Access control models and technologies, pp. 187–198. ACM (2014)
13. Fong, P.W.: Relationship-based access control: protection model and policy language. In: Proceedings of the First ACM Conference on Data and Application Security and Privacy, pp. 191–202. ACM (2011)
14. Fong, P.W., Siahaan, I.: Relationship-based access control policies and their policy languages. In: Proceedings of the 16th ACM Symposium on Access Control Models and Technologies, pp. 51–60. ACM (2011)
15. Garton, L., Haythornthwaite, C., Wellman, B.: Studying online social networks. J. Comput.-Mediat. Commun. **3**(1), JCMC313 (1997)
16. Gates, C.: Access control requirements for web 2.0 security and privacy. IEEE Web **2**(0) (2007)
17. Haass, J.C., Ahn, G.J., Grimmelmann, F.: ACTRA: a case study for threat information sharing. In: Proceedings of the 2nd ACM Workshop on Information Sharing and Collaborative Security, pp. 23–26. ACM (2015)
18. Haque, Md.F.: REBAC Model and TAXII Merged (2019). https://github.com/farhan071024/ReBACModel. https://github.com/farhan071024/TaxiiMerged

19. Iannacone, M.D., et al.: Developing an ontology for cyber security knowledge graphs. CISR **15**, 12 (2015)
20. Jagatic, T.N., Johnson, N.A., Jakobsson, M., Menczer, F.: Social phishing. Commun. ACM **50**(10), 94–100 (2007)
21. Johnson, C., Badger, M., Waltermire, D., Snyder, J., Skorupka, C.: Guide to cyber threat information sharing. Technical report, National Institute of Standards and Technology (2016)
22. Lane, J., Stodden, V., Bender, S., Nissenbaum, H.: Privacy, Big Data, and the Public Good: Frameworks for Engagement. Cambridge University Press, Cambridge (2014)
23. Mansfield-Devine, S.: Ransomware: taking businesses hostage. Netw. Secur. **2016**(10), 8–17 (2016)
24. Meadows, C.A.: Analyzing the Needham-Schroeder public key protocol: a comparison of two approaches. In: Bertino, E., Kurth, H., Martella, G., Montolivo, E. (eds.) ESORICS 1996. LNCS, vol. 1146, pp. 351–364. Springer, Heidelberg (1996). https://doi.org/10.1007/3-540-61770-1_46
25. Miller, J.J.: Graph database applications and concepts with Neo4j. In: Proceedings of the Southern Association for Information Systems Conference, Atlanta, GA, USA, vol. 2324 (2013)
26. Pandove, K., Jindal, A., Kumar, R.: Email spoofing. Int. J. Comput. Appl. **5**(1), 27–30 (2010)
27. Sandhu, R.S., Samarati, P.: Access control: principle and practice. IEEE Commun. Mag. **32**(9), 40–48 (1994)
28. Syed, Z., Padia, A., Finin, T., Mathews, L., Joshi, A.: UCO: a unified cybersecurity ontology. In: Workshops at the Thirtieth AAAI Conference on Artificial Intelligence (2016)
29. Thornburgh, T.: Social engineering: the dark art. In: Proceedings of the 1st Annual Conference on Information Security Curriculum Development, pp. 133–135. ACM (2004)

Decepticon: A Hidden Markov Model Approach to Counter Advanced Persistent Threats

Rudra Prasad Baksi[✉] and Shambhu J. Upadhyaya

University at Buffalo, SUNY, Buffalo, NY 14260, USA
{rudrapra,shambhu}@buffalo.edu

Abstract. Deception has been proposed in the literature as an effective defense mechanism to address Advanced Persistent Threats (APT). However, administering deception in a cost-effective manner requires a good understanding of the attack landscape. The attacks mounted by APT groups are highly diverse and sophisticated in nature and can render traditional signature based intrusion detection systems useless. This necessitates the development of behavior oriented defense mechanisms. In this paper, we develop Decepticon (Deception-based countermeasure) a Hidden Markov Model based framework where the indicators of compromise (IoC) are used as the observable features to aid in detection. This framework would help in selecting an appropriate deception script when faced with APTs or other similar malware and trigger an appropriate defensive response. The effectiveness of the model and the associated framework is demonstrated by considering ransomware as the offending APT in a networked system.

Keywords: Advanced Persistent Threats (APT) · Computer security · Cyber-security · Hidden Markov Model (HMM) · Ransomware

1 Introduction

Advanced Persistent Threats (APT) are a form of quiet invaders [20] and are a big nuisance to industries and government organizations. They silently perform reconnaissance, quietly invade, and keep a communication channel open in order to communicate with the command and control (C&C) centers. The attackers control the behavior of the malware from the C&C centers. APTs carry out *targeted attacks* to achieve their goal. They are quite persistent in their efforts of achieving the goals and in doing so they might come with a contingency plan to which they resort to upon discovery [2]. Such type of attacks has become prevalent and frequent, owing to the fact that malware-as-a-service (MaaS) are easily available, which provide the attackers with the necessary framework and infrastructure to create attacks [14,22]. APTs come in different forms and formats. In this paper we focus on the mitigation of ransomware that qualifies as an APT [2].

© Springer Nature Singapore Pte Ltd. 2020
S. K. Sahay et al. (Eds.): SKM 2019, CCIS 1186, pp. 38–54, 2020.
https://doi.org/10.1007/978-981-15-3817-9_3

According to FireEye, 4,192 attacks were detected in a particular year, which were mounted by groups that can confidently be classified as APT groups [4]. They were also able to detect 17,995 different infections by APT groups. The attacks thereafter have been increasing by leaps-and-bounds. RSA Security LLC suffered financial losses of about \$66.3 Million when it became a victim of an APT attack [31]. According to a study by Ponemon Institute, the average financial losses suffered by a company owing to the damaged reputation after an APT often amounts to \$9.4 Million [16]. WannaCry, Petya and NotPetya are ransomware campaigns that graduated to become APTs and wreaked havoc and collected huge amounts of ransom causing considerable financial losses to the victims [2]. WannaCry collected ransom in BitCoins. According to certain reports, between May 12, 2017 and May 17, 2017, the attackers collected \$75,000 to \$80,000 in ransoms [7,28]. With time the cost of financial damage suffered by the companies is expected to go higher up. Both industries and government organizations are known to suffer significantly. In case of government agencies, the damage could be beyond mere financial losses; the attacks might even threaten national security.

These aforementioned factors and incidents outline a great threat to the critical infrastructure as a whole, be it government or industry. The problems are intense and the attacks are adaptive in nature, requiring a holistic approach to address them. On the contrary, it is not necessary to put the entire defense framework into the same defense mode every time the system comes under attack because deploying a sophisticated defense mechanism indiscreetly to fend off attacks will severely affect performance and degrade the quality of service (QoS). The idea is to deploy the most sophisticated countermeasure against the most severe form of attack. Lesser sophisticated countermeasures taking care of the less severe attacks would not only be economical but also might help in preserving the quality of service (QoS) of the system. In the same vein, system security through different forms of information isolation has been studied for quite sometime [19]. Isolation can be achieved through software or hardware [18]. But with advanced attacks from APT groups which are highly adaptive in nature, they have been successful in attacking physically isolated systems as well. One such example is the Stuxnet campaign that took place in the Iranian nuclear facility [3,9,13]. Therefore, a need for a new form of defensive strategy arose. Researchers have looked into various approaches to repel highly sophisticated attacks. One of the approaches is the use of *deception* as a defense tool.

In this paper, the aforementioned research ideas, namely, *isolation* and *deception*, are used to confront intricate attacks arising from APT groups. The paper puts forward a basic architecture, which deceives the attacker into believing in its success, while surreptitiously triggering a fix to thwart the attack. To make the defense-system cost-effective, the defender must have knowledge about the attack scenario. The information about the status of a malware helps a defender to develop an efficient attack averting strategy. This paper presents Decepticon, a Hidden Markov Model (HMM) based deceptive countermeasure which uses indicators of compromise (IoC) that will serve as observable features for detection and mitigation of APTs. The major contributions of the paper are the design of a hardware-based defense framework and a HMM-based ransomware type APT detection tool. The framework is a special case of the Kidemonas architecture [1] and uses the concept of smart-box from [21] for surreptitious reporting and triggering of defensive scripts on being attacked. The paper is organized as follows. Section 2 discusses some related work in this area. Section 3 presents the new deception architecture. Section 4 describes the HMM based detection system. Section 5 discusses the architecture's usage in detection and mitigation of APTs. Finally, Sect. 6 concludes the paper and paves way for future work.

2 Preliminaries and Related Work

In this section, some preliminaries are given on malware, APT, TPM hardware, deception and HMM, which are used to develop the Decepticon architecture in Sect. 3. Related work on these topics is also briefly reviewed.

Malware created by the APT groups do not carry out the attacks in a single stage. The "Cyber Kill Chain" framework developed by Lockheed Martin describes an APT through a seven stage life cycle [11]. The model describes the beginning of the attack through a *reconnaissance* phase wherein the malware gathers information about the system. This is followed by the *weaponization* phase, thereupon creating a remote access malware that can be controlled by the attacker. The *delivery* phase denotes the intrusion of the malware into the system. In the *exploitation* phase, the malware exploits the vulnerabilities that exist in the system. The *installation* phase signifies the escalation of privileges on the part of the malware and installation of back-doors to maintain a communication with the command and control (C&C) centers to receive further instructions. The *command and control* phase implies the access of the target system gained by the attackers from the C&C centers. Finally, in the *actions on objective* phase, the intruder mounts the final assault on the system. LogRythm describes an APT through a five stage life cycle [17]. Lancaster University describes APT through a three stage life cycle [26]. Baksi and Upadhyaya [2] describe APT through the characteristics exhibited by a sophisticated malware.

Ransomware are a type of malware which infiltrate a system and hold critical data for a ransom. Primarily there are three simpler types of ransomware, namely *the locker, the crypto* and *the hybrid* [32]. The locker variant of the ransomware locks the entire system and denies the user access to the system. The crypto form of the malware, targets specific files and/or folders and encrypts them, thereby denying the user any access to those encrypted resources. The hybrid version of ransomware possesses the capabilities of both types of ransomware. It can encrypt and lock targeted resources and/or the entire system. But the ransomware under consideration in this paper is a more advanced form of malware. In addition to possessing the features of ransomware, they are more sophisticated to have a contingency plan of attack on being discovered [2]. They also perform the attack through multiple stages and generally are controlled by the attackers from the C&C centers. They qualify as APTs.

The TPM or the Trusted Platform Module is a hardware component designed following the guidelines of the security consortium, the Trusted Computing Group [30]. The TPM comes with essential cryptographic potential. It can generate cryptographic keys, both symmetric and asymmetric keys. It also has the capability of generating random numbers when required and can store cryptographic credentials. It also provides hashing capabilities. The primary functionalities of TPM include verification of platform integrity, safeguarding encryption keys, and preservation of password and user credentials. Figure 1 gives a simplified schematic of the TPM version 1.2 specifications of which are laid down by the Trusted Computing Group (TCG). TPMs today come in different incarnations which depends on the type of device and the manufacturer. Intel Software Guard Extension (Intel SGX) and ARM TrustZone are versions of TPM like hardware components which come with certain functionalities in addition to the ones already mentioned for TPMs [8,12,29,33]. They provide a Trusted Execution Environment, which are generally outside the purview of high-priority OS instructions but can be accessed using the user credentials. Therefore, in general it can be assumed, even if the OS is compromised, that the hardware component is outside the purview of the attacker.

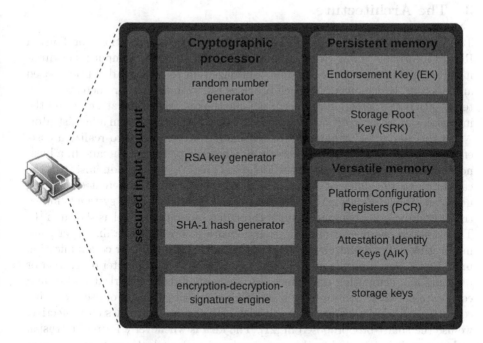

Fig. 1. A simplified schema of TPM [24]

Deception can often be considered as a potential weapon against sophisticated attacks and it is an important area of research. In [5], the authors use deception as a potential weapon to fight against denial of service (DoS) attacks.

The authors have analyzed the deceptive strategy using a game-theoretic model based on the signaling game with perfect Bayesian equilibrium (PBE) to investigate the implications of deception to counter the attacks. Deception as a defensive strategy has been used in [23], wherein the authors have used deceptive measures to lure the attackers to high-interaction honeypots for designing a malware detection system.

Hidden Markov Models (HMM) have been historically been used for speech recognition [15,25]. It has also been applied for handwritten character and word recognition [6]. The biggest advantage that comes with HMM is that, in a process wherein the stages are not visible to the observer, certain observable features can be used to predict the stage of the process at a certain instance. Owing to this advantage, HMM-based techniques have often been used for the analysis of sophisticated malware. Metamorphic virus can be an annoyance. A metamorphic virus is capable of changing its code and become a new variant of itself without changing the functionalities. The changes are not exactly visible to the observer and therefore observable characteristics play an important role in the analysis. HMM has been used for detection and analysis of such metamorphic viruses [27].

3   The Architecture

The Trusted Computing Group (TCG) laid down the specifications for Trusted Platform Module (TPM) with an idea of creating a trusted computing environment [30]. These specifications were capitalized on to create a deception based architecture, Kidemonas [1], which provides isolation to malware detection systems so that the detection can occur outside the purview of the attacker and the intrusion can be surreptitiously reported to the user or the system administrator.

In this paper the capabilities of Kidemonas are extended to realize a cost-effective system to detect intrusions from advanced persistent threats. In a business enterprise type environment, Kidemonas gives the system administrator the capability to run different forms of intrusion detection on different computing units, and the information regarding intrusion is shared with the system administrator and the other computing units through a separate channel as shown in [1]. This is called the peer communication network comprising of a link-layer communicating unit present on each computing unit called the peer communication unit (PCU). A computing unit in this scenario refers to a computer or a server or basically any computing unit which forms a node in the networked system in a corporate network monitored by a single user or a single group of users working collectively for the same purpose. To make the defense strategies cost-effective, we use the smart-box proposed in [21]. The idea is whenever a form of intrusion is detected, it is reported to the system administrator silently, who in turn uses the smart-box to trigger an appropriate defensive response from the repository. The repository is a storage unit for defense strategies that could be triggered to defend the system at the event of an attack on the system. The defense strategies range from simply blocking certain processes to defending against intricate attacks. The smart-box on learning from the nature of the attack and the status of the malware can trigger an effective response which would be economical in terms of time and resources being used. Smart-box is the decision making unit regarding defensive strategies depending upon the characteristics of the malware.

Figure 2 represents the hardware based defense architecture, and we call it Decepticon. The aim is to deceive ransomware type APTs. Kidemonas [1] is a more generic architecture to counter any APT, Decepticon is a customized version to have a HMM based ransomware detection tool (which is subsumed under the Enclave in the figure and discussed in the next section), and a smart-box to trigger defensive actions depending upon the severity of the attack. If the attack is determined to be of a simple nature, the smart-box triggers a simple response to counter it, and if the attack is sophisticated in nature, then it triggers an elaborate response.

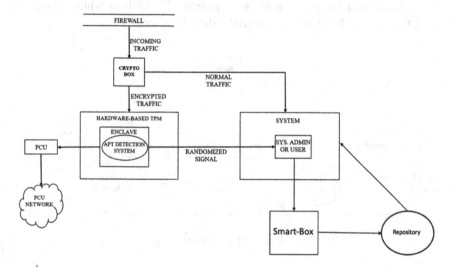

Fig. 2. Decepticon architecture

The firewall (Fig. 2) performs signature based detection. If the malware is able to get past the firewall along with the legitimate traffic, it reaches the crypto-box. The crypto-box makes a copy of the incoming traffic and sends the normal traffic to the system. The copied traffic is encrypted and sent to the hardware-based TPM. The encryption is performed using the public-key of the endorsement key of the hardware-based TPM. In the TPM, the ciphertext is decrypted using the private-key component of the endorsement key of the TPM. The analysis of the traffic is done by the HMM based detection tool. Any form of intrusion being detected is sent to the peer communication unit (PCU) and from there to the PCU network, so as to inform every node in the networked system about the form of intrusion. The PCU network is accessible only through the PCU, which in turn is accessible through the hardware-based TPM. At the same time, a surreptitious reporting is done to the user or the system administrator.

The system administrator then uses his/her storage root keys (SRK) to gain access to the TPM to gain knowledge and the nature of the intrusion that has taken place.

The security of the entire system relies on the fact that the private key component of the endorsement key of the TPM, which was created when it was manufactured, never leaves the TPM. The security also relies on the fact that the storage root keys (SRK) created by the user, when he/she took the ownership of the TPM, is kept safely guarded.

Figure 3 shows a snapshot of a networked system in a corporate network. This representation shows multiple computing units connected to a single access point. Each computing unit is connected to other computing units through the PCU network, which is also used to inform each other of any form of intrusion in the system. Figure 3 shows different versions of detection tools running on different computing units; some of them running Decepticon while others are running the generic Kidemonas style APT detection tools.

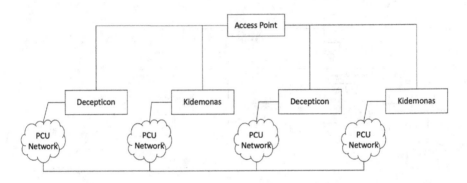

Fig. 3. The system

4   The Ransomware Detection Model

The threat model under consideration in this paper primarily deals with ransomware which qualify as advanced persistent threats. This means that the attack mounted would be highly sophisticated and persistent in nature. Such attacks can render the traditional signature based intrusion detection systems useless. To deal with APTs that have no prior history, behavior-oriented defense systems are a necessity. APTs are generally mounted in multiple stages unlike the more common threats. The knowledge of the stage in which an APT is currently in, is a utilitarian information for the defender to make an informed decision about the defense strategy. These attacks are mounted by the quiet invaders [20] and they subtly graduate through different stages. Therefore, the difficulty arises in figuring out the status of the malware. One can look into the behavioral changes and using those as observable can help make an informed decision. To help the defender in making that informed decision, we develop a Hidden Markov Model (HMM) based intrusion detection tool. This tool will help the defender discern the status of the malware with certain probability, which would define its confidence in choosing the defensive action.

The proposed HMM has N number of hidden states and M number of observables. The model can be denoted by $\lambda = (A, B, \pi)$, where

- A is an $N \times N$ matrix that gives the transition probabilities, characterizing the transition of each hidden state to another. Hence, it is called the transition matrix.
- B is an $N \times M$ that gives the emission probabilities for each hidden state. Hence, it is called the emission probability matrix.
- π is a $1 \times N$ matrix that contains the initial probability distribution for each of the hidden states.

This detection model strictly deals with ransomware. It intends to figure out whether a malware is a ransomware or not, and if it is a ransomware then is it a ransomware that has graduated to become an APT. Moreover, the model also investigates that if the ransomware is an APT then is it still pursuing its attack as a ransomware or would resort to a contingency plan of attack. Taking all these into consideration we formulate the model using the following parameters:

- The value of N is 4 which denotes that there are 4 hidden states being considered in this model $Z = \{z_1, z_2, z_3, z_4\}$
- The value of M is 5 which denotes that the number of observable random variables is 5, stated by $X = \{x_1, x_2, x_3, x_4, x_5\}$
- α_{ij} denotes the transition probability of the malware from i^{th} latent state to j^{th} latent state, where $i \in \{1, 4\}$ and $j \in \{1, 4\}$
- β_{ir} denotes the emission probability of ith latent state manifesting r^{th} observable behavior, where $i \in \{1, 4\}$ and $r \in \{1, 5\}$

The hidden or latent states of the malware are as follows:

- The first state z_1 is where it is just a malware, regardless of the fact whichever form of malware it graduates to.
- The second state z_2 is where the malware becomes a ransomware.
- The third stage z_3 is the one wherein the ransomware has graduated to become an APT.
- The fourth and the final hidden state in this model is denoted by z_4, wherein the attacker chooses to execute the contingency plan of attack instead of mounting a ransomware attack on the victim. This is an important stage, wherein a ransomware, which has graduated to become an APT, is choosing to execute a contingency plan of attack.

The hidden states of the malware are often outside the purview of the defender's intrusion detection system and hence, the term hidden state, which entailed the use of Hidden Markov Model based intrusion detection model for ransomware. For the model, as discussed earlier, the observable behavioral states are used to ascertain the status of the malware. The set of observable states is given by $X = \{x_1, x_2, x_3, x_4, x_5\}$. Following are the details regarding individual observable state used to design the model:

- x_1: Reconnaissance
- x_2: Interaction with honeypots or real-databases which are of high value
- x_3: Backdoor implants and/or back-channel traffic
- x_4: If the strategy of "Campaign Abort" exists
- x_5: Existence of any other contingency plan of attack

Figure 4 shows the HMM based ransomware detection model. Now that we have our latent and observable stages, and the associated parameters, we can determine the transition probability matrix A and the emission probability matrix B. With the aforementioned parameters we have the following:

$$A = \begin{bmatrix} \alpha_{11} & \alpha_{12} & \alpha_{13} & \alpha_{14} \\ \alpha_{21} & \alpha_{22} & \alpha_{23} & \alpha_{24} \\ \alpha_{31} & \alpha_{32} & \alpha_{33} & \alpha_{34} \\ \alpha_{41} & \alpha_{42} & \alpha_{43} & \alpha_{44} \end{bmatrix}$$

$$B = \begin{bmatrix} \beta_{11} & \beta_{12} & \beta_{13} & \beta_{14} & \beta_{15} \\ \beta_{21} & \beta_{22} & \beta_{23} & \beta_{24} & \beta_{25} \\ \beta_{31} & \beta_{32} & \beta_{33} & \beta_{34} & \beta_{35} \\ \beta_{41} & \beta_{42} & \beta_{43} & \beta_{44} & \beta_{45} \end{bmatrix}$$

Transition Probability:

$$T(ij) = p(z_{k+1} = j | z_k = i)$$

where $i \in \{1, 2, 3, 4\}$ and $j \in \{1, 2, 3, 4\}$

Emission Probability:

$$\varepsilon_i(x) = p(X_k = x | z_k = i)$$

where $\varepsilon_i(x)$ is the probability distribution on X and $i \in \{1, 2, 3, 4\}$

Initial Probability Distribution:

$$\pi(i) = p(z_1 = i)$$

where $i \in \{1, 2, 3, 4\}$

The joint probability distribution is given by:

$$p(z_1, ..., z_4, x_1, ..., x_5) = \pi(1) \prod_{k=1}^{3} T(z_{k+1} | z_k) \prod_{n=1}^{5} \varepsilon_z(x_n)$$

The transition probabilities considered for this paper are updated as in the following matrix:

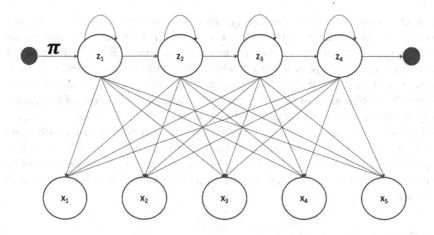

Fig. 4. HMM based ransomware detection model

$$A = \begin{bmatrix} \alpha_{11} & \alpha_{12} & 0 & 0 \\ 0 & \alpha_{22} & \alpha_{23} & 0 \\ 0 & 0 & \alpha_{33} & \alpha_{34} \\ 0 & 0 & 0 & \alpha_{44} \end{bmatrix}$$

The transition probability from stage z_1 to stage z_3 is 0 owing to the fact that it has to first go through stage z_2 as it will portray the features of ransomware anyway. If it portrays features of any other form of malware, then it stays in this stage as the detection of other forms of malware is outside the scope of this model. Similarly, the transition probability of stage z_1 to stage z_4 is also zero, as the malware cannot directly make a transition to the final stage without becoming a ransomware first. According to the assumption made in this model, effectively the malware can remain in some other form of malware or become a ransomware.

The transition probability of stage z_2 to z_1 is assumed to be zero. The basis for the assumption is, if the model can depict characteristics of some other form of malware, which is not a ransomware, then it is effectively stage z_4. Hence, any behavior of this type is categorized under phase z_4. The same reasoning applies to the transition probabilities of stages z_3 to z_1 and stage z_4 to z_1. The transition probability of stage z_2 to z_4 is 0, owing to the fact that in stage z_2 it is already a ransomware, and if the attacker is planning to execute a contingency plan of attack then it is effectively stage z_3 as it has already graduated to become an APT [2].

The transition probabilities of stages z_3 to z_2 and stage z_4 to z_2 are assumed to be 0. In stage z_3 the ransomware has graduated to become an APT. On reaching this stage, the ransomware will execute ransomware type APT attack and/or will abort the campaign upon discovery. In stage z_4 the ransomware type APT has decided to execute some other form of attack as a contingency plan of action owing to a belief of being discovered by the defender. The assumption here is that once a ransomware has graduated to become an APT, it cannot be considered as a simple ransomware, even though it executes a ransomware style attack and/or resort to a contingency plan of attack. Even if the attacker executes a contingency plan of attack which effectively is a ransomware attack, then there is a high possibility that the newer form of ransomware attack would be somewhat different from the primary form of attack, and therefore we assume this as an alternate form of attack and the model denotes the stage to be z_4.

The emission probability matrix and the initial distribution probabilities are not left to any assumption because the attack distribution probabilities as well as the probabilities with which the observable features might be visible depending on the type of resources, the system, the attack framework and the duration of the attack.

5   Discussion

The Decepticon architecture makes the system scalable in nature and easy to use due to its reliance on commercial off-the-shelf components (COTS) such as the TPM. In a corporate environment, where multiple systems are connected to a single gateway, Kidemonas style systems make the environment more secured and scalable in nature. In such an environment, all systems are connected to each other through the PCU network. This also gives the environment the capability to run different types of intrusion detection system on different systems. The information regarding any intrusion is conveyed to all other systems in the networked environment through the PCU network. The PCU network is outside the purview of the attacker, owing to the fact that it doesn't use the regular communication network.

The scalability of Kidemonas style architecture helps in future proofing of the entire system. If needed more computing units can be added to the entire system which would be secure in nature. The transition and emission probabilities once calculated, would provide the defender with valuable information about the malware that would help the user to trigger a cost-effective response from the repository through a smart-box. The biggest advantage for the defender is *awareness, security* and cost-effective *countermeasure*. Once the model is put to application in the real world, it would yield numerical values for the transition and emission probability matrices. This helps the defender to make an informed decision, without compromising the quality of service of the system.

A crucial feature manifested by APTs is the existence of a contingency plan of attack [2]. A simple ransomware can be taken care of with the existing infrastructure and defense strategies. But a ransomware type APT might come with a *contingency plan*. A contingency plan of attack is an alternate attack strategy, which the attacker might resort to, if it believes that the defender is able to thwart the primary attack campaign. The type of alternate campaign the attacker might resort to can be completely different from the primary attack strategy. If the attacker is spooked, it can execute the contingency plan and that can inflict unwanted but significant damage to the victim. This warranted the need for a probabilistic behavioral oriented detection tool and a surreptitious intrusion reporting architecture, which has been presented in this paper.

We further illustrate the utility of our research using WannaCry as a use case. WannaCry is a ransomware type APT [2]. The series of attacks carried out by WannaCry in 2017 is known as "WannaCry Campaign." The attack started on May 12, 2017 and ended on May 17, 2017. Over this period, the attackers earned somewhere between \$75,000 to \$80,000 from ransom [28]. To begin with, the first things to look for would be the observable features.

- x_1 in this case would flag any process or program searching for the *EternalBlue* vulnerabilities if at all they exist in the system.
- x_2 would flag any process that are actually interacting with the SMBv1 vulnerabilities [28]. It can also denote any process that is interacting with honeypots with similar vulnerabilities.
- x_3 feature manifests the existence of *DoublePulsar* back-door implant tool in the system and/or existence of back-channel communication between the malware and its command and control (C&C) centers.
- x_4 feature denotes the "Campaign Abort" strategy by the malware if it finds itself in a sand-boxed environment.
- x_5 feature is a bit tricky to predict or discern before it has actually been manifested by the attackers. In the context of WannaCry this can be the DDoS attack mounted on the server that hosted the "Kill-Switch" [10].

Once we have the observable features, we can use the tool to predict the hidden/latent states for the WannaCry Campaign.

- z_1 denotes the stage where it can be any malware.
- z_2 denotes the stage where it has manifested the features of being a ransomware.
- z_3 signifies the stage where the ransomware has qualified to become an APT with primary intention of executing ransomware attack or aborting the campaign upon discovery (which in this case is "Do Nothing" strategy when the malware "believes" that it is being run in a sand-boxed environment).
- z_4 manifests the intention of the attacker of executing some other form attack as a contingency plan of attack. In the context of WannaCry the contingency plan of attack is the DDoS attack mounted in the server hosting "Kill-Switch."

Through detailed experiments, the transition probability matrix, the emission probability matrix and the initial distribution matrix can be calculated and put to application in the real world scenario. Every time the status of the malware is detected, a cost-effective countermeasure could be deployed. In the context of WannaCry, following are the countermeasures that could be employed once the status of the malware is known:

- When it is at the stage of malware, simple patching of the system would help. Microsoft had release a patch update as soon as it had learned of the vulnerability.

– When the malware is graduating to become a ransomware then backing-up of the important databases would help.
– As the ransomware graduates to become an APT, blocking back-door traffic along with patching the system as well as maintaining a back-up of the database would help. Also triggering the "Kill-Switch" might help.
– In the final stage, APT proceeds to execute the contingency plan of attack which in this case is the DDoS attack mounted on server hosting the "Kill-Switch." The countermeasure in this case is all the countermeasures applicable for the previous stage as well as another defensive action would be to protect the server which hosts the "Kill-Switch."

The idea is to anticipate the state of the malware and take preventive action. For this purpose, one can use a classifier. Using the feature set for a given state, one can do online prediction of the state of the malware. But a Hidden Markov Model (HMM) based IDS would also be able to provide more behavioral data regarding the malware and in case of an APT, the behavioral pattern of the attacker can be logged and analyzed through the probability matrices. The Decepticon architecture is scalable in nature as shown in Fig. 3. Therefore, it is safe to assume there will be multiple nodes in a networked environment and each of them would be running a Kidemonas or a Decepticon type IDS individually. The intrusion detection happens outside the purview of the attacker. The paper doesn't claim that the APT detection system would be successful all the time. There can be advanced form of attacks, which might defeat the IDS itself, wherein the IDS fails to identify the attack and gives out false negative. In that case, the system comes under attack. But once the attack has occurred, a copy of the malware still exists on the Decepticon architecture. That malware can then be analyzed and attacks on systems with similar vulnerabilities can be thwarted. As shown in Fig. 5, if one system is under attack, the information is communicated to the other nodes in the networked environment through the PCU network and preventive action can be taken to save the remaining nodes. The probability matrix can be updated for future use. The detection system can be trained on past attacks, extracting features and updating the probability matrices. When the IDS gives out false positives, then also the performance is not affected as it happens outside the system.

There can be a classifier which does online predictions. As shown in Fig. 6, given the feature set at time $t + 1$ and the behavior observed till time t (the behavior observed through the feature sets manifested for the respective states) and the states observed till time t, the classifier can predict the state of the malware at time $t + 1$. This would be immensely helpful in tailoring a preventive action against the malware. But the HMM based IDS can do more than that. It can be trained using similar attacks originating from different APT groups and/or can be trained on different attacks originating from the same APT group. This would not only help the defender to ascertain the state of the malware but also would give an insight regarding the behavior of the malware and/or the attacker.

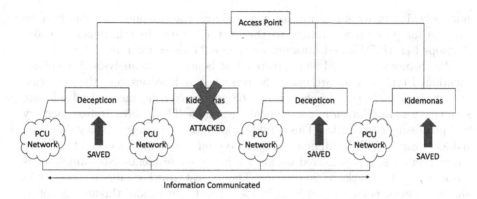

Fig. 5. A scenario wherein one system is under attack

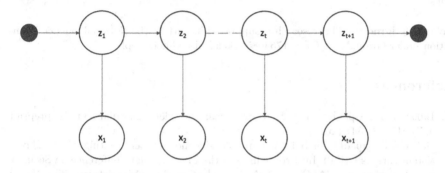

x_i : **Feature Set**
z_i : **States**

Fig. 6. Classifier based on-line predictive model

As illustrated above, our model shows the way the countermeasures become more sophisticated as and when the malware advances to the higher stages. The calculation of the transition probability and the emission probability matrices as well as the initial probability distribution is not done in this paper due to lack of real world data. The HMM based detection tool and the surreptitious reporting of the intrusion information by the Decepticon architecture pave the way for better security in the corporate environments as well as in the mission critical systems.

6   Conclusion and Future Work

The paper presents an architecture which incorporates the idea of isolation for the purpose of security. It employs deception as a defense technique through the use of hardware-based TPM. The architecture uses deception to surreptitiously report the attack detection to the system administrator. This dupes the attacker into believing in its silent invasion while giving the defender valuable time to prepare for preventive strategy to thwart the attack. In this paper, we also developed an HMM based ransomware type APT detection tool.

The future work would be to create a test-bench for the analysis of the aforementioned type of malware using the proposed architecture and the detection system. Initially the experiments would be performed using customized software simulation tools. Currently commercially available TPMs have limited memory and processing capabilities. This would make running of process heavy detection models inside a TPM a difficult proposition, and hence, the choice of software simulation tools is a preferred option for initial experiments. No framework is without any drawbacks or limitations. The biggest drawback for the security in this framework is the existence of insider threat. An insider threat can defeat the system. This is another aspect that has to be taken care of in the future work.

Acknowledgment. This research is supported in part by the National Science Foundation under Grant No. DGE – 1754085. Usual disclaimers apply.

References

1. Baksi, R.P., Upadhyaya, S.J.: Kidemonas: the silent guardian. arXiv preprint arXiv:1712.00841 (2017)
2. Baksi, R.P., Upadhyaya, S.J.: A comprehensive model for elucidating advanced persistent threats (APT). In: Proceedings of the International Conference on Security and Management (SAM), pp. 245–251. The Steering Committee of The World Congress in Computer Science, Computer Engineering and Applied Computing (2018)
3. Bencsáth, B., Pék, G., Buttyán, L., Felegyhazi, M.: The cousins of stuxnet: Duqu, flame, and gauss. Future Internet **4**(4), 971–1003 (2012)
4. Bennett, J.T., Moran, N., Villeneuve, N.: Poison ivy: assessing damage and extracting intelligence. FireEye Threat Research Blog (2013)
5. Çeker, H., Zhuang, J., Upadhyaya, S., La, Q.D., Soong, B.-H.: Deception-based game theoretical approach to mitigate DoS attacks. In: Zhu, Q., Alpcan, T., Panaousis, E., Tambe, M., Casey, W. (eds.) GameSec 2016. LNCS, vol. 9996, pp. 18–38. Springer, Cham (2016). https://doi.org/10.1007/978-3-319-47413-7_2
6. Chen, M.Y., Kundu, A., Zhou, J.: Off-line handwritten word recognition using a hidden Markov model type stochastic network. IEEE Trans. Pattern Anal. Mach. Intell. **16**(5), 481–496 (1994)
7. Clark, Z.: The worm that spreads WanaCrypt0r. Malwarebytes Labs, May 2017. https://blog.malwarebytes.com/threat-analysis/2017/05/the-worm-that-spreadswanacrypt0r/
8. Costan, V., Devadas, S.: Intel SGX explained. IACR Cryptol. ePrint Arch. **2016**(086), 1–118 (2016)
9. Falliere, N., Murchu, L.O., Chien, E.: W32. Stuxnet dossier. White paper, Symantec Corporation, Security Response **5**(6), 29 (2011)
10. Greenberg, A.: Hackers are trying to reignite WannaCry with nonstop botnet attacks. Wired Security, May 2017. https://www.wired.com/2017/05/wannacry-ransomware-ddos-attack/

11. Hutchins, E.M., Cloppert, M.J., Amin, R.M.: Intelligence-driven computer network defense informed by analysis of adversary campaigns and intrusion kill chains. Lead. Issues Inf. Warfare Secur. Res. **1**(1), 80 (2011)

12. Jang, J., et al.: PrivateZone: providing a private execution environment using arm trustzone. IEEE Trans. Depend. Secure Comput. **15**(5), 797–810 (2016)

13. Langner, R.: Stuxnet: dissecting a cyberwarfare weapon. IEEE Secur. Priv. **9**(3), 49–51 (2011)

14. Leonard, C.: 2015 threat report. Websense Security Labs (2015)

15. Ljolje, A., Levinson, S.E.: Development of an acoustic-phonetic hidden Markov model for continuous speech recognition. IEEE Trans. Sig. Process. **39**(1), 29–39 (1991)

16. Ponemon Institute LLC: The state of advanced persistent threats. Ponemon Institute Research Report, December 2013

17. LogRhythm: The APT lifecycle and its log trail. Technical report, July 2013

18. Lorch, J.R., Wang, Y.M., Verbowski, C., Wang, H.J., King, S.: Isolation environment-based information access, 20 September 2011. US Patent 8,024,815

19. Madnick, S.E., Donovan, J.J.: Application and analysis of the virtual machine approach to information system security and isolation. In: Proceedings of the Workshop on Virtual Computer Systems, pp. 210–224. ACM, New York (1973). https://doi.org/10.1145/800122.803961

20. Mehresh, R.: Schemes for surviving advanced persistent threats. Faculty of the Graduate School of the University at Buffalo, State University of New York (2013)

21. Mehresh, R., Upadhyaya, S.: A deception framework for survivability against next generation cyber attacks. In: Proceedings of the International Conference on Security and Management (SAM). p. 1. The Steering Committee of The World Congress in Computer Science, Computer Computer Engineering and Applied Computing (2012)

22. Messaoud, B.I., Guennoun, K., Wahbi, M., Sadik, M.: Advanced persistent threat: new analysis driven by life cycle phases and their challenges. In: 2016 International Conference on Advanced Communication Systems and Information Security (ACOSIS), pp. 1–6. IEEE (2016)

23. Pauna, A.: Improved self adaptive honeypots capable of detecting rootkit malware. In: 2012 9th International Conference on Communications (COMM), pp. 281–284. IEEE (2012)

24. Piolle, E.: Simplified schema of a trusted platform module (TPM). Wikipedia, September 2008. https://commons.wikimedia.org/wiki/File:TPM.svg

25. Rabiner, L.R.: A tutorial on hidden Markov models and selected applications in speech recognition. Proc. IEEE **77**(2), 257–286 (1989)

26. Rashid, A., et al.: Detecting and preventing data exfiltration (2014)

27. Kumar Sasidharan, S., Thomas, C.: A survey on metamorphic malware detection based on hidden Markov model. In: 2018 International Conference on Advances in Computing, Communications and Informatics (ICACCI), pp. 357–362. IEEE (2018)

28. Secureworks: WCry Ransomware Campaign. Secureworks Inc., May 2017. https://www.secureworks.com/blog/wcry-ransomware-campaign

29. Shepherd, C., et al.: Secure and trusted execution: past, present, and future-a critical review in the context of the internet of things and cyber-physical systems. In: 2016 IEEE Trustcom/BigDataSE/ISPA, pp. 168–177. IEEE (2016)

30. TCG: TPM main specification. Trusted Computing Group, March 2011. https://trustedcomputinggroup.org/tpm-main-specification/

31. Vukalović, J., Delija, D.: Advanced persistent threats-detection and defense. In: 2015 38th International Convention on Information and Communication Technology, Electronics and Microelectronics (MIPRO), pp. 1324–1330. IEEE (2015)
32. Zakaria, W.Z.A., Abdollah, M.F., Mohd, O., Ariffin, A.F.M.: The rise of ransomware. In: Proceedings of the 2017 International Conference on Software and e-Business, pp. 66–70. ACM (2017)
33. Zhao, C., Saifuding, D., Tian, H., Zhang, Y., Xing, C.: On the performance of Intel SGX. In: 2016 13th Web Information Systems and Applications Conference (WISA), pp. 184–187. IEEE (2016)

A Survey on Ransomware Detection Techniques

C. V. Bijitha$^{(\boxtimes)}$ ⓘ, Rohit Sukumaran, and Hiran V. Nath ⓘ

Department of Computer Science and Engineering,
National Institute of Technology Calicut, Kozhikode, Kerala, India
{bijitha_p180078cs,rohit_b150264cs,hiranvnath}@nitc.ac.in

Abstract. Ransomware is among the most dangerous malware prevailing in today's world. Once infected, the malware either encrypts the data or lock the system screen, and prevents the owner from accessing his data and system until some ransom money is paid, resulting in multi-million dollars of cyber-extortion annually. Additionally, there is no guarantee that the owner would regain access to the seized data after payment is made. Ransomware attacks keep troubling the cybersecurity community; researchers are working towards developing efficient techniques for the detection and prevention of ransomware attacks. In this paper, we are attempting to review the existing solutions based on the methodology adopted and validate them using specific performance metrics.

Keywords: Anti-ransomware · Ransomware detection · Malware · Security attacks · Survey

1 Introduction

Communication was revolutionized with the introduction of the Internet, and some menaces accompanied those benefits. Thus, cybersecurity experts have to offer efficient tools and techniques to secure data and assets of its potential end-users from malicious software, which comes in a variety of forms. Malicious software or malware is the generic term used to describe any program intended to ravage the computer system and induces loss to its owners. They generally cover viruses, worms, ransomware, Trojans, rootkits, spyware and many more. Among those, ransomware is a recent interest to malware writers.

2016 was marked as a remarkable year in the history of malware, especially ransomware. It turned out to be the time with most successful ransomware attacks, distinguished as the 'year of ransomware' [1]. Private and public sectors enterprises, including the health care industry, were affected along with individual users. WannaCry [2] is a popular name among people once, regarded as one of the most notorious and successful ransomware attacks infecting thousands of users around the globe. User data was encrypted, and bitcoins were demanded as ransom [3]. Cryptowall [4], CryptoLocker [5], Locky [6], and GandCrab [7] are a few other celebrated names in the list.

© Springer Nature Singapore Pte Ltd. 2020
S. K. Sahay et al. (Eds.): SKM 2019, CCIS 1186, pp. 55–68, 2020.
https://doi.org/10.1007/978-981-15-3817-9_4

Gazet [8] defines ransomware as: "*A kind of Malware that demands payment in exchange for a stolen functionality.*" Thus ransomware is characterized by a specific form of malicious activity, i.e., it steals an essential function of the infected system, denying users access to that function, and finally, demanding a ransom for the user to regain access to the particular function.

Ransomware can be either File-Lockers (Crypto-ransomware), or Screen-Lockers. File-Lockers encrypt files on the system, making them inaccessible until the victim pays a ransom to the hacker, to decrypt their files. This is a common variety of ransomware that most anti-ransomware efforts concentrate on. Screen-Lockers, on the contrary, do not intervene with data but instead prevent you from navigating through your system by either locking their desktop or showing a pop-up that never closes.

According to Scaife et al. [9], based on the method of action, file-lockers, in turn, can be of classified into three types, Namely Class A, Class B and Class C, or equivalently Type I, Type II and Type III. Class A ransomware opens the file, reads it, writes the encrypted content in place and then closes it. Class B ransomware extends class A. It moves the file out of the directory first, then performs class A actions, then moves the file back to the original directory. The file name after alteration may not be the same as the filename before. Class C ransomware reads the file, writes the encrypted content to another newly created file and then deletes or overwrites the original file.

As ransomware is growing as a widespread and convenient mode of attacking, variety of ransomware families are launched every year. It is predicted that by the end of 2019, companies have to face ransomware attacks in every 14 s [10]. Moreover, 75% of the Canadian companies affected with ransomware stood ready to pay the ransom, followed by 58% in the UK and 22% in Germany [11]. As long as the firms and individuals are willing to pay for their data, attacks are likely to persist. As a consequence, the security research community has undertaken the challenges in identifying ransomware attacks and preventing them. A variety of techniques are available in the literature. When stronger solutions are available, the offenders come up with even more potent malware. Reyptson [12], leakerlocker [13], Cerber [14] are a few ransomware struck recently. Hence investigations [15, 16] on ransomware, their detection, mitigation and prevention techniques hold significance and is happening among cybersecurity researchers today. Accordingly, we are conducting an independent study on state-of-the-art ransomware detection techniques, and analytical evaluation of their performance is presented.

The characteristics of ransomware detection techniques available in the literature are described in Sect. 2. The effectiveness of those methods are assessed and tabulated in Sect. 3 and finally concluded in Sect. 4.

2   Ransomware Detection Techniques

Fighting against ransomware is not easy for several reasons. The malicious users show much interest in ransomware as it is manageable to create or acquire them

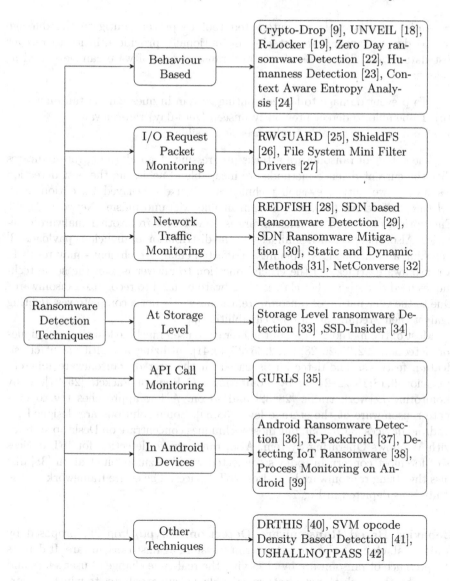

Fig. 1. Ransomware detection technique categories

easily, attack naive users (who does not care about taking a backup of their data) and earn money. The operations of ransomware are no different from benign software; the differentiation is not easy, causing the ransomware to act without getting detected [9]. Hence, techniques to automatically detect ransomware, more precisely zero-day attacks is the need of the hour.

Anti-Ransomware is an automated tool to prevent/mitigate the damage caused due to ransomware attacks and optionally provide utilities to recover lost data if any. The goals of any anti-ransomware software can be stated as follows:

(i) To prevent damage to the computing system in question via ransomware
(ii) To be able to detect previously unseen (zero-day) ransomware
(iii) To be as unnoticeable to the user as possible

The extent of ransomware attacks progressing at an alarming rate indicates that the current defence methods are incapable of achieving the best detection results. As we notice, evasion techniques [17] like - Delayed Execution, Self-deleting/Self-destruction, Polymorphism and Metamorphism, Network Traffic Encryption, etc.- used by ransomware is no different from other malware categories. Also, there is much similarity in the distribution of malicious payloads [3] - clicking a malicious link, opening an affected email attachment - may result in a ransomware attack. So the crucial question to answer is, can the same techniques used to detect other classes of malware be used to recognize ransomware? Due to the very nature of ransomware, the answer is not a complete yes, fighting against them, require additional capabilities [3].

Most of the methodologies in the literature used machine learning techniques for detection [22, 25, 26, 28, 31, 32, 35–37, 40, 41], utilizing a multitude of classification features. The detection is based on the user or ransomware inherent behavior [9, 18, 19, 22–24] or by monitoring I/O Request Packets [25–27], or by monitoring network traffic [28–32] and so on. A few approaches try to mitigate ransomware at the storage level [33, 34]. Some solutions are designed for Android devices [36, 37, 39], but most techniques concentrate on Desktop systems with Windows Operating System. Also, ransomware detection for IoT devices is of foremost concern in today's connected world. Azmoodeh et al. in [38] discuss thwarting ransomware in android IoT devices. The entire framework for the study is as depicted in Fig. 1.

Behavior Based Ransomware Detection: CryptoDrop [9], proposed by Scaife et al. claims to be an early-warning system against ransomware. It detects the presence of ransomware by observing the real-time change of user's files and data. The approach also suggests specific file system attributes to which, majority of the crypto-ransomware acts. To this end, they have identified file type changes, similarity hashes and Shannon Entropy as the three primary indicators; and file deletion and file type funnelling as the two secondary indicators, achieving much better performance. A notable limitation is, CryptoDrop is incapable of distinguishing encryption activities of user and ransomware.

UNVEIL [18] automatically generates an artificial user environment to mimic the typical user environment, detecting file lockers as well as screen lockers. The realised file system activity monitor is system-wide and uses the Windows filesystem Mini-filter Driver framework. It sets callbacks on each I/O request and monitors I/O buffer data entropy using Shannon Entropy as well as per-process file access patterns to look for suspicious activities. File-access patterns include combinations of read, write, delete patterns that crypto-ransomware typically use in their encryption schemes.

R-Locker [19] attempts for early detection of ransomware with strategies to eventually prevent from further damages. R-Locker, rooted in deception technology [20, 21], implements the honey file trap as a FIFO pipe, and the ransomware is blocked once it starts reading the file. The features incorporated in R-Locker are highly dependent on how the OS deals with the Reader-Writer problem. Moreover, the method does not require pre-training or experience; claiming effective against zero-day attacks. As attacks incidence with new and novel variants of ransomware is increasing, Al-rimy et al. in [22] also present a methodology which can recognise the so-called zero-day attacks. Both behavioural detection, as well as anomaly detection approaches, are used in tandem. A behavioural model is a group of classifiers with SVM which constitute the base estimators. The results of the classifiers are combined using the majority voting strategy. The anomaly based-estimator was built using a one-class SVM trained with data from benign applications only. The results of the two are combined using OR logic.

The method explained in [23] introduces a detection method based on the users file operating characteristics. The idea is to differentiate between 'ransomwareness' and 'humanness'. The 'humanness' factor is hinged on the idea that, when the user edits a document, it lets the file content be displayed on a window in the desktop. On the other hand, 'ransomwareness' assumes that the encryptor does not expose any file content and subsequent operations. The fundamental idea used in [24] is that when files are encrypted by ransomware, the entropy of the file header is significantly higher than encryption by a regular, trusted process. This information is coupled with context awareness to ascertain whether the user or the ransomware is performing file encryption.

Ransomware Detection Based on I/O Request Packet Monitoring: Mehnaz et al. introduce RWGuard [25], which can detect crypto-ransomware in real-time with three monitoring techniques - decoy monitoring, file change monitoring, and process monitoring. File changes are observed using metrics like similarity, entropy, file type changes and file size changes. Those changes over a threshold value are sent for further assessments. Also, the file classification module classifies file encryption as benign or malicious by learning the usage of built-in crypto-tool and profiling user encryption behaviour.

To detect ransomware at runtime, ShieldFS [26] uses a supervised classifier trained with I/O Request Packet (IRP) data collected from both clean and infected machines. The classifier uses two different models: process-centric: trained on the processes individually. System-centric: trained considering the IRP data as coming from a single process. ShieldFS uses an array of such classifiers each one trained at a different level of the percentage of files accessed. ShieldFS also implements a cryptographic primitive detector which scans the committed pages of any process classified as suspicious or malicious and searches for traces of a cipher and further tries to extract the symmetric key if one can be found.

Rather than focusing on the detection of ransomware, the methodology discussed in [27] attempts to mitigate the damages caused by ransomware, thereby ensuring integrity and availability of the data. I/O Request Packets to user files are monitored. The mini-filter driver prevents read/write access of user files by processes other than the user-defined default applications of each file type. The driver also classifies renaming of file extensions as unsafe. It is likely to have false positives; but, drivers lack flexibility.

Ransomware Detection Based on Network Traffic Monitoring: RedFish [28] uses a network traffic analyzer device to monitor the traffic of shared storage devices in a corporate network to detect ransomware activity. As we know, reading and writing exercise, deleting or overwriting the contents are among the fundamental activities concerning ransomware. So the device detection algorithm here considers the minimum number of files deleted, the maximum period during which deletion occurs and minimum average network throughput (reads + writes) for detection as features. These parameters are then tuned using training sets consisting of traffic traces from both uninfected and infected networks.

A Software-Defined Networking (SDN) based detection approach is proposed by Cabaj et al. in [29] and [30]. In [29] they claim that the analysis of HTTP messages and their volume are enough to detect ransomware attacks. An HTTP traffic analyzer that is part of an SDN controller extracts and pre-processes HTTP packets by reassembling them and obtaining size, server and IP information. The results were supported by only two crypto-ransomware families, namely CryptoWall and Locky.

In [31], a hybrid approach combining static and dynamic analysis against ransomware affecting desktop computers is suggested. In the static approach, trigger scripts, along with honey-files, based on deception technology [20], are placed in the artificial environment to detect when the ransomware is modifying the files. Also, Network packets are monitored, and parameters are extracted from the packet headers and matched against a dataset which is trained to identify malicious behaviour. An extension to the Static network analysis using a larger dataset with more parameters is presented as the dynamic analysis approach. It should be noted that the method is incapable of recovering the victim files.

In NetConverse [32], a machine learning approach considering the network traffic using the Decision Tree classifier is discussed. Ransomware network traffic is observed and kept track of the characteristics of packets generated by the infected machine.

Ransomware Detection at Storage Level: Ransomware detection mechanism in storage devices, especially in a flash-based storage device is discussed in [33]. An access-pattern-based detector that can detect type I ransomware, works in conjunction with a custom buffer management policy used by SSD's to manage their read and write buffers is proposed. The buffer management policy keeps track of reads and writes to the same location to check for ransomware activity. The method fails when read-write buffers are relatively small.

Baek et al. in [34] proposed a new method to safeguard the system against ransomware inside NAND flash-based SSDs called SSD-Insider. They have used block address, size, and type of an IO request to an SSD as features to capture the characteristics of ransomware. Moreover, have utilized binary decision tree using ID3 for detecting ransomware. Also introduced the design of a new FTL (Flash Translation Layer) for the recovery of infected files utilizing the NAND flash's inherent property of delayed deletion. The entire process incurs extra overhead to the SSD system.

Ransomware Detection Based on API Call Monitoring: GURLS [35] is a supervised learning method based on the Regularized Least Square algorithm. This method is trained on data where the frequency of API calls and strings are used as the feature. The best performance was guaranteed with Radial Basis Function kernel. Linear kernel, when used resulted in false positives, where the entire benign class, was misclassified as ransomware.

Ransomware Detection in Android Devices: Ferrante et al. [36] proposes a hybrid approach combining static and dynamic analysis techniques to mitigate ransomware attacks in Android devices. The static analysis approach considers the frequency of opcodes used, and the dynamic approach considers memory usage, CPU usage, network usage and system call statistics. The binary classifier is trained using 2-grams of opcode sequences as inputs obtained from ransomware samples set and only trusted samples set. Dynamic analysis is done by extracting data from execution logs of processes at runtime, and the behaviour is classified as ransomware or not again using a binary classifier.

R-PackDroid [37] is an ransomware detection technique meant for Android phones. The method is also supported by machine learning with system API packages and uses Random Forest Classifier.

Azmoodeh et al. in [38] propose a method of detecting ransomware specifically in android IoT devices, by classifying applications to benign or malicious based on the power consumption patterns. The k-Nearest Neighbors classifier with k=1 offered maximum accuracy when Dynamic Time Warping measure is used as the Similarity measure. When the power usage patterns vary significantly, it is not feasible to use the of conventional classification methods like NN, KNN and SVM with Euclidean method as the distance measure.

The proposed technique in [39] file directories are monitored for abnormal activities based on memory usage, processor usage and I/O rates. The method is tested against only single custom ransomware created by the authors.

Other Techniques: In [40], a Deep Ransomware Threat Hunting and Intelligence System (DRTHIS) is proposed to classify executables as malicious and benign and then map the ransomware to its family. Deep learning techniques like

Long Short-Term Memory (LSTM)and Convolutional Neural Network (CNN) with softmax algorithm is employed for classification.

A crypto-ransomware detection mechanism by the static analysis of benign and malicious executables is proposed in [41]. The density histograms of opcodes extracted from those executables are used as the feature and have applied SMO classifier available with the WEKA toolkit.

UShallNotPass [42] relies on the idea that ransomware requires better sources of random numbers to provide secure encryption. Modern operating systems render pseudo-random number generator functions to its applications to deliver randomness. So the strategy discussed here is to control the access PRNG APIs and prevents unauthorized applications from calling and using them. However, the hackers can bypass this system with an alternate source of randomness like requesting their C&C servers or use anonymous VPNs like TOR.

3   Discussions

Premature ransomware detection techniques are based on signature matching and still widely used by many anti-virus software. If the anti-virus database does not include the signature for malicious behaviour, the new malware remains undetected. As we know, it is not that hard today for the malicious software developers to create new ransomware variants and bypass detection. So, concentrating on detection of ransomware behaviours rather than typical malware samples is essential [34].

Ransomware authors are tenacious; they come with novel techniques for evasion [17] and new tactics for forcing victims to pay the ransom. Just like programmers use obfuscation techniques to preserve their intellectual properties, the hackers also obfuscate or pack their programs to hide the logic and remain undetected during analysis. One such latest revealed packing technique is RarSFX [45]. A new variant of Cerber [14] was packaged with SFX, helpful in evading machine learning approaches. Details furnished in Sect. 2 indicates that most of the ransomware mitigation methods rely on machine learning techniques. Effectiveness of detection techniques with obfuscated malware using machine learning is under question [43]; the absolute faith in those algorithms won't be the right choice for ransomware detection. Moreover, none of the methods discussed guarantee a foolproof system with 100% detection, including zero-day ransomware attacks. Another significant difficulty for the researcher is the availability of standard dataset for training. Most strategies are built on top of a subset of available samples and claim the highest accuracy, which makes the comparison of results pointless.

Methods that rely on network traffic monitoring is based on the presumption that the ransomware communicates with its Command and Control (C&C) servers for any purpose, like to get the encryption key [28]. Those detection methods are destined to fail if malware does not contact any server but use a local key (but is likely to get revealed during analysis). Some ransomware hides their network traffic by using proxy servers to contact C&C servers. Such proxy

Table 1. Performance comparison of various ransomware detection techniques

Anti ransomware solutions	Ransomware type	TPR (%)	FPR (%)	File recovery support	Overhead
Crypto-Drop [9]	File Locker	100	1	No	1–16 ms
UNVEIL [18]	File Locker, Screen Locker	96.3	0	No	Not mentioned
R-Locker [19]	File Locker	100	0	No	0
Zero Day ransomware Detection [22]	File Locker	99%	2.4%	No	Not mentioned
Humanness Detection [23]	File Locker	–	–	No	Not mentioned
Context Aware Entropy Analysis [24]	File Locker	100%	0%	Yes	Not mentioned
RWGUARD [25]	File Locker	100	0.1	Yes	1.9
ShieldFS [26]	File Locker	99–100	0–0.2	Yes	0.3–3.6x
File System Mini Filter Drivers [27]	File Locker	100	0	Not Required	Not mentioned
REDFISH [28]	File Locker	100	0	Yes	None
SDN based Ransomware Detection [29]	File Locker, Screen Locker	97–98	1–5	No	Not mentioned
SDN Ransomware Mitigation [30]	File Locker	–	–	No	0
Static and Dynamic Methods [31]	File Locker	–	–	No	Not mentioned
NetConverse [32]	File Locker	95%	1–6%	No	Not mentioned
Storage Level ransomware Detection [33]	File Locker (type 1)	–	–	–	Not mentioned
SSD-Insider [34]	File Locker	100	0–5	Yes	147 ns–254 ns
GURLS [35]	File Locker, Screen Locker	87.7%	7.5%	No	Not mentioned
Android Ransomware Detection [36]	File Locker, Screen Locker	100	4	No	Not mentioned
R-Packdroid [37]	File Locker, Screen Locker	97%	2%	No	Varies with APK size
Detecting IoT Ransomware [38]	File Locker, Screen Locker	95.65	–	No	Not mentioned
Process Monitoring on Android [39]	File Locker	–	–	–	Not mentioned
DRTHIS [40]	File Locker	97.2%	2.7%	No	Not mentioned
SVM opcode Density Based Detection [41]	File Locker	95%	0–5%	No	Not mentioned
USHALLNOTPASS [42]	File Locker	94	–	Not required	None

servers could be blocked as in [29], but the use of DGA (Domain Generation Algorithm) can make the black-listing useless.

Ransomware detection techniques based on energy consumption pattern is confirmed to withstand anti-forensic techniques, as malware power consumption characteristics are not as straightforward as modifying the function calls [38]. Also, it is to be noted that the overhead and time lag between executing subsequent operations and identifying anomalies by different modules extend the room for ransomware to conquer the system. Remarkably lightweight approaches are anticipated but are intricate to accomplish.

The use of a virtual environment for detection is tricky these days. Because today's smart malware does not reveal their intended malicious behaviour when a virtual environment is detected, causing analysis impossible. Then like UNVEIL [18], extra effort has to be taken to create files with meaningful names of various extensions, typically in use (.doc, .ppt, .xls, .txt, etc.) with semi-meaningful content and placed in intuitively logical directories with meaningful timestamps. Still, the success probability is limited. Once the attacker identifies the presence of decoys or honeypots, it seems to avoid it, possibly feeds them with incorrect information. Such deception techniques fall before that ransomware which alters only the user-created files, not system files [18]. Deception technology is more advanced and active approach compared to honeypots, performing detection and defence with automation in the data processing. It is capable of providing maximum accuracy with minimal human intervention [20].

Another critical aspect to consider here is how to distinguish between user encryption and ransomware encryption [25]. The file's significant change by a user should be accepted and be used to train user behaviour, helping to avoid false positives because of users normal file operations. Studies reveal that ransomware utilizes standard cryptosystems as well as customized versions during attacks [44]. The malicious users go for custom-made cryptosystems to evade detection and make data recovery complicated [44]. As we already said, obfuscation or packing reveals no useful during static and dynamic analysis, making detection almost impossible. Hence only a few techniques could identify cryptographic primitives in obfuscated programs; their degraded performance makes them ineffective for real-time protection.

Evaluation Metrics: As we already stated in Sect. 2, anti-ransomware solutions have specific goals to achieve. With these goals in mind, evaluation metrics must be decided upon to assess the effectiveness of proposed solutions.

- True Positive Rate (TPR):- It is the ratio of the number of samples correctly classified as ransomware to the total number of ransomware samples.
- False Positive Rate (FPR):- It is the ratio of the number of benign samples wrongly identified as ransomware to the total number of benign samples.
- Performance Overhead:- The time delay incurred either in seconds or percentage by the anti-ransomware system when running.

The suggested matrices consolidated in Table 1 show how successful the anti-malware solutions are in classifying the given collection of executable files as 'ransomware' or 'benign.'

4 Conclusion

Our study reveals that machine learning techniques are the most popular in ransomware detection; no method guaranteed 100% detection along with zero-day attacks. Most of them used at least one kind of monitoring method such as file monitoring, process monitoring, network monitoring or system API monitoring. Majority of the solutions are aimed solely for desktop, particularly windows. As most people believe, backing up of data is not a practical countermeasure against ransomware attacks. Solutions based on deception technology is also not fool-proof, not popular among naive users and is comparatively expensive. Also, powerful ransomware could closely monitor the user behaviour, and alters only those files involving user activities, avoiding honey files.

A compelling ransomware detection framework must strive to attain close to 100% TPR along with zero-day detection, close to 0% FPR with minimal performance overhead. The study reveals that the solutions inadequate in that perspective. The problem may lie in modelling the problem of detecting a ransomware attack. Intuitively, it seems that this may best be achieved by modelling it as a pattern recognition problem on the behaviour of running processes on the system. On the other hand, One may choose to protect the systems resources from any anomalous behaviour. However, this tends to get in the way of the user quite often. Machine Learning techniques expect to offer better results. However, More research is needed to determine which features correctly distinguish ransomware from benign behaviour. Along with monitoring activities of ransomware, equal attention is required on features of benign applications to construct a better detector.

References

1. 2016: Year of the ransomware attacks. http://techgenix.com/2016-ransomware/. Accessed 15 Aug 2019
2. Mohurle, S., Patil, M.: A brief study of Wannacry threat: ransomware attack 2017. Int. J. Adv. Res. Comput. Sci. **8**(5), 1938–1940 (2017)
3. Kharraz, A., Robertson, W., Kirda, E.: Protecting against ransomware: a new line of research or restating classic ideas? IEEE Secur. Priv. **16**(3), 103–107 (2018). https://doi.org/10.1109/MSP.2018.2701165
4. Ransom: Cryptowall. https://www.symantec.com/security-center/writeup/2014-061923-2824-99. Accessed 15 Aug 2019
5. CryptoLocker ransomware. https://www.secureworks.com/research/cryptolocker-ransomware. Accessed 15 Aug 2019
6. Look into locky ransomware. https://blog.malwarebytes.com/threat-analysis/2016/03/look-into-locky/. Accessed 15 Aug 2019

7. Ransom: GandCrab. https://www.symantec.com/security-center/writeup/2018-013106-5656-99. Accessed 15 Aug 2019
8. Gazet, A.: Comparative analysis of various ransomware virii. J. Comput. Virol. **6**(1), 77–90 (2010)
9. Scaife, N., Carter, H., Traynor, P., Butler, K.R.B.: CryptoLock (and drop it): stopping ransomware attacks on user data. In: 2016 IEEE 36th International Conference on Distributed Computing Systems (ICDCS). IEEE, June 2016
10. Global ransomware damage costs predicted to hit $11.5 billion by 2019. https://cybersecurityventures.com/ransomware-damage-report-2017-part-2/. Accessed 15 Aug 2019
11. What is ransomware? And how to help prevent it 27 terrifying ransomware statistics & facts you need to read. https://phoenixnap.com/blog/ransomware-statistics-facts. Accessed 15 Aug 2019
12. Ransom: Reyptson. https://www.symantec.com/security-center/writeup/2017-072703-4612-99. Accessed 11 Oct 2019
13. Ransom: Cerber. https://www.symantec.com/security_response/earthlink_writeup.jsp?docid=2016-030408-0817-99. Accessed 11 Oct 2019
14. LeakerLocker ransomware discovered in Google play store apps. https://www.tritium-security.com/blog/tag/Apps. Accessed 11 Oct 2019
15. Aurangzeb, S., Aleem, M., Iqbal, M., Islam, A.: Ransomware: a survey and trends. J. Inf. Assur. Secur. **12**, 48 (2017). (ESCI - Thomson Reuters Indexed), ISSN 1554-1010
16. Al-rimy, B., Maarof, M., Shaid, S.: Ransomware threat success factors, taxonomy, and countermeasures: a survey and research directions. Comput. Secur. **74** (2018). https://doi.org/10.1016/j.cose.2018.01.001
17. Dargahi, T., Dehghantanha, A., Bahrami, P.N., Conti, M., Bianchi, G., Benedetto, L.: A cyber-kill-chain based taxonomy of crypto-ransomware features. J. Comput. Virol. Hacking Tech. **15**(4), 277–305 (2019). https://doi.org/10.1007/s11416-019-00338-7
18. Kharaz, A., Arshad, S., Mulliner, C., Robertson, W., Kirda, E.: UNVEIL: a large-scale, automated approach to detecting ransomware. In: 25th USENIX Security Symposium (USENIX Security 2016), Austin, TX, pp. 757–772. USENIX Association (2016)
19. Gomez-Hernandez, J.A., Álvarez-Gonzaalez, L., Garcıa-Teodoro, P.: R-Locker: thwarting ransomware action through a honeyfile-based approach. Comput. Secur. **73**, 389–398 (2018)
20. Almeshekah, M.H., Spafford, E.H.: Cyber security deception. In: Jajodia, S., Subrahmanian, V.S.S., Swarup, V., Wang, C. (eds.) Cyber Deception, pp. 25–52. Springer, Cham (2016). https://doi.org/10.1007/978-3-319-32699-3_2
21. Practical honeypots - a list of open-source deception tools that detect threats for free. https://www.smokescreen.io/blog/. Accessed 15 Aug 2019
22. Al-rimy, B.A.S., Maarof, M.A., Prasetyo, Y.A., Shaid, S.Z.M., Ariffin, A.F.M.: Zero-day aware decision fusion-based model for crypto-ransomware early detection. Int. J. Integr. Eng. **10**(6), 82–88 (2018)
23. Honda, T., Mukaiyama, K., Shirai, T., Ohki, T., Nishigaki, M.: Ransomware detection considering user's document editing. In: 2018 IEEE 32nd International Conference on Advanced Information Networking and Applications (AINA). IEEE, May 2018
24. Jung, S., Won, Y.: Ransomware detection method based on context-aware entropy analysis. Soft. Comput. **22**(20), 6731–6740 (2018). https://doi.org/10.1007/s00500-018-3257-z

25. Mehnaz, S., Mudgerikar, A., Bertino, E.: RWGuard: a real-time detection system against cryptographic ransomware. In: Bailey, M., Holz, T., Stamatogiannakis, M., Ioannidis, S. (eds.) RAID 2018. LNCS, vol. 11050, pp. 114–136. Springer, Cham (2018). https://doi.org/10.1007/978-3-030-00470-5_6

26. Continella, A., et al.: ShieldFS: a self-healing, ransomware-aware filesystem. In: Proceedings of the 32nd Annual Conference on Computer Security Applications, ACSAC 2016, pp. 336–347. ACM, New York (2016)

27. Bottazzi, G., Italiano, G.F., Spera, D.: Preventing ransomware attacks through file system filter drivers. In: Second Italian Conference on Cyber Security, Milan, Italy (2018)

28. Morato, D., Berrueta, E., Magana, E., Izal, M.: Ransomware early detection by the analysis of file sharing traffic. J. Netw. Comput. Appl. **124**, 14–32 (2018)

29. Cabaj, K., Gregorczyk, M., Mazurczyk, W.: Software-defined networking-based crypto ransomware detection using HTTP traffic characteristics. Comput. Electr. Eng. **66**, 353–368 (2018)

30. Cabaj, K., Mazurczyk, W.: Using software-defined networking for ransomware mitigation: the case of cryptowall. IEEE Netw. **30**(6), 14–20 (2016)

31. Netto, D.F., Shony, K.M., Lalson, E.R.: An integrated approach for detecting ransomware using static and dynamic analysis. In: 2018 International CET Conference on Control, Communication, and Computing (IC4). IEEE, July 2018

32. Alhawi, O.M.K., Baldwin, J., Dehghantanha, A.: Leveraging machine learning techniques for windows ransomware network traffic detection. In: Dehghantanha, A., Conti, M., Dargahi, T. (eds.) Cyber Threat Intelligence. AIS, vol. 70, pp. 93–106. Springer, Cham (2018). https://doi.org/10.1007/978-3-319-73951-9_5

33. Paik, J.-Y., Choi, J.-H., Jin, R., Wang, J., Cho, E.-S.: A storage-level detection mechanism against crypto-ransomware. In: Proceedings of the 2018 ACM SIGSAC Conference on Computer and Communications Security, CCS 2018. ACM Press (2018)

34. Baek, S.H., Jung, Y., Mohaisen, A., Lee, S., Nyang, D.: SSD-insider: internal defense of solid-state drive against ransomware with perfect data recovery. In: 2018 IEEE 38th International Conference on Distributed Computing Systems (ICDCS). IEEE, July 2018

35. Harikrishnan, N.B., Soman, K.P.: Detecting ransomware using GURLS. In: 2018 Second International Conference on Advances in Electronics, Computers and Communications (ICAECC). IEEE, February 2018

36. Ferrante, A., Malek, M., Martinelli, F., Mercaldo, F., Milosevic, J.: Extinguishing ransomware - a hybrid approach to android ransomware detection. In: Imine, A., Fernandez, J.M., Marion, J.-Y., Logrippo, L., Garcia-Alfaro, J. (eds.) FPS 2017. LNCS, vol. 10723, pp. 242–258. Springer, Cham (2018). https://doi.org/10.1007/978-3-319-75650-9_16

37. Scalas, M., Maiorca, D., Mercaldo, F., Visaggio, C.A., Martinelli, F., Giacinto, G.: R-PackDroid: practical on-device detection of Android ransomware. CoRR, abs/1805.09563 (2018)

38. Azmoodeh, A., Dehghantanha, A., Conti, M., Choo, K.-K.R.: Detecting crypto-ransomware in IoT networks based on energy consumption footprint. J. Ambient. Intell. Hum. Comput. **9**(4), 1141–1152 (2017). https://doi.org/10.1007/s12652-017-0558-5

39. Song, S., Kim, B., Lee, S.: The effective ransomware prevention technique using process monitoring on Android platform. Mob. Inf. Syst. **2016**, 1–9 (2016)

40. Homayoun, S., et al.: DRTHIS: deep ransomware threat hunting and intelligence system at the fog layer. Futur. Gener. Comput. Syst. **90**, 94–104 (2019)

41. Baldwin, J., Dehghantanha, A.: Leveraging support vector machine for opcode density based detection of crypto-ransomware. In: Dehghantanha, A., Conti, M., Dargahi, T. (eds.) Cyber Threat Intelligence. AIS, vol. 70, pp. 107–136. Springer, Cham (2018). https://doi.org/10.1007/978-3-319-73951-9_6

42. Genç, Z.A., Lenzini, G., Ryan, P.Y.A.: No random, no ransom: a key to stop cryptographic ransomware. In: Giuffrida, C., Bardin, S., Blanc, G. (eds.) DIMVA 2018. LNCS, vol. 10885, pp. 234–255. Springer, Cham (2018). https://doi.org/10.1007/978-3-319-93411-2_11

43. Nath, H.V., Mehtre, B.M.: Static malware analysis using machine learning methods. In: Martínez Pérez, G., Thampi, S.M., Ko, R., Shu, L. (eds.) SNDS 2014. CCIS, vol. 420, pp. 440–450. Springer, Heidelberg (2014). https://doi.org/10.1007/978-3-642-54525-2_39

44. Kharraz, A., Robertson, W., Balzarotti, D., Bilge, L., Kirda, E.: Cutting the gordian knot: a look under the hood of ransomware attacks. In: Almgren, M., Gulisano, V., Maggi, F. (eds.) DIMVA 2015. LNCS, vol. 9148, pp. 3–24. Springer, Cham (2015). https://doi.org/10.1007/978-3-319-20550-2_1

45. Ransomware Recap: tougher tactics and evasion techniques. https://www.trendmicro.com/vinfo/us/security/news/cybercrime-and-digital-threats/ransomware-recap-tougher-tactics-and-evasion-techniques. Accessed 11 Oct 2019

Security and Artificial Intelligence

Indian New Currency Denomination Identification System with Audio Feedback Using Convolution Neural Networks for Visually Challenged and Elderly People

Padma Vasavi Kalluru[✉] [ID]

Shri Vishnu Engineering College for Women, Bhimavaram, India
padmavasaviece@svecw.edu.in

Abstract. The visually challenged people lack the ability to perform activities for daily living in general and instrumental daily living activities in particular. The major problems faced by visually challenged people and elderly people with low vision in pursuing money transactions are to distinguish between an original and fake currency note and identify the correct denomination of the given currency note. This paper proposes a hand held portable device that implements a currency recognition algorithm developed using customized Convolution neural networks. The proposed device has the ability to distinguish between original and fake currency notes and recognize the denomination of the currency notes. Further, it sends the information regarding the currency denomination by an audio feedback to the visually challenged user thus enabling him to do money transactions on his own. The performance of the proposed system is verified under real time by giving it to the actual user and the accuracy of the proposed system is found to be 97.4% executed within 10 s of time.

Keywords: Currency recognition · Visually challenged · Convolution neural networks · Classification

1 Introduction

According to the statistics of World Health Organization, approximately 1.3 Billion people across the globe are suffering from one or the other forms of visual impairments. Of them around 188.5 Million people suffer from mild vision problems while 217 Million people have moderate to severe vision problems and 36 Million people are totally blind [1]. Further, according to the findings of Times of India, of the 36 Million People from the world over 15 Million blind people are from India [2].

The visually challenged people lack the ability to perform activities for daily living in general and instrumental daily living activities (like walking, reading, driving using the phone, making money transactions) in particular. The major problems faced by visually challenged people and elderly people with low vision in pursuing money transactions are to distinguish between an original and fake currency note and identify the correct denomination of the given currency note. Generally, the visually challenged persons try to identify the currency denomination with the help of the dimensions of the note and tactile marks that can be felt by touch. The elderly people with low vision can identify the denomination if the notes have contrast colours and large fonts.

In India "Notex" is the popular cheap and simple device used for detection of currency note denomination. It is a flexible scale with groves which can be wrapped around the wrist. When the currency note is placed on the scale the user detects the currency denomination based on the grove it is ended with. However, it cannot distinguish between original and fake notes and is suitable only for old Indian currency.

Gogoi proposed an automatic currency denomination recognition system in [3]. In their work they have segmented the features like dominant colour and aspect ratio of the note. Then they extracted the unique id of the currency note by making use of Fourier descriptors. Finally, the unique shapes on each currency note are classified by using Artificial Neural Networks. Raval in their work "I CuRe" developed an IoT application for helping visually challenged people in recognizing Indian currency notes [4]. Barani developed a hand held device for segregation of different denominations by making use of IR sensors placed at different positions to determine the length of the currency note [5]. Deepak proposed a system that identifies fake notes and recognizes the denomination by extracting the features using a Gray Level Co-Occurrence Matrix (GLCM). They have used probabilistic neural networks algorithm for classification [6]. Mittal developed an Indian Bank note recognition system using deep neural networks [7].

However, after demonetization in 2016, Reserve Bank of India (RBI) has introduced new currency notes in India. The physical size of the new notes is totally different from their old counterparts. For the visually challenged people the more the physical dimensions of the note the high is the denomination of the currency. But, the size of the Five Hundred rupee note and Two-Thousand-rupee note are smaller than the size of the older notes with lower denominations like the Hundred Rupee note. Further, the size of the new Two Hundred Rupees note and old Twenty rupees note are almost the same. So, the above-mentioned algorithms have become virtually obsolete to identify the new currency of India.

To overcome the above-mentioned problems, RBI has introduced angular bleed lines in the new currency notes to distinguish among the available denominations of currency. They also have introduced intaglio or raised printings of Mahatma Gandhi and Ashoka pillar emblem to distinguish between original and fake note. In spite of all the care taken by the RBI the visually challenged people still feel it difficult to recognize the denominations because, the bleed lines get worn out with the time and intaglio is suitable for a polymer currency and not for paper currency.

So, RBI has come up with an initiative that invites an innovative device that can help visually challenged people in identifying the denomination of the currency note [8]. This paper aims at fulfilling the challenge by developing a hand held portable device that implements a currency recognition algorithm developed using Convolution neural networks. The proposed device has the ability to distinguish between original and fake currency notes and recognize the denomination of the currency notes. Further, it sends the information regarding the currency denomination by an audio feedback to the user. The rest of the paper is organized as follows: Sect. 2 describes the Indian new currency notes to understand the significant features to be extracted for classification and recognition. Section 3 discusses the proposed system that distinguishes between original and fake note, classifies the currency according to their denomination and provides an audio feedback to the user. The experiments and results that validate the performance of the proposed system are presented in Sect. 4. Finally, Sect. 5 concludes the paper.

2 Indian New Currency Features

The Reserve Bank of India has released new currency in 2016 and the denominations of the new Indian Currency notes are: 10, 20, 50, 100, 200, 500 and 2000. The features of each of these currency notes as given by Reserve Bank of India are described in this section. Each of the currency note can be distinguished from each other by the color theme of the currency and the motif at the reverse side of the currency note illustrating the cultural heritage of India. The 10 rupees note is chocolate brown in color with the motif of Konark temple, the 20 rupees note is having Greenish Yellow color with Motif of Ellora caves. The 50 Rupees note is having a color theme of Fluorescent Blue with a subject of Hampi with Chariot. The 100 rupees note has lavender color with a theme of Rani ki Vav and the 500 rupees note is gray in color with a theme of Red Fort. The 2000 rupees note is lavender in color with a motif of Mangalyaan described on it [9].

The other feature that distinguishes each currency note from the other is its dimensions which are given in Table 1.

Table 1. Dimensions of Indian new currency notes

S. no.	Currency note	Dimensions in mm
1	10 Rupees	63 × 123
2	20 Rupees	63 × 129
3	50 Rupees	66 × 135
4	100 Rupees	66 × 142
5	200 Rupees	66 × 146
6	500 Rupees	66 × 150
7	2000 Rupees	66 × 166

To distinguish between the original and fake currency note the RBI has given the following security features for all the currency notes. The illustration of the security features provided to the currency notes in the obverse side is shown in Fig. 1. The security features are provided both on obverse and reverse side of the note. The details of each of the security features on the obverse side of the note are listed below:

1. See through register with denomination numeral
2. Latent image of the denomination numeral
3. Denomination numeral in Devanagari
4. Portrait of Mahatma Gandhi
5. Windowed security thread
6. Guarantee Clause, Governor's signature with promise clause and RBI emblem
7. Portrait and electro type of water mark

8. Number panel with numerals growing from small to big
9. Denomination in numerals with Rupee symbol
10. Ashoka pillar emblem on the right
11. Circle with denomination numeral in raised print
12. Bleed lines

Fig. 1. Security features on the obverse side of the currency note

The security features provided by RBI on the reverse side of the currency note is shown in Fig. 2 for illustration. The details of the security features on the reverse side of the note are listed below:

1. Year of Print
2. Swachh Bharat Logo with slogan
3. Language Panel
4. Motif of Indian Heritage
5. Denomination numeral in Devanagari

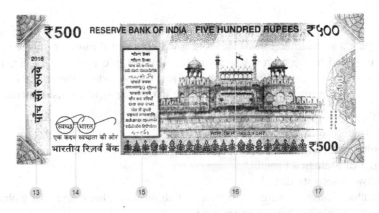

Fig. 2. Security features on reverse side of the currency note

In the proposed work, all the features of the currency notes are taken into consideration to train a convolution neural network for recognizing the currency note. The next section presents the details of the proposed methodology.

3 Proposed Indian Currency Recognition System

As shown in Fig. 3, the visually challenged person places the currency note in the portable hand held device that captures the image of the currency note. The image thus acquired is processed by image processing algorithms for noise removal, adjustment of illumination and then the features of the note are extracted. The features are then given for a Convolution network which is pretrained with the features of the currency note. The Convolution neural network recognizes the original note and classifies into one among the seven classes of the currency denomination. The note denomination then will be announced by a speaker in English with Indian accent or in any regional language as chosen by the user.

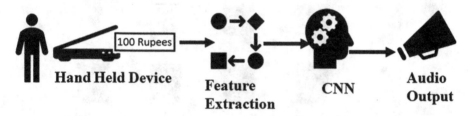

Fig. 3. Concept diagram of Indian Currency Recognition System (ICRS)

The proposed currency recognition system with audio feedback uses Convolution Neural Network with one input layer 13 hidden layers and one output layer as shown in Fig. 5. The CNN is designed to classify the currency notes with utmost accuracy and in minimum time possible to aid the visually challenged people.

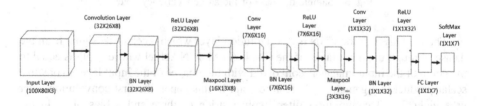

Fig. 4. Convolution neural network architecture for proposed ICRS

The input layer of the CNN as shown in Fig. 4 consists of a color image of size 100 × 80 × 3. The dataset included the images of the currency notes with denominations of 10, 20, 50, 100, 200, 500 and 2000. A hundred images of each denomination are captured by making use of mobile phone camera under different lighting conditions like indoor, outdoor, dim light and bright light. The currency notes chosen were new bank notes, used, worn out and crumpled ones. The original size of each image captured is 1280 × 1280 × 3 which makes the resolution of each image to approximately be 2 MP. The size of the images is then resized to 100 × 80 × 3 to be suitable for the size of the input layer of the Convolution Neural Network used in the methodology. The size of the database collected following the above procedure consisted of a total of 700 images. To improve the accuracy of the classification, the data set is augmented by subjecting it to random rotations, horizontal and vertical flips. The dataset thus acquired is centered towards the origin by subtracting the mean from each of the channels and then is normalized by dividing with its standard deviation. This process is called "Zero Center Normalization" and is performed to ensure all the data dimensions are approximately of the same size which in turn helps the proposed CNN to learn at a faster rate.

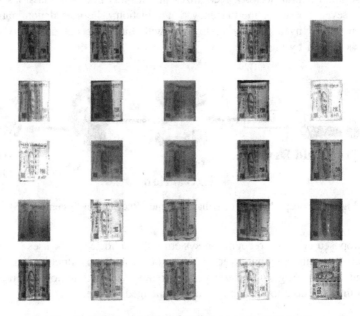

Fig. 5. Sample database of Indian new currency notes

The next layer of the CNN is a convolution layer which receives its signal from the dataset through the input layer of the CNN. An M × N kernel whose depth is equal to the depth of the input images is convolved with the images of the input layer to obtain a scalar product that generates the feature map. In this paper, the first convolution layer uses eight 3 × 3 convolution filters with a stride of three and a bias of 1. In the proposed CNN architecture, there are 33 × 26 × 8 activations in the first convolution layer. A Batch Normalization (BN) layer is used after the first convolution layer to improve the stability of the convolution neural network. The BN layer normalizes the output of the convolution layer by subtracting the batch mean and dividing with its standard deviation. The number of activations of the BN layer and Convolution layer are same as each other. A Rectified Linear Unit (ReLU) layer comes after the BN layer of the CNN. ReLU layer is used to transform the weighted sum of the input from the node to its activation or output. As this layer uses a rectified linear activation function it is given this name. A rectified linear activation is a piecewise linear function which gives the output same as the input if the value of the input is greater than zero or is positive and the output becomes zero otherwise. ReLU activation is used in this paper owing to its computational simplicity, representational sparsity and linear behavior. The next layer used is a "Max Pooling layer", which is a sample discretization layer, used to down sample the image data. It uses a sliding filter with stride same as the size of the filter. The filter is applied to the image data to output the maximum value in each sub region of the convolution process. In this paper, a filter of size 2×2 with a stride of 2 is used in the first max pool layer. The layers from convolution layer to the Maxpool layer are repeated for three times to improve the accuracy of classification and recognition of currency notes. The output layer of the CNN consists of Fully Connected layer followed by a Soft max layer for classifying the denomination of currency into one of the seven classes. The fully connected layer has the highest number of parameters which are obtained by the product of the parameters in the current layer and the previous layer in addition to the bias parameter.

The label of the identified denomination is checked among the pre-recorded voices stored in the Raspberry Pi processor and the corresponding audio message is given out through the ear phones connected to the audio port of the processor. This whole process enables the visually challenged person to know the denomination of the currency note and makes it possible to make money transactions.

4 Experiments and Results

The MATLAB simulations to recognize the currency denomination are carried out on a 'GeForce MX150' CUDA device with a clock rate of 1.5 GHz. The real time implementation is done on a quad core Raspberry Pi ARM Cortex processor using Python programming.

The training uses a Stochastic Gradient Descent approach with an initial learning rate of 0.001 for a maximum batch size of 10 and the training is carried out for a maximum of six epochs with a validation frequency of 3. The currency note recognition is tested by segregating the data set into training and test data sets with different percentages ranging from 90% training data, 10% test data to 50% training data and 50% test data. The classification results of currency recognition with 90% training data and 10% test data are shown in Fig. 6.

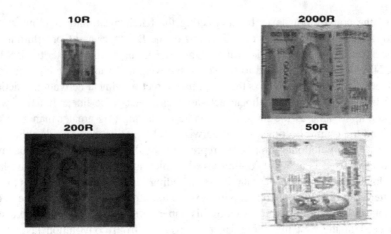

Fig. 6. Classification result with 90% training data and 10% test data

The training and validation of the proposed network with 90% training data is shown in Fig. 7.

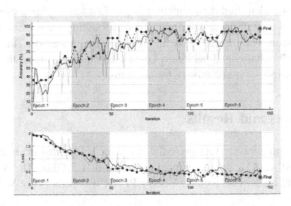

Fig. 7. Training and validation of CNN with 90% training data and 10% testing data

From Fig. 7, it is observed that the validation accuracy of the proposed CNN for 90% training data is 96%. The Confusion Matrix obtained for the classification of currency notes shown in Fig. 6 is shown in Fig. 8.

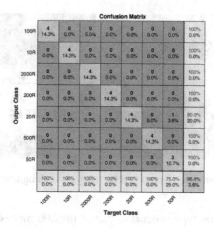

Fig. 8. Confusion matrix for 90% training data and 10% testing data

From the confusion matrix in Fig. 7 it is understood that the over all testing accuracy is 96.43% and the performance of the CNN is weak in classifying 20 rupees denomination. So, experiments are carried out with different sets of training and test data percentages and the corresponding testing and validation accuracies are given in Table 2.

Table 2. Testing and validation accuracy of proposed CNN

Training data (%)	Validation accuracy (%)	Testing accuracy (%)	Execution time (seconds)
90	96.43	96.4	9
80	83.93	94.6	9
70	86.9	97.6	10
60	75.89	93.8	11
50	85.7	92.5	12

From Table 2 it is observed that the performance of the CNN is better with 70% training data and 30% test data as it gives 97.6% testing accuracy with an execution time of 10 s. So, the proposed system uses this data to recognize the currency denomination and labels it. The label is then checked with the prestored mp3 files in the SD card of the Raspberry pi processor. So, the sound file with matched label is announced through the ear phones connected to the system. The prototype of the proposed system is shown in Fig. 9.

Fig. 9. Prototype of proposed currency note recognition system

The length of the prototype is equal to that of the 200 rupees note and the width is equal to that of the old 100 rupees note. A camera is placed on the top to capture the image of the currency note is processed for recognition and the denomination value is heard from the ear phones. The performance of the proposed system is tested with real users at Center for Visually Challenged, Bhimavaram and is found to be working well according to the requirements of the user.

5   Conclusion

In this paper, an Indian new currency denomination detection system using a custom-made Convolution Neural Networks is proposed. The proposed CNN architecture is able to classify the seven different classes of denomination with 97% testing accuracy and within 10 s of execution time. The identify denomination is given as an audio feedback so that the visually challenged and elderly people can identify the currency notes for their market transactions. The proposed system is tested with the actual end user and the results are found to be satisfactory. At present, the execution time of the recognition is 10 s, in future attempts will be made to reduce the execution time to 2 s as per the requirements of Reserve Bank of India.

References

1. Bourne, R.R.A., et al.: Magnitude, temporal trends, and projections of the global prevalence of blindness and distance and near vision impairment: a systematic review and meta-analysis. Lancet Glob. Health **5**(9), e888–e897 (2017). Vision Loss Expert Group
2. https://timesofindia.indiatimes.com/india/india-changes-definition-of-blindness-opts-for-who-criteria/articleshow/58262184.cms
3. Gogoi, M., Ali, S.E., Mukherjee, S.: Automatic Indian currency denomination recognition system based on artificial neural networks. In: 2nd International Conference on Signal Processing and Integrated Networks, Noida, India (2015)
4. Raval, V., Shah, A.P.: iCuｎe—an IoT application for Indian currency recognition in vernacular languages for visually challenged people. In: 2017 7th International Conference on Cloud Computing, Data Science & Engineering – Confluence, pp. 577–581 (2017)

5. Barani, S.: Currency identifier for Indian denominations to aid visually impaired. In: International Conference on Circuits, Power and Computing Technologies, Nagercoil, India (2015)
6. Deepak, M.P., Prajwala, N.B.: Identification of fake notes and denomination recognition. In: International Conference on Communication and Signal Processing, India, 3–5 April 2018 (2018)
7. Mittal, S., Mittal, S.: Indian banknote recognition using convolutional neural network, pp. 1–6 (2018). https://doi.org/10.1109/iot-siu.2018.8519888
8. https://m.economictimes.com/wealth/save/rbi-to-make-it-easier-for-visually-impaired-to-identify-bank-notes/articleshow/64479283.cms
9. https://www.rbi.org.in/Scripts/ic_banknotes.aspx

Secure and Energy-Efficient Key-Agreement Protocol for Multi-server Architecture

Trupil Limbasiya[✉] and Sanjay K. Sahay

BITS Pilani, Goa Campus, Zuarinagar, India
limbasiyatrupil@gmail.com, ssahay@goa.bits-pilani.ac.in

Abstract. Authentication schemes are practiced globally to verify the legitimacy of users and servers for the exchange of data in different facilities. Generally, the server verifies a user to provide resources for different purposes. But due to the large network system, the authentication process has become complex and therefore, time-to-time different authentication protocols have been proposed for the multi-server architecture. However, most of the protocols are vulnerable to various security attacks and their performance is not efficient. In this paper, we propose a secure and energy-efficient remote user authentication protocol for multi-server systems. The results show that the proposed protocol is comparatively ∼44% more efficient and needs ∼38% less communication cost. We also demonstrate that with only two-factor authentication, the proposed protocol is more secure from the earlier related authentication schemes.

Keywords: Authentication · Energy · Multi-server · Security

1 Introduction

In today's emerging world, the Internet has become more and more popular for its various facilities, and it is extensively used in government organizations, smart city applications, education sectors, business, private sectors, etc. Further, there are many applications in which users should get diverse services from different systems remotely, e.g., banking system, healthcare, smart agriculture, smart grid, home automation, etc. Consequently, the network has become highly sophisticated and demanding. Hence, it is not easy to fulfill all users' requirements at the same time, and it leads to the provision of multi-server based system through which applicants can get services any time without any interruption.

In general, server and user should authenticate each other before transmitting/delivering resources to prevent various attacks in a public environment. Therefore, a secure and efficient authentication scheme is required to confirm the legitimacy of the server and a user. In most of the systems, both (user and server) practice the authentication process before starting a communication [1–4]. Figure 1 shows a user-server connection representation for a multi-server

© Springer Nature Singapore Pte Ltd. 2020
S. K. Sahay et al. (Eds.): SKM 2019, CCIS 1186, pp. 82–97, 2020.
https://doi.org/10.1007/978-981-15-3817-9_6

environment in which various users are connected to different servers to obtain facility. These servers are typically synchronized with each other, and a user has a smart card to get authenticated by the server. In this scheme, a user cannot connect to multiple servers at the same time, but he/she can establish a connection with different servers alternatively as shown in Fig. 1.

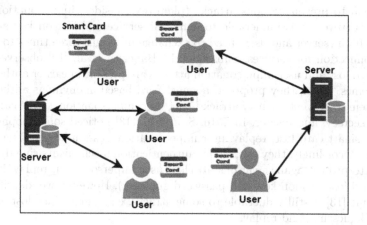

Fig. 1. User-server mutual authentication overview in multi-server based structure

1.1 Related Works

Li et al. [5] suggested an authentication system based on an artificial neural networks to resist a replay attack for the multi-server architecture. Lin et al. [6] recommended a new authentication protocol to protect a modification attack and a replay attack. Tsaur et al. [7] noticed that an off-line password guessing is feasible in their previous scheme and thus, they designed an improved authentication method to prevent an off-line password guessing attack. However, they [5–7] used the Diffie–Hellman key exchange concept for the encryption and decryption. Therefore, these schemes are vulnerable to man-in-the-middle, impersonation attacks. Besides, they requires high computational time to perform all necessary operations.

Juang [8] suggested a mutual authentication and key agreement system for the multiple server framework with low computation and communication cost. Besides, this scheme has various merits, i.e., only one-time registration, no need of a verification table, freely chosen password by a user, mutual authentication, low communication and computation cost. However, they used the symmetric key concept to design an authentication protocol [8] and thus, there is a key challenge to share the encryption/decryption key between the server and a user. Besides, the encrypted secret key is saved in a smart card. For all these reasons, the scheme [8] is vulnerable to smart card lost, replay, impersonation, and man-in-the-middle attacks.

Liao and Wang [9] proposed an authentication protocol to resist distinct attacks (replay, insider, server spoofing, and stolen verifier). However, Hsiang and Shi [10] found a server spoofing attack is feasible in [9] as discussed in [10]. To overcome server spoofing and session key attacks, they [10] suggested an enhanced remote user authentication method for the multi-server structure. In 2014, Lee et al. [11] came up with an extensive chaotic based authentication mechanism to prevent various attacks (plain-text, insider, impersonation, and replay). However, it is vulnerable to denial of service and session key attacks. Besides, both (server and user) need to exchange messages three times to establish a connection for services. Subsequently, Banerjee et al. [12] observed that smart card lost and user impersonation attacks are present in earlier authentication schemes. Then, they proposed a smart card-based anonymous authentication system to prevent security attacks, e.g., user impersonation, smart card lost, forward secrecy, and insider. In 2016, Sun et al. [13] noticed some loopholes in [12], i.e., smart card lost, replay, user impersonation, session key, and password guessing. Accordingly, they advised an authentication mechanism using dynamic identity to protect against various attacks (user impersonation, replay, insider, smart card lost, session key, and password guessing). However, we identify that the scheme [13] is still vulnerable to some attacks, e.g., smart card lost, off-line password guessing, and replay.

Li et al. [14] found security concerns (no single registration, no password update support, and spoofing) in [11] and proposed a chaotic based key-agreement scheme for enhancing security features. However, Irshad et al. [16] found security drawbacks (password guessing, stolen smart card, and user impersonation) in [14]. In addition, they proposed an advanced system to resist identified security concerns in [16]. However, Irshad et al.'s scheme [16] requires high computational time, storage cost, and communication overhead. Jangirala et al. [15] noticed some security issues in earlier system and advised an extended authentication protocol to enhance security. They also stated that the scheme [15] is resistant to multiple attacks (password guessing, stolen smart card, replay, man-in-the-middle, server spoofing, and forgery), but this scheme is weak in performance. Recently, Ying and Nayak [17] suggested a remote user authentication mechanism for multi-server architecture using self-certified public key cryptography to improve performance results, but this protocol is susceptible to different attacks, i.e., smart card lost, impersonation, replay, password guessing, session key disclosure, and insider. Moreover, comparatively it requires more computational resources.

1.2   Contributions

From the literature survey [11–17], we notice that most of authentication methods are vulnerable to different security attacks and they need more computational resources for the implementation. Thus, we understand that a secure and efficient remote user verification protocol is required for the multi server-based system to provide on-time services and to resist against various security attacks.

Therefore, we propose an energy-efficient and more secure remote user authentication scheme, and our contributions are as follows in this paper.

- Design an advanced energy-effective mutual authentication protocol.
- Security discussions to check strengths against different attacks, e.g., password guessing, replay, impersonation, insider, session key disclosure, smart card lost, and man-in-the-middle.
- Present performance analysis for the proposed method and do the comparison with relevant authentication schemes for different performance measures.

The paper is structured as follows. In Sect. 2, we explain the system architecture and the adversary model is described in Sect. 3. In Sect. 4, we propose an advanced authentication protocol using a smart card for multi-server based system. Section 5 discusses performance and security analysis of the suggested system. Then, we do a comparison of the suggested protocol with other related authentication schemes in terms of security and performance. We summarize our conclusions in Sect. 6.

2   System Architecture

The registration authority (RA), smart cards, smart card readers, and servers are components in the multi-server system. Users access resources from the server after proving their legitimacy and this data access can be carried out using a smart card through a smart card reader. The RA is a trusted authority in order to register a new user and to provide a legal smart card to that user. Servers are used to provide resources to the legal users and it is highly configured in security, processing power, and storage. A smart card is used to store some important values and these parameters help its owner to get resources/services from the server. In general, a smart card is used to establish a secure connection between a user and the server or to update a user password. The multi-server architecture based system is classified into three phases as (1) registration (2) login and authentication (3) password update. The registration phase is initiated by a new user to become a legitimate person of the system via a secure medium. The login and authentication phase is executed in the interest of a user to access resources from the server over a public channel. The password update phase is performed to change/update a user password via an insecure channel. Figure 2 shows an extensive system model overview for different phases by involving different actors.

3   Adversary Model

We consider an adversary model according to [2–4] for mutual authentication system between a user and the server in a public environment. Accordingly, an attacker has the following capabilities.

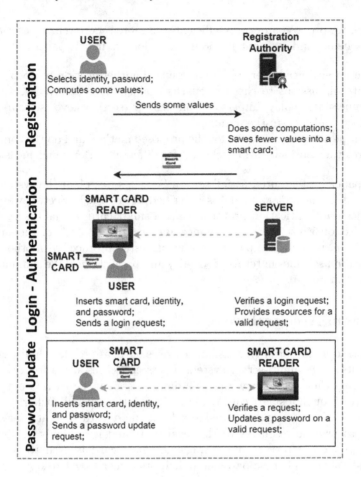

Fig. 2. The system architecture

- An adversary can read/delay/re-transmit packets (transferred over a public channel).
- An attacker has the ability to extract parameters from a smart card. And this is feasible after stealing a smart card or getting a lost smart card.
- An adversary can modify messages, which are transmitted through an insecure medium.
- An attacker can send a forged login request in a polynomial time.

4   The Proposed Scheme

We suggest an energy-efficient remote user authentication protocol for multi-server based system to resist various security attacks. The proposed scheme consists of four phases, (1) server registration, (2) user registration, (3) login and authentication, and (4) user password update as follows. Table 1 shows different notations.

Table 1. List of different symbols

Notations	Explanations
U_i	A user i
ID_i	U_i's identity
PW_i	U_i's password
S_j	A server j
SC_i	U_i's smart card
SCR_k	A smart card reader k
$N_i/N_j/b/p_i$	Random nonce
x/y	A server's secret key
y_i	U_i's secret key generated by RA
SK_{U_i}	A session key at U_i end
SK_{S_j}	A session key at S_j side
$List_{ID_i}$	The list of user identities
$List_{F_i}$	The list of computed values F_i
$\mathcal{A}$	An adversary/attacker
$\oplus$	Bit-wise XOR operation
$\|$	Concatenation operation
$h(\cdot)$	One-way hash function
ΔT_a	A threshold delay fixed at time a
T_b	Generated time-stamp at time b

4.1 Server Registration

In the multi-server architecture, different servers should be registered with the registration authority (RA) via an online secure channel. The server registration process is as follows.

1. A server (S_j) chooses an identity (ID_{S_j}) and password (PWD_{S_j}), and random nonce (x_j). Then, S_j computes $\alpha_j = h(ID_{S_j}\|PWD_{S_j}\|x_j)$ and sends $\{ID_{S_j}, \alpha_j\}$ to the RA.
2. The RA confirms the availability of ID_{S_j} and if it is, then the RA does $\beta_j = \alpha_j \oplus ID_{S_j}$, and saves β_j, α_j, $List_{ID_i}$, $List_{F_i}$ in the S_j's secure storage.

4.2 User Registration

A new user (U_i) of the system should enroll with the registration authority (RA) once to become a legal user over a secure channel. U_i gets a smart card (SC_i) after completing the registration process successfully and this SC_i helps to get logged into the system for services. This phase is also shown in Fig. 3.

1. U_i selects ID_i, PW_i, p_i and calculates $A_i = p_i \oplus h(ID_i\|PW_i)$, $B_i = h(PW_i\|p_i)$. Then, U_i sends $\{ID_i, A_i, B_i\}$ to the RA over a secure channel.

2. The RA generates a random nonce (say q_i for U_i) and enumerates $C_i = A_i \oplus h(q_i||x)$, $D_i = C_i \oplus B_i \oplus ID_i$, $E_i = A_i \oplus B_i \oplus h(q_i||x)$, $F_i = ID_i \oplus A_i \oplus C_i$. After that, it saves A_i, D_i, E_i, $List_{IDs_j}$ into SC_i and F_i into the database securely. Next, the RA sends SC_i to U_i via a secure medium.

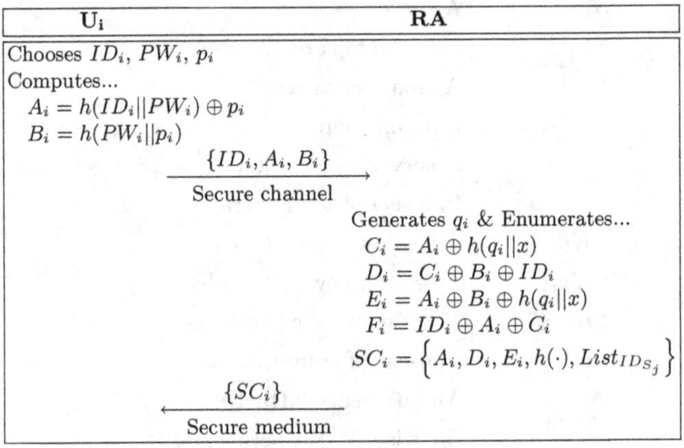

U_i	RA
Chooses ID_i, PW_i, p_i	
Computes...	
$\quad A_i = h(ID_i||PW_i) \oplus p_i$	
$\quad B_i = h(PW_i||p_i)$	
$\xrightarrow{\quad \{ID_i, A_i, B_i\} \quad}$	
Secure channel	
	Generates q_i & Enumerates...
	$\quad C_i = A_i \oplus h(q_i||x)$
	$\quad D_i = C_i \oplus B_i \oplus ID_i$
	$\quad E_i = A_i \oplus B_i \oplus h(q_i||x)$
	$\quad F_i = ID_i \oplus A_i \oplus C_i$
	$\quad SC_i = \left\{ A_i, D_i, E_i, h(\cdot), List_{IDs_j} \right\}$
$\xleftarrow{\quad \{SC_i\} \quad}$	
Secure medium	

Fig. 3. The proposed registration phase

4.3   Login and Authentication

When U_i wants to access service(s) from the server (S_j), this phase is executed between a smart card reader (SCR_k) and S_j. For this, U_i/SCR_k performs following steps. Figure 4 presents the proposed login and authentication phase.

1. U_i puts SC_i, ID_i, and PW_i into SCR_k. Then, SCR_k computes $p_i' = h(ID_i||PW_i) \oplus A_i$, $B_i' = h(PW_i||p_i')$, $C_i' = B_i' \oplus D_i \oplus ID_i$, $h(q_i||x) = C_i' \oplus A_i$, $E_i' = A_i \oplus B_i' \oplus h(q_i||x)$. Now, SCR_k checks the correctness by comparing E_i and E_i'. If both are equal, SCR_k generates N_i and enumerates $AID_i = ID_i \oplus IDS_j$, $G_i = N_i \oplus C_i' \oplus A_i$, $H_i = G_i \oplus h(SID_j||N_i||T_1)$, $I_i = N_i \oplus p_i' \oplus ID_i$, $J_i = h(G_i||H_i||I_i||p_i'||T_1)$. Then, it sends $\{ID_i, G_i, I_i, J_i, T_1\}$ to S_j publicly.
2. S_j confirms the validity of $\{ID_i, F_i, H_i, I_i, T_1\}$ by calculating $T_2 - T_1 \leq \Delta T_1$. If it is valid, then it computes $ID_i = \beta_j \oplus AID_i \oplus \alpha_j$, $N_i' = F_i \oplus G_i \oplus ID_i$, $H_i' = G_i \oplus h(SID_j||N_i'||T_1)$, $p_i' = N_i' \oplus ID_i \oplus I_i$, $J_i' = h(G_i||H_i'||I_i||p_i'||T_1)$. Further, S_j performs $J_i' \overset{?}{=} J_i$ for the verification. S_j continues to the next step in case of equality. Otherwise, it ends the session immediately.
3. S_j generates N_j and enumerates $K_j = N_i' \oplus N_j \oplus p_i'$, $M_j = h(K_j||N_i'||N_j||J_i'||T_2)$. Subsequently, it transfers $\{K_j, M_j, T_2\}$ to U_i.

4. SCR_k calculates $T_3 - T_2 \leq \Delta T_2$ to check its freshness. And it computes $N'_j = N_i \oplus K_j \oplus p'_i$, $M'_j = h(K_j||N_i||N'_j||J_i||T_2)$ and verifies M'_j by comparing with M_j. If it holds, then SCR_k and S_j generates a session key as $h(ID_i||SID_j||N_i||N_j||p'_i||H_i||\Delta T_1)$. Ultimately, SCR_k and S_j communicate based on this session key for a limited period.

4.4 Password Update

The password change is a facility for the system users to update their PW_i for different reason(s) later. For this, U_i should imitate following steps.

1. U_i inserts SC_i, ID_i, and PW_i into SCR_k. Then, SCR_k enumerates $p'_i = h(ID_i||PW_i) \oplus A_i$, $B'_i = h(PW_i||p'_i)$, $C'_i = B'_i \oplus D_i \oplus ID_i$, $h(q_i||x) = C'_i \oplus A_i$, $E'_i = A_i \oplus B'_i \oplus h(q_i||x)$. Now, SCR_k performs $E_i \overset{?}{=} E'_i$ to confirm equality. If it holds, SCR_k asks for a new password (PW_{New_i}) and computes $A_{New_i} = h(ID_i||PW_{New_i}) \oplus p'_i$, $B_{New_i} = h(PW_{New_i}||p'_i)$, $C_{New_i} = A_{New_i} \oplus h(q_i||x)$, $D_{New_i} = B_{New_i} \oplus ID_i \oplus C_{New_i}$, $E_{New_i} = A_{New_i} \oplus h(q_i||x) \oplus B_{New_i}$. After that, SCR_k replaces A_i, D_i, and E_i by A_{New_i}, D_{New_i}, E_{New_i} into SC_i. Finally, U_i will have updated SC_i.

5 Analysis of the Proposed Scheme

After proposing an advanced authentication system, we do analysis on this protocol to verify security robustness and performance efficiency. For this confirmation, we have discussed security analysis and performance analysis as below.

5.1 Security Analysis

We explain various security attacks and how the proposed system is resistant to different attacks. Then, we compare security robustness of the suggested scheme with other related authentication mechanisms [11–16].

Password Guessing. If an adversary ($\mathcal{A}$) can identify the correctness of a guessed password (PW'_i), then a password guessing attack is possible. SCR_k sends $\{ID_i, G_i, I_i, J_i, T_1\}$ to S_j over an open channel. Therefore, $\mathcal{A}$ has access to these parameters. To become a successful in this attack, $\mathcal{A}$ needs to compare PW'_i at least with one variable in which PW_i has been used and that parameter should be available publicly. G_i is computed using PW_i indirectly and thus, $\mathcal{A}$ has an opportunity to know correctness of PW'_i if he or she can get/derive/compute G'_i. For this, $\mathcal{A}$ requires N_i, C_i, A_i. However, N_i and p'_i are generated randomly at U_i end, and these random values are only known to U_i. Therefore, it is difficult to obtain A_i and N_i exactly. Further, $\mathcal{A}$ does not have essential credentials (B_i and D_i) to compute C_i. Hence, it is infeasible to derive G'_i by having only PW'_i. Consequently, $\mathcal{A}$ has no opportunity to compare G'_i. For this reason, $\mathcal{A}$ cannot apply a password guessing attack in the suggested system.

U_i/SCR_k	S_j
Inserts ID_i & PW_i	
Enumerates...	
$\quad p_i' = h(ID_i\|PW_i) \oplus A_i$	
$\quad B_i' = h(PW_i\|p_i')$	
$\quad C_i' = B_i' \oplus D_i \oplus ID_i$	
$\quad h(q_i\|x) = C_i' \oplus A_i$	
$\quad E_i' = A_i \oplus B_i' \oplus h(q_i\|x)$	
$E_i' \stackrel{?}{=} E_i$	
$\quad$ Generates N_i	
$\quad AID_i = ID_i \oplus ID_{S_j}$	
$\quad G_i = N_i \oplus C_i' \oplus A_i$	
$\quad H_i = G_i \oplus h(SID_j\|N_i\|T_1)$	
$\quad I_i = N_i \oplus p_i' \oplus ID_i$	
$\quad J_i = h(G_i\|H_i\|I_i\|p_i'\|T_1)$	
$\xrightarrow{\quad\{AID_i, G_i, I_i, J_i, T_1\}\quad}$	
Open Channel	
	$T_2 - T_1 \leq \Delta T_1$
	$ID_i = \alpha_j \oplus AID_i \oplus \beta_j$
	$N_i' = F_i \oplus G_i \oplus ID_i$
	$H_i' = G_i \oplus h(SID_j\|N_i'\|T_1)$
	$p_i' = N_i' \oplus ID_i \oplus I_i$
	$J_i' = h(G_i\|H_i'\|I_i\|p_i'\|T_1)$
	$J_i' \stackrel{?}{=} J_i$
	Generates N_j
	$K_j = N_i' \oplus N_j \oplus p_i'$
	$M_j = h(K_j\|N_i'\|N_j\|J_i'\|T_2)$
$\xleftarrow{\quad\{K_j, M_j, T_2\}\quad}$	
Open Channel	
$T_3 - T_2 \leq \Delta T_2$	
Calculates...	
$\quad N_j' = N_i \oplus K_j \oplus p_i'$	
$\quad M_j' = h(K_j\|N_i\|N_j'\|J_i\|T_2)$	
$M_j' \stackrel{?}{=} M_j$	
$SK_{U_i} = SK_{S_j} = h(ID_i\|SID_j\|N_i\|N_j\|p_i'\|H_i\|\Delta T_1)$	

Fig. 4. The proposed login and authentication

User Impersonation. A user impersonation attack is feasible if $\mathcal{A}$ has a favorable plan to create a fake login request, and it should be accepted by S_j. For this, $\mathcal{A}$ should know or compute ID_i, G_i, I_i, J_i in the proposed model. First of all, T_1 is used in H_i and J_i. Therefore, $\mathcal{A}$ needs to compute these variables (J_i and H_i) to forge a login request. As a result, s/he requires some amount of time to forge a request or generate a fake login request in future. Accordingly, s/he should use fresh time-stamp (say T_1'). In order to work out for forged parameters (J_i' and H_i'), $\mathcal{A}$ needs G_i, N_i, p_i'. Here, G_i is calculated as $N_i \oplus A_i \oplus C_i'$ and hence, $\mathcal{A}$ should know A_i and C_i' additionally. In the proposed method, N_i and p_i' are randomly generated numbers. Moreover, $\mathcal{A}$ is not able to enumerate C_i' and A_i due to unavailability of essential credentials (B_i, p_i', PW_i, and D_i). For these reasons, an adversary cannot obtain required credentials anyhow and thus, s/he is restricted to forge H_i and I_i. Additionally, S_j confirms the validity of a login request. As a result, $\mathcal{A}$ fails to make feasible a user impersonation attack in the proposed method.

Replay. In the proposed scheme, we have used the concept of a time-stamp to identify transaction time. Here, SCR_k sends $\{ID_i, J_i, G_i, I_i, T_1\}$ to S_j over an open medium and S_j transfers $\{M_j, K_j, T_2\}$ to SCR_k via an insecure channel. Thus, $\mathcal{A}$ can attempt to stop or delay this request/response. However, S_j confirms validity of $\{ID_i, G_i, I_i, J_i, T_1\}$ by executing $\Delta T_1 \leq T_2 - T_1$. Similarly, SCR_k proceeds further after verifying (by calculating ΔT_2) the reasonableness of $\{M_j, K_j, T_2\}$. If SCR_k does not get a response message from S_j within a reasonable time, then U_i understands that $\mathcal{A}$ has tried to interrupt $\{ID_i, J_i, I_i, G_i, T_1\}$ and after that, SCR_k terminates the session directly. It means that if $\mathcal{A}$ tries to perform a replay attack, it will be identified at the receiver side. Additionally, $\mathcal{A}$ cannot change T_1 in the request or T_2 in the response message because these time-stamps are used in H_i, J_i, M_j and these parameters are confirmed at the receiver end. Furthermore, $\mathcal{A}$ does not have essential credentials to calculate H_i, J_i, M_j. After these considerations, an adversary is not able to perform a replay attack in the advised protocol.

Smart Card Lost. This attack is applicable if $\mathcal{A}$ can deal with S_j mutually and successfully after sending a bogus login request. We assume that a legitimate user (U_i) can lose his/her SC_i or someone can steal SC_i. Therefore, $\mathcal{A}$ has knowledge of SC_i variables (A_i, D_i, E_i) and common channel parameters (ID_i, T_2, G_i, T_1, I_i, J_i, K_j, M_j) according to the suggested protocol for this attack. Here, $\mathcal{A}$ should compute a login request in such a way on which S_j should be agreed to process further. U_i sends $\{ID_i, J_i, I_i, G_i, T_1\}$ to S_j as a login message. These values are calculated as $J_i = h(G_i||H_i||I_i||p_i'||T_1)$, $I_i = N_i \oplus p_i' \oplus ID_i$, $H_i = G_i \oplus h(SID_j||N_i||T_1)$. Now, $\mathcal{A}$ needs G_i, N_i, p_i' for enumerating H_i' and J_i'. But $\mathcal{A}$ does not find any proficiency to obtain/calculate these credentials without knowing B_i, p_i', PW_i, N_i, and D_i (see Sect. 5.1.2). Additionally, S_j checks freshness of a received login request. If ($T_2 - T_1$) is beyond ΔT_1, then S_j discards that request immediately. Hence, $\mathcal{A}$ cannot proceed to generate a valid login request and this stops to an adversary for further process. In this fashion, the proposed model is protected against a smart card lost attack.

Session Key Disclosure. If $\mathcal{A}$ can generate/compute a valid session key, then there is a possibility of a session key disclosure attack. A session key is calculated as $SK_{U_i}/SK_{S_j} = h(ID_i||SID_j||N_i||N_j||p_i'||H_i||\Delta T_1)$ in the suggested scheme. Thus, $\mathcal{A}$ should know p_i', ΔT_1, N_i, H_i, and N_j in order to compute it illegally. We consider that ID_i and SID_j are identity values of U_i and S_j and thus, these variables are known to $\mathcal{A}$ generally. Next, ΔT_1 is the difference between T_2 and T_1. Hence, it is also available to an attacker. However, $\mathcal{A}$ does not have N_i, N_j, p'_i, and H_i. In the proposed method, p'_i, N_i, and N_j are random numbers and these are only known to U_i and S_j for a limited time and for this session only. Further, both (U_i and S_j) are agreed on N_j and N_i for a fixed period. Accordingly, it is hard to know/get these random values. In the proposed method, H_i is computed as $h(SID_j||N_i||T_1) \oplus G_i$ and therefore, $\mathcal{A}$ cannot calculate H_i correctly without having N_i. For these reasons, $\mathcal{A}$ is unable to proceed for a session key (SK_{S_j} / SK_{U_i}) anyway. After this analysis, a session key disclosure attack is not feasible in the proposed system.

Man-in-the-Middle. If a person can understand transmitted request/response messages in public environment, then this attack is considerable. In the proposed mechanism, SCR_k transmits $\{ID_i, J_i, G_i, I_i, T_1\}$ to S_j and S_j responses to SCR_k as $\{M_j, K_j, T_2\}$ through an open channel. Therefore, $\mathcal{A}$ can know ID_i, T_1, and T_2 based on these transactions. ID_i is a user's identity and it can be identifiable generally. T_2 and T_1 are time-stamps and these time-stamps are not profitable to $\mathcal{A}$ effectively because T_1 and T_2 are valid for a limited period only. Accordingly, both (S_j and U_i) do not consider T_1/T_2 for further process or do not accept any request/response beyond $\Delta T_1/\Delta T_2$. Next, $\mathcal{A}$ needs other vital credentials (e.g., PW_i, p'_i, N_i, $h(q_i||x)$) to understand G_i, J_i, and I_i. Similarly, $\mathcal{A}$ requires N_j, N_i, $h(q_i||x)$, G'_i for M_j and K_j. But $\mathcal{A}$ cannot obtain these private values based on public channel parameters. Consequently, an attacker fails to work out for a man-in-the-middle attack in the suggested method.

Insider. If an authorized user can compute a valid login request using his/her own credentials for another legal user, then an insider attack can be applied in the system. We consider two legitimate users (U_A and U_i) in the proposed scheme and U_A acts an adversary to impersonate U_i. U_A has his/her SC_A and s/he knows SC_A values (A_A, D_A, E_A). In general, U_i sends a login request to S_j via a public channel. Therefore, U_A has knowledge of ID_i, J_i, G_i, I_i, T_1. To get access of system resources behalf of U_i, U_A needs to compute a fake login request freshly and this request should be accepted by S_j to generate a session key mutually. For this, U_A should enumerate I_i, J_i, and G_i correctly so that S_j will be agreed on these values legitimately. U_A should know N_i, ID_i, p'_i (for I_i), G_i, H_i, I_i, p'_i (for J_i), and A_i, N_i, C_i (for G_i). We have already described that $\mathcal{A}$ cannot get N_i, A_i, C_i, p'_i, H_i (see Sect. 5.1.2). Similarly, U_A is not able to get relevant credentials. Additionally, a time-stamp is used in the suggested method. Next, q_i is a random nonce and it is not known to anyone in the proposed system. Further, q_i is concatenated with x and then, S_j has performed a one-way hash operation. Accordingly, it is difficult to know q_i of U_i. In this fashion, U_A fails to calculate a bogus login request. Thus, the suggested scheme can withstand to an insider attack.

Table 2 shows a comparison in terms of different security attributes. A smart card lost attack is feasible in [12–15]. Authentication schemes [11–13]

Table 2. Security features of various authentications protocols

Schemes	Security attributes								
	A1	A2	A3	A4	A5	A6	A7	A8	A9
Lee et al. [11]	✓	X	X	✓	✓	✓	✓	Yes	No
Banerjee et al. [12]	X	X	X	✓	X	X	X	Yes	No
Sun et al. [13]	X	X	X	X	✓	✓	X	Yes	No
Li et al. [14]	X	✓	X	X	X	✓	✓	Yes	No
Jangirala et al. [15]	X	X	X	X	✓	✓	✓	Yes	No
Irshad et al. [16]	★	✓	★	X	X	✓	✓	No	Yes
Ying and Nayak [17]	X	X	X	X	X	✓	X	Yes	No
Proposed	✓	✓	✓	✓	✓	✓	✓	Yes	No

A1: Smart card lost; A2: Impersonation; A3: Password guessing; A4: Replay; A5: Session key disclosure; A6: Man-in-the-middle; A7: Insider; A8: Two-factor authentication; A9: Three-factor authentication; ✓: Secure; X: Vulnerable; ★: Insecure without biometric-identity.

are vulnerable to an impersonation attack. An adversary has an opportunity to confirm a guessed password in [11–15] easily. The schemes [13–16]cannot withstand against a replay attack. A session key disclosure attack can be performed in [12,14], and [16]. Banerjee et al.'s scheme [12] is also weak against a man-in-the-middle attack. A legitimate person acts as an adversary to perform an insider attack in [12] and [13]. A biometric identity is used in [16] to enhance security but it fails to resist attacks (replay and session key disclosure). Additionally, if we consider that a biometric identity can be forged, then two other attacks (smart card lost and a password guessing) are partially possible in [16]. In this way, various authentication schemes [11–16] are insecure against various attacks. However, the proposed scheme can withstand against different security attacks as mentioned in Table 2. Further, the suggested protocol can achieve this security level using two-factor authentication only. Therefore, the proposed method is more secure compared to other schemes.

5.2   Performance Analysis

We explain different performance measure, i.e., execution time, storage cost, and communication overhead. Then, we present outcomes of various remote user authentication mechanisms based on these performance parameters.

Execution Time. It is depended on the total number of needed cryptographic operations to carry out the authentication procedure. In this computational cost, most of the verification schemes have used four different cryptographic functions, e.g., one-way hash $(T_{h(\cdot)})$, elliptic curve cryptography (T_{EC}), concatenation $(T_{||})$, chebyshev chaotic (T_{CC}), and Ex-OR $(T_{\oplus})$. Generally, these operations expect

Table 3. Execution Cost Comparison for different verification schemes

Schemes	Registration	Login and Authentication
Lee et al. [11]	$3T_{h(\cdot)}$ ($\approx$1.74 ms)	$11T_{h(\cdot)} + 6T_{CC}$ ($\approx$132.62 ms)
Banerjee et al. [12]	$7T_{h(\cdot)}$ ($\approx$4.06 ms)	$17T_{h(\cdot)}$ ($\approx$9.86 ms)
Sun et al. [13]	$6T_{h(\cdot)}$ ($\approx$3.48 ms)	$18T_{h(\cdot)}$ ($\approx$10.44 ms)
Li et al. [14]	$3T_{h(\cdot)}$ ($\approx$1.74 ms)	$19T_{h(\cdot)} + 6T_{CC}$ ($\approx$137.26 ms)
Jangirala et al. [15]	$7T_{h(\cdot)}$ ($\approx$4.06 ms)	$23T_{h(\cdot)}$ ($\approx$13.34 ms)
Irshad et al. [16]	$3T_{h(\cdot)}$ ($\approx$1.74 ms)	$29T_{h(\cdot)} + 6T_{CC}$ ($\approx$143.06 ms)
Ying and Nayak [17]	$4T_{h(\cdot)} + 2T_{EC}$ ($\approx$77.76 ms)	$9T_{h(\cdot)} + 7T_{EC}$ ($\approx$269.26 ms)
Proposed	$3T_{h(\cdot)}$ ($\approx$1.74 ms)	$10T_{h(\cdot)}$ ($\approx$5.80 ms)

some amount of time in the execution. We consider the running time based on a specific system configuration, i.e., the Ubuntu 12.04.1 32-bit OS, 2 GB RAM with Intel 2.4 GHz CPU [16]. The pairing-based cryptography library is inherited for cryptographic operations. After noting down a running time of these functions, we do not include a computing time for $T_{||}$ and $T_{\oplus}$ because they need highly negligible time to accomplish an operation compared to other functions (T_{EC}, T_{CC}, and $T_{h(\cdot)}$). Therefore, we consider only $T_{h(\cdot)}$, T_{EC}, and T_{CC} for the implementation time and these functions expect 0.58 ms (ms), 37.72 ms and 21.04 ms respectively. The comparability between varied authentication schemes ([11–16], and the suggested method) is appeared in Table 3. In general, the registration phase is executed once only but the login and authentication process is performed when a legitimate user wants access system resources. Therefore, we mainly focus on the execution time of the login and authentication phase. After looking requirement of different cryptographic functions in Table 3, Banerjee et al.'s scheme [12] takes less execution time (i.e., 9.86 ms) compared to other authentication methods [11,13–16], and [17]. Next, the scheme [13] requires 10.44 ms to complete the login and authentication phase. Although these protocols [12] and [13] are vulnerable to various attacks (see Table 2). However, the suggested method can be implemented in 5.80 ms and it is safe against different security attacks (see Sect. 5.1). Thus, the proposed protocol can be executed rapidly rather than other mentioned authentication systems.

Storage Cost. During the registration or the initialization phase, the registration authority stores some credentials into SC_i and for this, the system needs to reserve a specified number of bytes. An identity/random nonce variable needs 8 bytes, a chebyshev chaotic function requires 16 bytes, elliptic curve (EC) needs 64 bytes, and 32 bytes (SHA-2) are expected as a storage cost. Lee et al.'s scheme [11] requires 2 (one-way hash), 1 (time-stamp), and 3 (identity/normal) variables. Banerjee et al.'s model [12] and Sun et al.'s system [13] need 5 (one-way hash) and 1 (identity) variables individually. Li et al.'s mechanism [14] expects 1 (time-stamp), 3 (one-way hash), and 2 (identity/normal)variables. 5 (one-way hash) and 2 (normal) parameters are needed in [15]. Irshad et al.'s protocol [16] requires 3 (one-way hash), 3 (identity/normal), and 1 (chebyshev chaotic) variables. The protocol [17] requires 3 (EC), 2 (one-way hash), and 1 (random nonce).

However, the suggested system needs to save only four (computed using a one-way hash) and one (normal) parameters. Figure 5 shows required storage memory (in bytes) for various authentication models individually. In general, the system saves different credentials into the smart card once. Consequently, this is a one-time process only. Lee et al.'s scheme [11] needs 92 bytes in storage, which is ~19% less compared to the suggested method but the scheme [11] is weak to two security attacks (password guessing and impersonation) and it expects very high implementation time (see Table 3).

Communication Overhead. In the login and authentication procedure, both (sender and receiver) transmits different parameters in order to generate a common session key and therefore, they require to spend essential bytes as a communication overhead. An identity variable needs 8 bytes, EC requires 64 bytes, a chebyshev chaotic function expects 16 bytes, a time-stamp requires 4 bytes, and 32 bytes (*SHA-2*) are needed for a one-way hash during the communication. Lee et al.'s method [11] can be performed using 3 (chebyshev chaotic) and 5 (one-way hash) parameters. The schemes ([12] and [13]) require 7 (one-way hash) variables separately. Li et al.'s system [14] needs 1 (identity), 13 (one-way hash), and 4 (chebyshev chaotic) parameters. The scheme [15] can be carried out with 7 (one-way hash) variables. Irshad et al.'s system [16] expects 16 (one-way hash), 1 (identity), and 4 (chebyshev chaotic) parameters. Ying and Nayak's scheme [17] needs 5 (EC), 1 (identity), and 2 (one-way hash).

However, the proposed protocol can be implemented using only three (identity), three (one-way hash), and two (time-stamp) variables. The communication cost comparison is shown in Fig. 5. Lee et al.'s scheme [11] requires 208 bytes for communication but the communication overhead is ~38% less in the suggested protocol compared to [11]. Thus, the proposed method needs less energy to provide services.

Energy Consumption. During the authentication phase, the system takes a fixed amount of energy to execute various operations and to send different parameters. This is known as the energy consumption and it is measured in millijoule (mJ). The energy consumption is calculated as $EC_{EXE} = (V * I * t)$ for the execution cost and $EC_{CC} = (V * I * m)/(D_r)$ for communication cost. Where, V = voltage power, I = current, t = the execution time, m = message size, and D_r = data rate (6100 Kbps). If the authentication protocol takes low execution time and less communication overhead, then it consumes less energy compared to other authentication schemes. The proposed protocol needs 5.80 ms as the execution time and 128 bytes in the communication, which are less compared to other authentication mechanisms [11–13,15–17]. Therefore, the proposed scheme is also energy-efficient compared to other protocols.

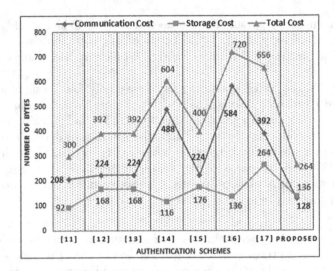

Fig. 5. Communication and storage cost demand for distinct authentication systems.

6 Conclusion

We have proposed a secure and energy-efficient remote user authentication protocol for the multi-server based system. Security analysis of the proposed system is done, and it is shown that our model resists various attacks, i.e., password guessing, impersonation, insider, man-in-the-middle, replay, smart card lost, and session key disclosure even without biometric identity. After analyzing the performance, the results show that the suggested scheme is implemented at least ~44% more efficiently compared to relevant schemes. Further, the proposed system comparatively requires ~42% less communication overhead and ~19% less storage space. Accordingly, the proposed method consumes less energy in the authentication process. To make the multi-server authentication mechanism more attack-proof, we are working to enhance the security and efficiency of the multi-server authentication system, by analyzing meet-in-the-middle and side-channel attacks, etc.

References

1. Lamport, L.: Password authentication with insecure communication. Commun. ACM **24**(11), 770–772 (1981)
2. Messerges, T.S., Dabbish, E.A., Sloan, R.H.: Examining smart-card security under the threat of power analysis attacks. IEEE Trans. Comput. **51**(5), 541–552 (2002)
3. Madhusudhan, R., Mittal, R.C.: Dynamic ID-based remote user password authentication schemes using smart cards: a review. J. Netw. Comput. Appl. **35**(4), 1235–1248 (2012)
4. Limbasiya, T., Doshi, N.: An analytical study of biometric based remote user authentication schemes using smart cards. Comput. Electr. Eng. **59**, 305–321 (2017)

5. Li, L.H., Lin, L.C., Hwang, M.S.: A remote password authentication scheme for multiserver architecture using neural networks. IEEE Trans. Neural Netw. **12**(6), 1498–1504 (2001)
6. Lin, I.C., Hwang, M.S., Li, L.H.: A new remote user authentication scheme for multi-server architecture. Future Gener. Comput. Syst. **19**(1), 13–22 (2003)
7. Tsaur, W.J., Wu, C.C., Lee, W.B.: An enhanced user authentication scheme for multi-server internet services. Appl. Math. Comput. **170**(1), 258–266 (2005)
8. Juang, W.S.: Efficient multi-server password authenticated key agreement using smart cards. IEEE Trans. Consum. Electron. **50**(1), 251–255 (2004)
9. Liao, Y.P., Wang, S.S.: A secure dynamic ID based remote user authentication scheme for multi-server environment. Comput. Stand. Interfaces **31**(1), 24–29 (2009)
10. Hsiang, H.C., Shih, W.K.: Improvement of the secure dynamic ID based remote user authentication scheme for multi-server environment. Comput. Stand. Interfaces **31**(6), 1118–1123 (2009)
11. Lee, C.C., Lou, D.C., Li, C.T., Hsu, C.W.: An extended chaotic-maps-based protocol with key agreement for multiserver environments. Nonlinear Dyn. **76**(1), 853–866 (2014)
12. Banerjee, S., Dutta, M.P., Bhunia, C.T.: An improved smart card based anonymous multi-server remote user authentication scheme. Int. J. Smart Home **9**(5), 11–22 (2015)
13. Sun, Q., Moon, J., Choi, Y., Won, D.: An improved dynamic ID based remote user authentication scheme for multi-server environment. In: Huang, X., Xiang, Y., Li, K.-C. (eds.) GPC 2016. LNCS, vol. 9663, pp. 229–242. Springer, Cham (2016). https://doi.org/10.1007/978-3-319-39077-2_15
14. Li, X., et al.: A novel chaotic maps-based user authentication and key agreement protocol for multi-server environments with provable security. Wirel. Pers. Commun. **89**(2), 569–597 (2016)
15. Jangirala, S., Mukhopadhyay, S., Das, A.K.: A Multi-server environment with secure and efficient remote user authentication scheme based on dynamic ID using smart cards. Wirel. Pers. Commun. **95**(3), 2735–2767 (2017)
16. Irshad, A., et al.: An enhanced and provably secure chaotic map-based authenticated key agreement in multi-server architecture. Arab. J. Sci. Eng. **43**(2), 811–828 (2018)
17. Ying, B., Nayak, A.: Lightweight remote user authentication protocol for multi-server 5G networks using self-certified public key cryptography. J. Netw. Comput. Appl. **131**, 66–74 (2019)

Access Control Models

A Formal Specification of Access Control in Android

Samir Talegaon[✉] and Ram Krishnan

University of Texas at San Antonio, San Antonio, USA
{samir.talegaon,ram.krishnan}@utsa.edu

Abstract. A formal specification of any access control system enables deeper understanding of that system and facilitates performing security analysis. In this paper, we provide a comprehensive formal specification of the Android mobile operating system's access control system, a widely used mobile OS. Prior work is limited in scope, in addition recent developments in Android concerning dynamic runtime permissions require rethinking of its formalization. Our formal specification includes two parts, the User-Initiated Operations (UIOs) and Application-Initiated Operations (AIOs), which are segregated based on the entity that initiates those operation. Formalizing ACiA allowed us to discover many peculiar behaviors in Android's access control system. In addition to that, we discovered two significant issues with permissions in Android which were reported to Google.

Keywords: Android · Permissions · Access control · Formal model

1 Introduction and Motivation

Android is a widely popular mobile OS; Android regulates access to its components and end-user resources with a permission based mechanism. A formal specification for access control in Android (AciA) facilitates a deeper understanding of the nature in which Android regulates app access to resources.Prior work targeting such formalization of the permission mechanism exists, but is limited in its scope since most of it is based on the older install time permission system [7,10,12,13]. Hence, detailed analysis and testing needs to be conducted to build this model, to enable a systematic review for security vulnerabilities.

Users install apps in Android which enable them to fully utilize the device features; and, permission based access control in Android (ACiA) works to regulate app access to sensitive resources. Android contains a wide variety of software resources such as access to the Internet, contacts on the phone, pictures and videos etc., and hardware resources such as Bluetooth, NFC, WiFi, Camera etc. The apps installed by the users require access to these resources for achieving full functionality and they request it from the OS. The OS in turn seeks user interaction to approve some of these requests and grant the necessary permissions to the apps [4,11]; this is illustrated in Fig. 1.

© Springer Nature Singapore Pte Ltd. 2020
S. K. Sahay et al. (Eds.): SKM 2019, CCIS 1186, pp. 101–125, 2020.
https://doi.org/10.1007/978-981-15-3817-9_7

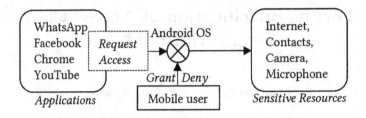

Fig. 1. Permission-based access control in Android

Formalization of ACiA is a non trivial task, and one that has received limited attention, apart from the fact that much of this work has limitations with respect to the current ACiA, due to the major changes in ACiA with the introduction of runtime permissions and non-holistic nature of the work. We believe that the formal specification of Android obtained from documentation as well as the source code has not been done comprehensively, that includes all the aspects of ACiA such as User Initiated Operations (UIO) and Application Initiated Operations (AIO). Our analysis also enables a holistic and systematic review of ACiA security policies and facilitates the discovery of loopholes in ACiA.

Our Contribution: We present a formal specification of ACiA that enables its analysis from the point of view of security. This model (ACiA$_\alpha$) sheds a light on the internal access control structure of the Android OS with respect to apps, permissions and uri permissions. Without such a model, finding and plugging individual security loopholes in ACiA becomes too complex and may not yield the results that can be obtained via a holistic approach. In order to be more precise and thorough, we have divided our ACiA$_\alpha$ formal specification into two parts, based on the initiating entity for that operation; UIOs and AIOs, initiated by users and apps respectively.

OUTLINE: In Sect. 2, we place our research amongst the current body of works and Sect. 3, describes ACiA formal specification. In Sect. 4, we present anomalies and quirks we discovered in ACiA that were revealed as a result of thorough testing and Sect. 5, describes conclusion and future work with respect to ACiA$_\alpha$. Finally, we end with Sect. 6 containing the references.

2   Related Work

ACiA has received some attention from prior works; a few such closely related works are described in this section. Shin et al. [13] build a model of ACiA and is one of the few works that come close to our work in modeling the ACiA, including UIOs and AIOs. However, they do not distinguish between multiple competing custom permission definitions, because Android permissions were designed differently at that time. Also, owing to the early nature of this work, it does not model dangerous runtime permissions nor does it include the uri-permissions used to facilitate inter app data sharing. Fragkaki et al. [12] also model ACiA,

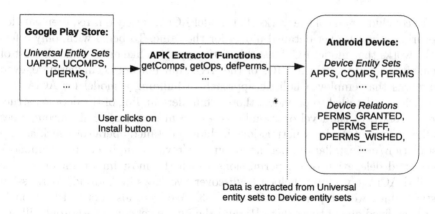

Fig. 2. Building blocks of the ACiA

but their work is centered largely around the uri-permission system. Android's UIOs are not discussed in the work including app installation, un-installation and the vital issue about multiple competing custom permission definitions. Hence, it is required to build a formal model of the ACiA with a holistic perspective, to obtain a deeper understanding of permissions in Android.

Betarte et al. [8–10] present a state-based model of ACiA, which is important owing to the analytical capabilities such a model can offer with respect to security. They define a model state as 8-tuples that record the current state for an Android device, which includes installed apps, permissions, runtime components, temporary and permanently delegated data permissions. They proceed by defining a valid state using 8 distinct conditions, including uniqueness of installed apps, validity of a delegated uri permission which is true is app that receives such a permission, is running, and, uniqueness of all resources on the device. Finally they show three example actions which are the launching of a component, reading of data by a runtime component from a content provider, and, delegation of a temporary uri permission. However, their work does not mention the UIOs along with the fact that apps from the same developer can define the same permissions into distinct permission-groups and protection-levels. Bagheri et al. [5,6] built a formal ACiA model, but, there is no distinction between defined custom permissions and effectively defined custom permissions. They refer to a compete model in the references, however, even in this model, the UIOs do not mention this distinction. In summary, even though the above works formalize both UIO and AIO operations of ACiA, they are limited in detail.

Tuncay et al. [14] identify that developers should always define custom permissions with the same particulars such as permission-group and protection-level; but, the UIOs proposed by them do not differentiate between multiple competing custom permission definitions. Apart from this, uri-permissions are not included in their model, so this model is insufficient to obtain a holistic understanding of ACiA.

To conclude, none of the works that model ACiA, satisfy our requirements for capturing a holistic yet detailed model for the same. To begin with, only a few of the works that model ACiA use a holistic approach like ours, while the rest of them either only model the UIOs or the AIOs, but not both. Furthermore, even the works that employ a holistic approach in building a model for ACiA, are insufficiently detailed to provide a thorough understanding of the detailed structure of ACiA, to the level of granularity we deem necessary. This encompasses all the aspects of Android permissions including detailed operations such as app installation/un-installation, permission grants/revocation, inter app component access and delegation of uri permissions which the most important ones. The detailed ACiA$_\alpha$ we built, helped us discover two flaws in Android's permission system which were reported to Google [1,3]. We were also notified by Google that they fixed one of those flaws [1], and the future versions of Android will not have that flaw.

3   Formal Specification of Access Control in Android

ACiA$_\alpha$ was built by reading the developer/source code documentation [2,4], reading the source code itself and verifying our findings via inter-app tests. The ACiA$_\alpha$ model is specified below.

In the normal course of action, the Android user downloads many apps from the Google Play Store. App data such as app names, permissions, app component names are stored at Google and on an Android device. The data stored by Google is mimicked by Universal Sets, whereas, the data stored on an Android device, is mimicked by Device Sets. To install the apps the OS uses many different APIs which we summarize as APK Extractor Functions, and, as shown in the Fig. 2, these functions assist in the installation procedure by extracting the required data from the Universal sets. Upon successful installation, all the necessary device entity sets and relations are updated as shown in Table 4 (InstallApp operation). Similarly, to facilitate app uninstallation, the helper functions enable us to extract data from the device sets and relations for their removal. Many other operations take place during the normal course of working of an app, and, this is portrayed by the UIOs and AIOs that mimic built-in methods such as RequestPermission, GrantPermission, GrantUriPermission etc.

3.1   Building Blocks of ACiA$_\alpha$

ACiA$_\alpha$ operations utilize certain element sets, functions and relations that are listed in Tables 1, 2 and 3. Table 1 shows primary data sets from the Google Play Store (Universal Entity Sets - column 1) and a generic Android device (Device Entity Sets - column 2).

Universal Sets. The Universal Sets are designed to mimic the data structures of the Google Play Store and begin with the letter "U"; they are populated by Google along with app developers and are assumed to be immutable for the purposes of this paper.

Table 1. ACiA entity sets

Universal entity sets	Device entity sets
UAPPS	APPS
UCOMPS	COMPS
UAUTHORITIES	AUTHORITIES
UPERMS	PERMS
USIG	-
UPGROUP	PGROUP
UPROTLVL	PROTLVL
-	DATAPERMS
-	URI
-	OP

Table 2. APK extractor functions

getComps: UAPPS $\rightarrow 2^{\text{UCOMPS}}$
getOps: UCOMPS $\rightarrow 2^{\text{OP}}$
getAuthorities: UAPPS $\nrightarrow 2^{\text{UAUTHORITIES}}$
getCompPerm: UCOMPS $\times$ OP $\nrightarrow$ PERMS
appSign: UAPPS $\rightarrow$ USIG
defPerms: UAPPS $\nrightarrow 2^{\text{UPERMS}}$
defPgroup: UAPPS $\nrightarrow 2^{\text{UPGROUP}}$
defProtlvlPerm: UAPPS $\times$ UPERMS $\nrightarrow$ UPROTLVL
defPgroupPerm: UAPPS $\times$ UPERMS $\nrightarrow$ UPGROUP
wishList: UAPPS $\nrightarrow 2^{\text{UPERMS}}$

Table 3. ACiA relations and convenience functions

APP_COMPS $\subseteq$ APPS $\times$ COMPS	ownerApp: COMPS $\rightarrow$ APPS
	appComps: APPS $\rightarrow 2^{\text{COMPS}}$
COMP_PROTECT $\subseteq$ COMPS $\times$ OP $\times$ PERMS	requiredPerm: COMPS $\times$ OP $\nrightarrow$ PERMS
	allowedOps: COMPS $\rightarrow 2^{\text{OP}}$
AUTH_OWNER $\subseteq$ APPS $\times$ AUTHORITIES	authoritiesOf: APPS $\rightarrow 2^{\text{AUTHORITIES}}$
PERMS_DEF $\subseteq$ APPS $\times$ PERMS $\times$ PGROUP $\times$ PROTLVL	defApps: PERMS $\rightarrow 2^{\text{APPS}}$
	defPerms: APPS $\rightarrow 2^{\text{PERMS}}$
	defPgroup: APPS $\times$ PERMS $\nrightarrow$ PGROUP
	defProtlvl: APPS $\times$ PERMS $\rightarrow$ PROTLVL
PERMS_EFF $\subseteq$ APPS $\times$ PERMS $\times$ PGROUP $\times$ PROTLVL	effApp: PERMS $\rightarrow$ APPS
	effPerms: APPS $\rightarrow 2^{\text{PERMS}}$
	effPgroup : PERMS $\nrightarrow$ PGROUP
	effProtlvl : PERMS $\rightarrow$ PROTLVL
DPERMS_WISHED $\subseteq$ APPS $\times$ PERMS	wishDperms: APPS $\rightarrow 2^{\text{PERMS}}$
PERMS_GRANTED $\subseteq$ APPS $\times$ PERMS	grantedPerms: APPS $\rightarrow 2^{\text{PERMS}}$
GRANTED_DATAPERMS $\subseteq$ APPS $\times$ URI $\times$ DATAPERMS	grantNature: APPS $\times$ URI $\times$ DATAPERMS $\rightarrow$ {**SemiPermanent, Temporary, NotGranted**}
	uriPrefixCheck: APPS $\times$ URI $\times$ DATAPERMS $\rightarrow \mathbb{B}$

Table 4. Helper functions

userApproval: APPS $\times$ PERMS $\rightarrow \mathbb{B}$
brReceivePerm: COMPS $\rightarrow$ PERMS
corrDataPerm: PERMS $\rightarrow 2^{\text{URI} \times \text{DATAPERMS}}$
belongingAuthority: URI $\rightarrow$ AUTHORITIES
requestApproval: APPS $\times$ APPS $\times$ URI $\rightarrow 2^{\text{DATAPERMS}_b}$
grantApproval: APPS $\times$ APPS $\times$ URI $\times 2^{\text{DATAPERMS}} \rightarrow \mathbb{B}$
prefixMatch: APPS $\times$ URI $\times$ DATAPERMS $\rightarrow \mathbb{B}$
appAuthorized: APPS $\times$ URI $\times$ DATAPERMS $\rightarrow \mathbb{B}$

- UAPPS: the universal set of applications available in the app store (any app store e.g.: Google Play store, Amazon app store).
- UCOMPS: the universal set of components for all the applications from the app store.
- UAUTHORITIES: the universal set of authorities for all the content providers that are defined by all the applications from the app store. An authority is an identifier for data that is defined by a content provider.
- UPERMS: the universal set of permissions consisting of pre-defined system-permissions and application-defined custom permissions from the app store.
- USIG: the universal set of application signatures from the app store.
- UPGROUP: the universal set of permission-groups for pre-defined system permissions as well as application-defined custom permissions for all applications from the app store.
- UPROTLVL: the set of all pre-defined permission protection-levels on an Android device. The protection-level of a permissions corresponds to the significance of the information guarded by it and consists of a base protection-level and additional protection-flags. For the purposes of this paper we only consider the base protection-levels i.e.: **normal**, **dangerous** and **signature**.

Device Sets. The Device Sets are designed to mimic the data structures of a generic Android device and are populated by the device itself in accordance with pre-defined policies from Google.

- APPS: the set of all pre-installed system applications and user-installed custom applications on an Android device; this set includes the stock Android system as well, defined as a single element. So, APPS ⊆ UAPPS for any given Android device (realistically).
- COMPS: the set of all the components belonging to the pre-installed system applications and user-installed custom applications on an Android device. So, COMPS ⊆ UCOMPS on a given Android device.
- AUTHORITIES: the set of all authorities belonging to all applications (pre-installed system applications and user-installed applications) that are installed on an Android device.
- PERMS: the set of all application-defined custom permissions and pre-defined system permissions on an Android device. Note that, PERMS ⊆ UPERMS on a given Android device.
- PGROUP: the set of all application-defined custom permission-groups and pre-defined system permission-groups on an Android device. Note that UPGROUP ⊆ PGROUP on a given Android device.
- PROTLVL: the set of all protection levels present on the device which are the same for any Android device. Note that, PROTLVL = UPROTLVL on a given Android device.
- DATAPERMS: the set of all data-permissions that applications with content providers can grant to other applications, to provide permanent or temporary access to their data. There are two types of data-permissions in Android; base data-permissions and modifier data-permissions. We denote

the base data permissions as $DATAPERMS_b$ and the modifier data permissions as $DATAPERMS_m$. So, $DATAPERMS_b$ = {**dpread, dpwrite**} and $DATAPERMS_m$ = {**mpersist, mprefix, none**} and therefore, DATAPERMS = $DATAPERMS_b$ × $DATAPERMS_m$ = {(**dpread, none**), (**dpwrite, none**), (**dpread, mpersist**), (**dpread, mprefix**), (**dpwrite, mpersist**), (**dpwrite, mprefix**)} for a given Android device.

- URI: the set of all data addresses that applications with content providers can define, which includes certain pre-defined addresses from system applications.
- OP: the set of all operations that may be performed on any Android component. Note that the component types for Android are - Activity, Service, Broadcast Receiver and Content Provider; and, this set is pre-populated by Google. This means that any operations that may be performed on any components installed on a given Android device have to be chosen from this set. Examples of operations that can be performed on components include: *startActivity* on an Activity, *startService* on a Service, *sendBroadcast* on a Broadcast Receiver, and, *create, read, update* and *delete* (CRUD) operations on a Content Provider (this is not an exhaustive list of operations).

APK Extractor Functions. Functions that retrieve information from an application that is about to be installed on the device; evidently, the relations maintained in the device are not useful for these functions. We call these functions APK Extractor Functions. These are shown in Table 2.

- getComps, a function that extracts the set of components belonging to an application from the universal set of components.
- getOps, a function that extracts the set of allowed operations for a given component, based on the type of that component.
- getAuthorities, a partial function that extracts the set of authorities that are defined by an application. An application can define multiple unique authorities and no two authorities from any two applications can be the same.
- getCompPerm, a partial function that maps application components and operations they support, to the permissions that other applications are required to posses, to perform these operations. To obtain the set of valid operations on any given component, we use the function getOps on that component. Apart from this, a component may not be protected by any permission, and in such a case, the component can be freely accessed by any installed applications (the decision of allowing inter-application component access for any application is made by the developer of that application). If a component is protected by a permission that is not defined on the given Android device, other applications may not perform any operations on such a component (auto deny).
- appSign, a function that extracts the signature of an application from the universal set of signatures. This function is used to match application signatures in the pre-requisite condition for granting of signature permissions (i.e.: permissions with the protection level - signature).
- defPerms, a function that extracts the custom-permissions that are defined by an application, from the UPERMS. When any application gets installed,

it can define new permissions that are distinct from the pre-installed system permissions and are used to regulate access to its components by other installed applications.

- defPgroup, a function that extracts the custom permission groups that are defined by an application, from the UPGROUP. When any application gets installed, it can define new permission-groups that are distinct from the pre-installed permission-groups and are used to mitigate the number of permission prompts shown to the user (a permission prompt is an application asking for certain permission).

- defProtlvlPerm, a function that extracts a protection level for a permission as defined by an application. Protection-level is defined for all permissions by some applications, and different applications may define distinct protection-levels for the same permission[1]. Note that, $\forall ua \in$ UAPPS, $\forall up \in$ UPERMS, $\forall pl_1 \neq pl_2 \in$ UPROTLVL. defProtlvlPerm$(ua, up) = pl_1 \Rightarrow$ defProtlvlPerm$(ua, up) \neq pl_2$.

- defPgroupPerm, a partial function that extracts the permission-group for some permissions if defined by an application. Permission-group may be defined for some permissions by some applications, and different applications may define distinct permission-groups for the same permission (see footnote 1). Note that, $\forall a \in$ UAPPS, $\forall p \in$ UPERMS, $\forall pg_1 \neq pg_2 \in$ UPGROUP. defPgroupPerm$(ua, up) = pg_1 \Rightarrow$ defPgroupPerm$(ua, up) \neq pg_2$.

- wishList, a function that extracts a set of permissions wished by an application, from the UPERMS; this contains all those permissions that the application may ever need in its lifetime.

Device Relations and Convenience Functions. The Device Relations are derived from the Device Sets and portray the information stored by an Android device to facilitate access control decisions. Any relation is always pre-defined for built-in applications and system-permissions, but needs to be updated for user-installed applications and application-defined custom-permissions. Convenience functions query existing relations maintained on the device; evidently, these functions fetch information based on applications that are already installed on the device. These are listed in Table 3.

- APP_COMPS, a one-to-many relation mapping application to it's components. Note that, $\forall a_1 \neq a_2 \in$ APPS, $\forall c \in$ COMPS. $(a_1, c) \in$ APP_COMPS $\Rightarrow (a_2, c) \notin$ APP_COMPS

---

[1] (Two scenarios) Scenario A: Multiple applications from the same developer define the same permission into distinct permission-levels and/or permission-groups; this is a valid condition, but, only the first application's definition of the permission counts whereas the rest are ignored.

Scenario B: Multiple applications from different developers define the same permission into distinct permission-levels and/or permission-groups; this condition is invalid, since only one developer is allowed to define a new permission at any given time. However, once that application gets uninstalled, other applications from different developers are able to define the same permission!

- **ownerApp**, a function mapping application component to their owner application. Note that, a component can only belong to a single application. So, $\forall c \in \text{COMPS.}$ $(\text{ownerApp}(c), c) \in \text{APP\_COMPS.}$
- **appComps**, a function mapping an application to a set of its components. This function is used while an application is being uninstalled, to get the components of the application to be removed from the device. Formally, $\text{appComps}(a) = \{c \in \text{COMPS} \mid (a, c) \in \text{APP\_COMPS}\}.$

- COMP_PROTECT, a relation that maintains the permissions that are required for operations to be performed on application components. Note that, as it pertains to broadcasts, the sender as well as the receiver may require permissions, however, this relation only maintains the permissions protecting receiving components. To obtain permissions that are required by senders of broadcasts (to be granted to receivers), a helper function brReceivePerm defined in the following subsection can be used. So, $\forall c \in \text{COMPS}, \forall op \in \text{OP}, \forall p_1 \neq p_2 \in \text{PERMS.}$ $(c, op, p_1) \in \text{COMP\_PROTECT} \Rightarrow ((c, op, p_2) \notin \text{COMP\_PROTECT} \wedge p_1 = \text{getCompPerm}(c, op))$

  - **requiredPerm**, a function that gives the permission that an application component is required to have, to initiate an operation with another component. Note that two components from the same application do not normally need these permissions. So, $\forall c \in \text{COMPS}, \forall op \in \text{OP.}$ $(c, op, \text{requiredPerm}(c, op)) \in \text{COMP\_PROTECT}$
  - **allowedOps**, a function that gives the set of operations that can be performed on a component. Since not all components support all the operations, $\text{allowedOps}(c) = \{op \in \text{OP} \mid (c, op, p) \in \text{COMP\_PROTECT} \wedge p \in \text{PERMS}\}$

- AUTH_OWNER, a one-to-many relation that maps the authorities to their owning applications on a given device. If an application tries to re-define an already defined authority on an Android device, it will not get installed on that device. Note that, $\forall a_1 \neq a_2 \in \text{APPS}, \forall auth \in \text{AUTHORITIES.}$ $(a_1, auth) \in \text{AUTH\_OWNER} \Rightarrow ((a_2, auth) \notin \text{AUTH\_OWNER} \wedge auth \in \text{getAuthorities}(a))$

  - **authoritiesOf**, a function that give the authorities of a certain application that is installed on an Android device. So, $\text{authoritiesOf}(a) = \{auth \in \text{AUTHORITIES} \mid (a, auth) \in \text{AUTH\_OWNER}\}$

- PERMS_DEF, a relation mapping user-installed applications, the custom-permissions defined by these applications, the permission-group and the protection-level of such permissions as defined by the respective applications. Note that, $\forall a \in \text{APPS}, \forall p \in \text{PERMS}, \forall pg_1 \neq pg_2 \in \text{PGROUP}, \forall pl_1 \neq pl_2 \in \text{PROTLVL.}$ $(a, p, pg_1, pl_1) \in \text{PERMS\_DEF} \Rightarrow ((a, p, pg_2, pl_1) \notin \text{PERMS\_DEF} \wedge (a, p, pg_1, pl_2) \notin \text{PERMS\_DEF})$

  - **defApps**, a function that returns a set of applications that define a permission. When an application is uninstalled, this function is used to retrieve the set of application that define a certain permissions, thus facilitating the decision of permission removal. So, $\text{defApps}(p) = \{a \in \text{APPS} \mid (a, p, pg, pl) \in \text{PERMS\_DEF}\}$

- **defPerms**, a function that gives the set of permissions that are defined by an installed application. This function is used while an application is uninstalled from a device, to obtain the set of permissions defined by that application so that they may be removed from the device. So, $\text{defPerms}(a) = \{p \in \text{PERMS} \mid (a,\ p,\ pg,\ pl) \in \text{PERMS\_DEF}\}$
- **defPgroup**, a partial function that gives the permission-group for a permission as defined by an installed application. Note that, not all permissions that are defined by applications are categorized into permission-groups. So, $\forall a \in \text{APPS},\ \forall p \in \text{PERMS},\ \forall pg \in \text{PGROUP}.\ \text{defPgroup}(a,\ p) = pg \Rightarrow ((a,\ p,\ pg,\ pl) \in \text{PERMS\_DEF} \wedge pl \in \text{PROTLVL})$
- **defProtlvl**, a function that gives the protection-level for a permission as defined by an installed application. When an application from a certain developer is uninstalled from a device and another application from the same developer is still installed on the device, this function is used to transfer the permission definition to that of the remaining application. So, $\forall a \in \text{APPS},\ \forall p \in \text{PERMS},\ \forall pl \in \text{PROTLVL}.\ \text{defProtlvl}(a,\ p) = pl \Rightarrow ((a,\ p,\ pg,\ pl) \in \text{PERMS\_DEF} \wedge pg \in \text{PGROUP})$
- PERMS_EFF, a relation mapping all the pre-installed system applications and user-installed custom applications on a device, the permissions defined by them, the permission-groups and protection-levels of such permissions. In case of multiple apps attempting to re-defined a permission on a device, Android follows a first come first serve policy, thus only accepting the definition of the first app that is installed. This relation reflects the effective definition of permissions, as defined by system, system applications or user-installed applications. Note that, $\forall a \in \text{APPS},\ \forall p_1 \neq p_2 \in \text{PERMS},\ \forall pg_1 \neq pg_2 \in \text{PGROUP},\ \forall pl_1 \neq pl_2 \in \text{PROTLVL}.\ (a,\ p_1,\ pg_1,\ pl_1) \in \text{PERMS\_EFF} \Rightarrow (a,\ p_2,\ pg_1,\ pl_1) \notin \text{PERMS\_EFF} \wedge (a,\ p_1,\ pg_2,\ pl_1) \notin \text{PERMS\_EFF} \wedge (a,\ p_1,\ pg_1,\ pl_2) \notin \text{PERMS\_EFF}$
  - **effApp**, a function that gives the pre-installed system application, the Android OS, or the user-installed application that defined a permission. This function is used during the signature matching process required to be completed before any application is installed. So, $\forall p \in \text{PERMS}.\ (\text{effApp}(p),\ p) \in \text{PERMS\_EFF}$
  - **effPerms**, a function that gives the set of permissions as effectively defined by the system, a system application or a user-installed custom application. This function is used while an application is uninstalled from a device, to obtain the set of permissions defined by that application so that they may be removed from the device. So, $\text{effPerms}(a) = \{p \in \text{PERMS} \mid (a, p, pg, pl) \in \text{PERMS\_EFF} \wedge pg \in \text{PGROUP} \wedge pl \in \text{PROTLVL}\}$
  - **effPgroup**, a function that maps a permission to its permission-group. This function is used when making access control decisions to auto grant certain requested dangerous permissions. Note that, $\forall p \in \text{PERMS}.\ \text{effPgroup}(p) = pg \Rightarrow ((a, p, pg, pl) \in \text{PERMS\_EFF} \wedge pg \in \text{PGROUP} \wedge pl \in \text{PROTLVL})$

- **effProtlvl**, a function mapping a permission to its protection level on an Android device. This function is used to obtain permission protection-levels used during permission granting process. Note that, $\forall p \in$ PERMS. effProtlvl(p) = pl $\Rightarrow$ (a, p, pg, pl) $\in$ PERMS_EFF $\wedge$ pg $\in$ PGROUP $\wedge$ pl $\in$ PROTLVL)

– DPERMS_WISHED, a many-to-many relation mapping applications to the dangerous permissions requested by them in the manifest. Since normal and signature permission grants happen at install time, only dangerous permissions are a part of this relation. Note that, $\forall a \in$ APPS, $\forall p \in$ PERMS. $(a, p) \in$ DPERMS_WISHED $\Rightarrow p \in$ wishList(a) $\wedge$ effProtlvl(p) = dangerous

  - **wishDperms**, the mapping of an application to a set of dangerous permissions requested by it in the manifest. Formally, wishDperms(a) = $\{p \in$ PERMS $| (a, p) \in$ DPERMS_WISHED$\}$.

– PERMS_GRANTED, a many-to-many relation mapping applications to the permissions granted to them. Note that, $\forall a \in$ APPS, $\forall p \in$ PERMS. $(a,p) \in$ PERMS_GRANTED $\Rightarrow p \in$ wishList(a)

  - **grantedPerms**, the mapping of an application to the a set of permissions granted to it. Formally, grantedPerms(a) = $\{ p \in$ PERMS $| (a, p) \in$ PERMS_GRANTED$\}$.

– GRANTED_DATAPERMS, a relation mapping applications to the data permissions granted to them. Data permissions are granted to applications by the applications that own that data permission.

  - **grantNature**, a function that gives the nature of a data permission grant to an application. Such a nature can be Permanent, Temporary and Not Granted (when the data permission was not granted to that application); a permanent permission grant survives device restarts whereas a temporary permission grant is revoked once the application is shut down. So, $\forall a \in$ APPS, $\forall uri \in$ URI, $\forall dp_b \in$ DATAPERMS$_b$, $\forall dp_m \in$ DATAPERMS$_m$, $\forall dp \in$ DATAPERMS.
    grantNature(a, uri, dp) = **SemiPermanent** $\Rightarrow$ (dp_m = mpersist $\wedge$ (a, uri, dp) $\in$ GRANTED_DATAPERMS) $\vee$
    grantNature(a, uri, dp) = **Temporary** $\Rightarrow$ ($dp_m = \emptyset \wedge$ (a, uri, dp) $\in$ GRANTED_DATAPERMS) $\vee$
    grantNature(a, uri, dp) = **NotGranted** $\Rightarrow$ (a, uri, dp) $\notin$ GRANTED_DATAPERMS

  - **uriPrefixCheck**, a function that checks the data-permission for an application against a prefix match given by the data-permission modifier **mprefix**. Since data-permissions can be granted on a broad scale, this modifier makes it possible for the application to receive access to all the sub-URIs that begin with the specific URI that has been granted. For example, if any data-permission is granted consisting of the **mpersist** modifier for a URI to an application such as content://abc.xyz/foo, then, that application receives access to all the URIs that are contained in the granted URI such as content://abc.xyz/foo/bar or content://abc.xyz/foo/bar/1 and so on. So, $\forall a \in$ APPS, $\forall uri \in$ URI, $\forall dp_b \in$ DATAPERMS$_b$, $\forall dp_m \in$ DATAPERMS$_m$, $\forall dp = (dp_b, dp_m) \in$ DATAPERMS. uriPrefixCheck(a, uri, dp) $= \mathbb{T} \Rightarrow (dp_m = \mathbf{mprefix} \wedge$ prefixMatch(a, uri, dp))

Helper Functions. The Helper functions facilitate access control decisions by extracting data from the Android device and abstracting away complicated details for the Android device without compromising details about the Android permission model. These are listed in Table 4.

- userApproval, a function that gives the user's choice on whether to grant a permission for an application.
- brReceivePerm, a function that gives a permission that is required to be possesed by an application component in order to receive broadcasts from this component. Note that broadcast receivers from the same application do not need this permission.
- corrDataPerm, a function that obtains the correlated data address and data permission for a system level permission.
- belongingAuthority, a function that obtains the authority to which the given URI belongs. At any given time a URI can belong to only a single authority.
- requestApproval, an application-choice function that provides the data-permissions for the URIs that are requesting by one application and granted by the other application; only if conditions mentioned below are met, otherwise it returns a null set. Note that, $\forall a_2 \neq a_1 \in$ APPS, $\forall uri \in$ URI, $\forall dp \in$ DATAPERMS. requestApproval$(a_2, a_1, uri) \neq \emptyset \Rightarrow$
$$\bigwedge_{dp \,\in\, \text{requestApproval}(a_1,\, a_1,\, uri)} \text{appAuthorized}(a_2,\, uri,\, dp)$$
- grantApproval, an application-choice boolean function that provides the data-permissions for the URIs that are chosen to be delegated by one application to another ; only if conditions mentioned below are met, otherwise it returns a null set. Note that, $\forall a_1 \neq a_2 \in$ APPS, $\forall uri \in$ URI, $\forall dp \in$ DATA PERMS. grantApproval$(a_1, a_2, uri) = \mathbf{T} \Rightarrow$
$$\bigwedge_{dp \,\in\, \text{grantApproval}(a_1,\, a_2,\, uri)} \text{appAuthorized}(a_2,\, uri,\, dp)$$
- prefixMatch, a boolean function that matches an application, a uri and a data-permission to one of the **mprefix** data-permissions using the relation GRANTED_DATAPERMS.
- appAuthorized, a boolean function to check if an application has a certain data-permission with respect to the provided URI. So, $\forall a \in$ APPS, $\forall uri \in$ URI, $\forall dp \in$ DATAPERMS. appAuthorized(a, uri, dp) $\Rightarrow$ (a, uri, dp) $\in$ GRANTED_DATAPERMS $\vee$ ownerOf$\big($belongingAuthority$(uri)\big)$ $= a \vee \quad \exists p \in$ grantedPerms$(a). (uri,\ dp) \in$ corrDataPerm$(p) \vee$ uriPrefixCheck(a, uri, dp)

Understanding the ACiA$_\alpha$ operations

- Updates on Administrative operations are assumed to be in order, this means that they need to be executed in the order in which they are listed.
- The universal and on device sets are the building blocks of the relations, however, in this model, the sets and the relations need to be updated individually. This means that when a relation is constructed from two sets (for example), updating the sets will not impact the relation in any way.

3.2   User Initiated Operations

ACiA$_\alpha$ - UIOs are initiated by the user or require their approval before they can be executed. Note that certain special apps that are signed with Google's or the platform signature are exempt from this requirement, since they have access to a broader range of "system only" permissions that may enable them to perform these operations without user intervention. Also to be noted that only the most important updates are discussed in this section, the detailed updates are available on Table 5. For each operation, the updates are assumed to be executed in-order.

- **AddApp:** This operation resembles the user clicking on "install" button on the Google Play Store, and upon successful execution, the requested app is installed on the device. It is required, for app installation to proceed, that any custom permission definitions either be unique or in case of multiple such definitions, that they are all defined by apps signed with the same certificate.
- **DeleteApp:** This operation resembles a user un-installing an app from the Settings application. For this operation to proceed there are no conditions that need to be satisfied.
- **GrantDangerPerm/GrantDangerPgroup:** These operations resemble the user granting a dangerous permission/permission-group to an app via the Settings app; and, the execution of this operation result in an app receiving a dangerous permission/permission-group respectively. It is required for the app to have requested atleast 1 such dangerous permission from the same permission-group in the manifest.
- **RevokeDangerPerm/RevokeDangerPgroup:** These operations resemble the user revoking a dangerous permission/permission-group from an app via the Settings app; and, their execution results in an app's dangerous permission/permission-group getting revoked. It is required that the application be granted to said permission/permission-group prior to execution of these operations.

3.3 Application Initiated Operations

The AIOs are initiated by the apps when attempting to perform several tasks such as requesting a permission from the user, granting a uri permission to another app, revoking a uri permission from all apps etc. With the exception of the **RequestPerm** operation, these operations do not require user interaction and can be completed by the Android OS.

- **RequestPerm:** This operation resembles an app requesting a dangerous system permission from the Android OS. Such a permission request is successful only if the user grants it to the app, or, the app requesting it already has

Table 5. ACiA$_\alpha$ User Initiated Operations

Operation: **AddApp**(ua : UAPPS)

Authorization Requirement: $\forall up \in$ PERMS $\cap$ defPerms(ua). appSign(effApp(up)) = appSign(ua) $\wedge$ getAuthorities(ua) $\cap$ $\bigcup_{a\ \in\ APPS}$ getAuthorities(a) = $\emptyset$

Updates:

APPS$'$ = APPS $\cup$ \{ua\}; COMPS$'$ = COMPS $\cup$ getComps(ua); APP_COMPS$'$ = APP_COMPS $\cup$ \{ua\} $\times$ getComps(ua)

AUTHORITIES$'$ = AUTHORITIES $\cup$ getAuthorities(ua);

AUTH_OWNER$'$ = AUTH_OWNER $\cup$ \{ua\} $\times$ getAuthorities(ua)

PERMS_DEF$'$ = PERMS_DEF $\cup$ $\bigcup_{up\ \in\ defPerms(ua)}$ $\Big\{\big(ua,\ up,\ \mathrm{defPgroupPerm}(ua,\ up), \mathrm{defProtlvlPerm}(ua,\ up)\big)\Big\}$

PERMS_EFF$'$ = PERMS_EFF $\cup$ $\bigcup_{up\ \in\ defPerms(ua)\ \setminus\ PERMS}$ $\Big\{\big(ua,\ up,\ \mathrm{defPgroupPerm}(ua,\ up), \mathrm{defProtlvlPerm}(ua,\ up)\big)\Big\}$

PERMS$'$ = PERMS $\cup$ defPerms(ua)

COMP_PROTECT$'$ = COMP_PROTECT $\cup$ $\bigcup_{c\ \in\ appComps(a);\ op\ \in\ getOps(c);\ p\ \in\ PERMS\ \cap\ getCompPerm(op,\ c)}$ \{(c, op, p)\}

PGROUP$'$ = PGROUP $\cup$ defPgroup(ua)

PERMS_GRANTED$'$ = PERMS_GRANTED $\cup$ $\bigcup_{\substack{a'\ \in\ APPS \\ up\ \in\ wishList(a')\ \cap\ PERMS\ such\ that \\ effProtlvl(up)\ =\ normal}}$ \{(a', up)\} $\cup$ $\bigcup_{\substack{a'\ \in\ APPS;\ up\ \in\ wishList(a')\ \cap\ PERMS\ such\ that \\ (effProtlvl(up)\ =\ signature\ \wedge \\ appSign(effApp(up))\ =\ appSign(a'))}}$ \{(a', up)\}

DPERMS_WISHED$'$ = DPERMS_WISHED $\cup$ $\bigcup_{\substack{a'\ \in\ APPS;\ up\ \in\ wishList(a')\ such\ that \\ effProtlvl(up)\ =\ dangerous}}$ \{(a', up)\}

Operation: **DeleteApp**(a : APPS)

Authorization Requirement: **T**

Updates:

COMP_PROTECT$'$ = COMP_PROTECT $\setminus$ $\bigcup_{\substack{c\ \in\ appComps(a) \\ op\ \in\ allowedOps(c) \\ p\ \in\ PERMS\ \cap\ getCompPerm(op,\ c)}}$ \{(c, op, p)\} $\cup$ $\bigcup_{\substack{a'\ \in\ APPS\ \setminus\ \{a\};\ c\ \in\ appComps(a') \\ op\ \in\ allowedOps(c) \\ p\ \in\ effPerms(a)\ \cap\ requiredPerm(c,\ op)}}$ \{(c, op, p)\}

AUTH_OWNER$'$ = AUTH_OWNER $\setminus$ \{a\} $\times$ authoritiesOf(a); AUTHORITIES$'$ = AUTHORITIES $\setminus$ authoritiesOf(a)

COMPS$'$ = COMPS $\setminus$ appComps(a); APP_COMPS$'$ = APP_COMPS $\setminus$ \{a\} $\times$ appComps(a)

PERMS$'$ = PERMS $\setminus$ $\Big($effPerms(a) $\setminus$ $\bigcup_{a'\in APPS\setminus\{a\}}$ defPerms(a')$\Big)$

PGROUP$'$ = PGROUP $\setminus$ $\Big($defPgroup(a) $\setminus$ $\bigcup_{a'\in APPS\setminus\{a\}}$ defPgroup(a')$\Big)$

PERMS_GRANTED$'$ = PERMS_GRANTED $\setminus$ $\Big($\{a\} $\times$ grantedPerms(a) $\cup$ $\bigcup_{a'\in APPS\setminus\{a\};\ p\ \in\ effPerms(a)}$ \{(a',p)\}$\Big)$

DPERMS_WISHED$'$ = DPERMS_WISHED $\setminus$ $\Big($\{a\} $\times$ wishDperms(a) $\cup$ $\bigcup_{a'\in APPS\ \setminus\ \{a\};\ p\ \in\ effPerms(a)}$ \{(a', p)\}$\Big)$

PERMS_EFF$'$ = $\Big($PERMS_EFF $\setminus$ $\bigcup_{p\ \in\ effPerms(a)}$ $\big\{\big(a,\ p,\ \mathrm{effPgroup}(p), \mathrm{effProtlvl}(p)\big)\big\}\Big)$ $\cup$ $\bigcup_{p\ \in\ effPerms(a')}$ $\big\{\big(a',\ p,\ \mathrm{defPgroup}(a',\ p), \mathrm{defProtlvl}(a',\ p)\big)\big\}$, where $a' \in$ defApps(p) $\setminus$ \{a\}

(continued)

Table 5. (*continued*)

$$PERMS\_DEF' = PERMS\_DEF \ \setminus \ \bigcup_{p \ \in \ defPerms(a)} \left\{ \left(a, \ p, \ defPgroup(a, p), \ defProtlvl(a, p) \right) \right\}$$

$$COMP\_PROTECT' = COMP\_PROTECT \ \cup \bigcup_{\substack{c \ \in \ appComps(a'); \ op \ \in \ allowedOps(c) \\ p \ \in \ PERMS \ \cap \ getCompPerm(op, c)}}^{a' \ \in \ APPS \ \setminus \ \{a\}} \{(c, \ op, \ p)\}$$

$$PERMS\_GRANTED' = PERMS\_GRANTED \ \cup$$

$$\bigcup_{\substack{a' \ \in \ APPS \ \setminus \ \{a\} \\ p \ \in \ wishList(a') \ \cap \ PERMS \ such \ that \\ effProtlvl(p) \ = \ normal}} \{(a', \ p)\} \ \cup \bigcup_{\substack{a' \ \in \ APPS \ \setminus \ \{a\} \\ p \ \in \ wishList(a') \ \cap \ PERMS \ such \ that \\ \left(effProtlvl(p) \ = \ signature \ \wedge \ appSign\left(effApp(p)\right) \ = \ appSign(a') \right)}} \{(a', \ p)\}$$

$$DPERMS\_WISHED' = DPERMS\_WISHED \ \cup \bigcup_{\substack{a' \ \in \ APPS \ \setminus \ \{a\}; \ p \ \in \ wishList(a') \ such \ that \\ effProtlvl(p) \ = \ dangerous}} \{(a', \ p)\}$$

$$APPS' = APPS \ \setminus \ \{a\}$$

Operation: **GrantDangerPerm**(a : APPS, p : PERMS)
Authorization Requirement: $p \in wishDperms(a)$
Update: $PERMS\_GRANTED' = PERMS\_GRANTED \ \cup \ \{(a,p)\}$

Operation: **GrantDangerPgroup**(a : APPS, pg : PGROUP)
Authorization Requirement: $\exists p \in wishDperms(a). \ effPgroup(p) = pg$
Update: $PERMS\_GRANTED' = PERMS\_GRANTED \ \cup \bigcup_{p \ \in \ wishDperms(a) \ such \ that \ effPgroup(p) \ = \ pg} \{(a,p)\}$

Operation: **RevokeDangerPerm**(a : APPS, p : PERMS)
Authorization Requirements: $p \in grantedPerms(a) \ \wedge \ p \in wishDperms(a)$
Update: $PERMS\_GRANTED' = PERMS\_GRANTED \ \setminus \ \{(a, \ p)\}$

Operation: **RevokeDangerPgroup**(a : APPS, pg : PGROUP)
Authorization Requirements: $\exists p \in grantedPerms(a). \ effPgroup(p) = pg \ \wedge \ p \in wishDperms(a)$
Update: $PERMS\_GRANTED' = PERMS\_GRANTED \ \setminus \bigcup_{p \ \in \ grantedPerms(a) \ such \ that} \{(a, \ p)\}$
$\left(effPgroup(p) \ = \ pg \ \wedge \ p \in wishDperms(a) \right)$

another permission from the same permission group. If successful, the app is granted the requested dangerous permission.

- **RequestDataPerm:** This operation denotes the uri-permission requests by apps. Such a request may be granted by apps only if they have the required access. Once this request is successful, the app requesting it is granted the uri-permission.
- **GrantDataPerm:** This operation resembles the uri-permission delegation by apps; and, it only succeeds if the app trying to grant the permissions has access to do so.
- **RevokeDataPerm:** This operation resembles the revocation of uri-permission from an installed app. Applications can revoke uri-permissions from other apps only if they have been granted such a permission via the manifest, or, is the owner app for that uri.
- **RevokeGlobalDataPerm:** This operation is similar to the **RevokeDataPerm** except that it revokes the uri-permissions from all applications on the device. Applications that receive access to the content provider may only invoke this function successfully.
- **CheckDataAccess:** This operation checks if a particular app has access to a uri. Uri permissions are delegated to apps by other app possessing those permissions.

Table 6. $ACiA_\alpha$ Application Initiated Operations

Operation: **RequestPerm**(a : APPS, p : PERMS)
Authorization Requirement: $(a, p) \in$ DPERMS_WISHED $\wedge$
$\Big(\big(\exists p' \in$ PERMS $\setminus \{p\}.$ $\texttt{effPgroup}(p') = \texttt{effPgroup}(p) \wedge (a, p') \in$ PERMS_GRANTED $\big)$ $\vee$
$\quad\quad\quad\quad\quad\quad\quad\quad\quad\quad\quad\quad\quad\quad\quad\quad\quad\quad\quad\quad\quad\quad\quad\quad\quad \texttt{userApproval}(a, p) \Big)$
Updates: PERMS_GRANTED$'$ = PERMS_GRANTED $\cup$ $\{(a, p)\}$
Operation: **RequestDataPerm**(a_{src} : APPS, a_{tgt} : APPS, uri : URI)
Authorization Requirement: $\texttt{requestApproval}(a_{src}, a_{tgt}, uri) \neq \emptyset$
Updates: GRANTED_DATAPERMS$'$ = GRANTED_DATAPERMS $\cup$
$\quad\quad\quad\quad\quad\quad\quad\quad\quad\quad\quad \bigcup_{dp \in \texttt{requestApproval}(a_{src}, a_{tgt}, uri)} \{(a_{src}, uri, dp)\}$
Operation: **GrantDataPerm**$\Big(a_{src}$: APPS, a_{tgt} : APPS, uri : URI, $dp : 2^{\text{DATAPERMS}} \Big)$
Authorization Requirement: $\texttt{grantApproval}(a_{src}, a_{tgt}, uri, dp)$
Updates: GRANTED_DATAPERMS$'$ = GRANTED_DATAPERMS $\cup$ $(a_{tgt}, uri) \times dp$
Operation: **RevokeDataPerm**(a_{src} : APPS, a_2 : APPS, uri : URI, dp : DATAPERMS)
Authorization Requirement 1: $\neg\psi$
Update 1: GRANTED_DATAPERMS$'$ = GRANTED_DATAPERMS $\setminus \{(a_{src}, uri, dp)\}$
Authorization Requirement 2: ψ
Update 2: GRANTED_DATAPERMS$'$ = GRANTED_DATAPERMS $\setminus \{(a_{tgt}, uri, dp)\}$
where ψ : $\equiv$ $a_{src} = \texttt{ownerOf}(\texttt{belongingAuthority}(uri))$ $\vee$
$\quad\quad\quad\quad\quad\quad \exists p \in \texttt{grantedPerms}(a_{src}). (uri, dp) \in \texttt{corrDataPerm}(p)$
Operation: **RevokeGlobalDataPerm**(a : APPS, uri : URI)
Authorization Requirement: ψ
Update: GRANTED_DATAPERMS$'$ = GRANTED_DATAPERMS $\setminus \bigcup_{a \in \text{APPS}} \{(a, uri, dp)\}$
Operation: **CheckDataAccess**(a : APPS, uri : URI, dp : DATAPERMS)
Authorization Requirement: $\texttt{appAuthorized}(a, uri, dp)$
Update: -
Operation: **CheckAccess**(c_{src} : COMPS, c_{tgt} : COMPS, op : OP)
Authorization Requirement:
$\texttt{ownerApp}(c_{src}) = \texttt{ownerApp}(c_{tgt})$ $\vee$
$\Big(op \in \texttt{allowedOps}(c_{tgt}) \wedge \texttt{requiredPerm}(c_{tgt}, op) \in \texttt{grantedPerms}(\texttt{ownerApp}(c_{src}))$ $\wedge$
$(op = \texttt{sendbroadcast} \wedge \texttt{brReceivePerm}(c_{src})) \Rightarrow \texttt{brReceivePerm}(c_{src}) \subseteq \texttt{grantedPerms}(\texttt{ownerApp}(c_{tgt})) \Big)$
Update: -
Operation: **AppShutdown**(a : APPS)
Authorization Requirement: **T**
Updates: GRANTED_DATAPERMS$'$ = GRANTED_DATAPERMS $\setminus$
$\quad\quad\quad\quad\quad\quad\quad\quad\quad\quad \bigcup_{\substack{(a, uri, dp) \in \text{GRANTED\_DATAPERMS such that} \\ \texttt{grantNature}(a, uri, dp) = \textbf{Temporary}}} \{(a, uri, dp)\}$

- **CheckAccess:** This operation resembles a component attempting to do an operation on another component; components may belong to the same or distinct apps. This operation can succeed if the app attempting to perform it has been granted the required permissions.
- **AppShutdown:** This operation resembles an app shutting down, so all the temporary uri-permissions granted to it are revoked unless they are persisted.

4   Experimental Setup and Observations

After we extract the model for ACiA using source code and developer documentation, testing was done via carefully designed inter app tests. These tests enabled the discovery of the flaws that are stated in this section, apart from helping us understand the intricate details of operations such as application installation, uninstallation, permission grants and revocation etc. A brief overview on the testing methodology is explained in the section below.

Rationale for Testing. Mathematical models mitigate ambiguity in access control; documentation and source codes can be open to interpretation. Differences in interpretation leads to a plunge in accuracy of stated operations, which in turn leads to inaccurate predictions based on that interpretation. Since our entire model for ACiA depends on reading the source code and documentation, testing was performed to ensure that our model is in line with the behavior of the Android OS and that of Android apps. Apart from this, we made several predictions based on the model, and then verified them using these tests, and it is this very methodical procedure that enabled us to discover flaws in the design of ACiA that were communicated to Google via its issue-tracker.

4.1   Experimental Setup

A simple three app base testing environment was designed, which was adapted for each individual test. The apps used for these tests were dummy apps with two activities and one service component. According to need, the apps were programmed to define a new permission using one of the available protection levels, or, into a hitherto undefined permission group.

Test Parameters. A total of four test parameters (TP) are considered (see Table 7) which include installation procedure for an app, uninstallation procedure for an all, installation sequence for multiple apps and uninstallation sequence for multiple apps.

For brevity, we demonstrate a few simple tests that we conducted to verify our findings using test apps as follows.

1. **Verifying authorization requirements for AddApp operation.** The AddApp operation mimics the app installation procedure in Android, and several checks are required to pass before the installation can proceed.

Checks found via the source code and documentation.

(a) If the app being installed defines a new permission, it is required that such a permission be unique and is not already defined on the device.
(b) In the case it is already defined, the app must come from the same developer as the one that defined the permission; this means their signatures must match.
(c) If the app being installed defines a new authority for a content provider, this authority must be unique.

Table 7. Test parameters used for ACiA_α model evaluation

TP1[a]	*Install Procedure* e.g.: $adb push and then use GUI for installation, or $adb uninstall
TP2	*Uninstall Procedure* e.g.: $adb uninstall, or Use GUI for uninstallation
TP3	*Install order* e.g.: install App1, App2, App3; or install App2, App1, App3; or install App3, App2, App1
TP4	*Uninstall order* e.g.: uninstall App3, App2, App1; or uninstall App1, App2, App3; or uninstall App2, App1, App3

[a]TP: Test Parameter

Verification Methodology. For this test, we designed three test apps that each define the same permission, however, two are signed with the same certificate, whereas the third is signed with a different certificate. Upon attempting installation we encountered the following.

Case for defining new permission (see Fig. 3): Apps 1 and 2 could be installed even though they re-defined the same permission, however, App3's installation could not proceed since it was signed with a certificate from a different developer.

Case for defining new authority (see Fig. 4): Apps 1 and 3 could be installed since they defined a unique authority, however, App 2's installation could not proceed since it attempted to re-define an authority that already existed on the device.

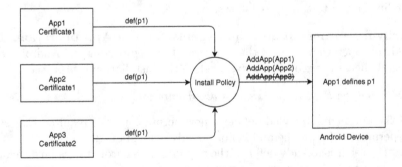

Fig. 3. App installation authorization requirement - new permission definition

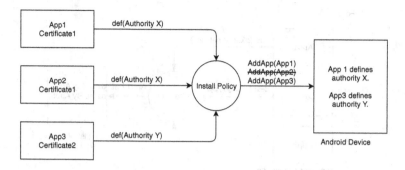

Fig. 4. App installation authorization requirement - unique authority

2. **Check whether permission definitions were changed in accordance to the apps that were present on a device.** The 3 above mentioned apps were designed to define a single permission, but into 3 distinct permission groups i.e.: pgroup1, pgroup2 and pgroup3. Upon installation of app1, the permission p1 was defined on the device into the permission-group "pgroup1"; following this, apps 2 and 3 were installed with no change in p1's permission-group (expected result). However, after app1 was uninstalled using the GUI uninstallation method, the permission definition of p1 changed randomly to "pgroup2" or "pgroup3"; this behavior was replicated using a combination of distinct sequences for TP3 and TP4 and each test yielded the same result. This meant that Android was randomly assigning permission definitions to apps, when the initial app defining such a permission was uninstalled (this means that a random app's definition of the permission would be enforced upon app1's uninstallation; once enforced, such a definition stays until that app gets uninstalled and so on). It is to be noted that this issue occurs during the GUI uninstallation method, and was not observed when apps were removed using the command line (something which only developers use anyway). This makes the issue more relevant, since users normally uninstall apps using the GUI and not the command line tools.

4.2 Observations from ACiA Acquired via Testing the ACiA$_\alpha$ Model

Our analysis of ACiA$_\alpha$ yields some interesting and peculiar observations; and, after a thorough review of the same, we derived the rationale behind these observations and make predictions based on them. Testing these predictions yield a number of potential flaws in ACiA, which were reported to Google [1,3], and, Google has said that [1] has been fixed and will be available in the future version of Android. We also present our rationales for these anomalies, wherever necessary. The model building phase for ACiA$_\alpha$ is quite complex due to the lengthy nature of Android's source code. Every important observation was verified using test-apps, and the final model is designed to capture all the important aspects

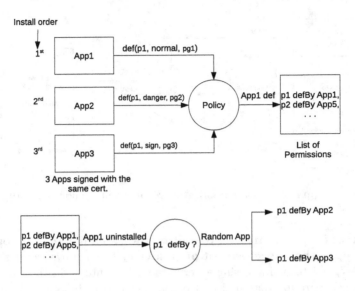

Fig. 5. Anomaly in Android custom permissions

of ACiA. Below we note a few such important observations and the related operations where they were encountered.

1. **Undefined behavior in case of competing custom permission definitions.** Android allows multiple definitions of the same permission (from apps signed with the same certificate) to co-exist on a device. The effective definition for such a permission is taken from the first app that defines it; any subsequent definitions of the same permission are ignored by Android. This can cause issues when that app that defined the permission is un-installed, since there is no order with which Android changes the definition of the permission, hence, the permission definition randomly jumps from the un-installed app, to any other app that defined the permission.

Explanation Using ACiA$_\alpha$ Model: This issue was encountered while testing ACiA, based on ACiA$_\alpha$ model and can be demonstrated via the Authorization Requirement of the **AddApp** operation (see Table 5), the PERMS_EFF updates in the **AddApp** and **DeleteApp** operations. While an app (App1) is being installed (see Fig. 5), Android checks to see if the custom permission defined by the app (p1) does not already exist on the device; when this check passes, the app gets installed (assume it passes). Then the relation PERMS_EFF gets updated to indicate App1 effectively defined the permission p1. Upon installing two additional apps (App2 and App3) that also define the same permission and are signed with the same certificate as App1, Android will ignore their definition of the permission p1; this is in line with how Android should work. Upon un-installation of App1, however, we can see that, in the operation **DeleteApp**, the relation PERMS_EFF gets modified after choosing a random permission from the set of permissions defined by any other app - in this case either App2 or App3.

Rationale: This random jump between permission definitions upon app un-installation is an unwanted behavior; and, may occur despite the fact that developers are expected to stick to the same definitions for any custom-permissions they define, since this is not enforced by Google.

Proposed Resolution: We believe that Android should remember the order of app installations and modify permission definitions in-order rather than take a random approach to the same; alternatively, keeping in line with highest protection level first, the permission definition that puts the permission into the higher protection level should be utilized by Android. This will enable developers to definitively know, which definition of a custom permission is active.

2. **Normal permissions are never re-granted after app un-installation.** According to Android, **normal** and **signature** permissions are defined to be install-time permissions by Android, so, when multiple apps define the same permission, app un-installation results in any new normal permissions to be not granted to apps. This is not the case with signature permissions, as they are automatically re-granted by Android.

Explanation Using $ACiA_\alpha$ Model: Consider two apps App1 and App2 that define a permission p1, where App1 defines this permission to be in the **normal** protection-level whereas App2 defines the same permission in the **dangerous** protection-level; since App1 got installed first, according to PERMS_EFF from the operation **AddApp** (see Table 5), its definition is effective i.e.: protection-level of p1 is **normal**. If, at this step, App1 is un-installed, App2's definition of the permission becomes active, this functions properly according to the model. However, App2 is not granted this per-mission nor do any other apps that may have requested this permission in their manifests prior to App1's un-install. This is not true for **signature** permissions that are granted upon signature match, nor does it apply to **dangerous** permissions that are requested at run-time by apps. To top it all, in the event that a developer defines a custom-permission without specifying any protection-level to it, the default protection-level applies that is **normal**, this further exacerbates the issue mentioned above and is particularly difficult for new developers. We have reported this issue to Google [1].

Rationale: We believe that this is an unwanted behavior, and the reason is that if a **signature** permissions are being granted in the above mentioned scenario, **normal** permissions should be granted as well since both these permissions are listed as install-time-granted permissions.

Proposed Resolution: We believe that Android should re-grant such converted **normal** permissions in the same way it re-grants the **signature** permissions, so that, the behavior of permissions can be correctly predicted by developers.

3. **Apps can re-grant temporary uri permissions to themselves permanently**. Android enables apps to share their data via content providers, temporarily (using intents with uri permissions), or semi-permanently (using the grantUriPermissions) method. Apart from this, apps can protect the entire content providers with a single (single permission for read and write) or double (one permission for read and one for write) permissions. When an app receives a temporary uri permission, it can even grant those permissions to any other apps temporarily or semi-permanently. This is clearly a flaw as no app can control this style of chain uri permission grants; this flaw is not exactly new and was discovered a few years ago [12].

Explanation Using ACiA$_\alpha$ Model: We can see from Table 6, the **GrantDataPerm** operation does not keep a record of the type of uri-permission grant (temporary or permanent). The authorization requirement for this operation is a simple boolean helper function from Table 4 - `grantApproval`. This is in line with how Android works, and, once the app shuts down, as can be seen from the operation **AppShutdown**, merely the temporarily granted permissions are revoked. The relation GRANTED_DATAPERMS (from Table 3) is responsible for keeping track of the types of uri-permission grants.

4. **Custom permission names are not enforced using the reverse domain style.** Although Google recommends developers to use the reverse domain style naming convention for defining custom-permissions, no formal regulation is done by Google. This can lead to unwanted behavior for the end-user when a new app fails to install, as it attempts to re-define a permission that already exists on the device (if this new app is from a different developer), confusing the user.

Rationale: Google's attempt at providing developers free reign over custom-permissions may backfire and cause an unaware user to be unable to install required apps. This issue should be rectified by Google by regulating custom-permission names (Fig. 6).

5. **Complex custom permission behavior upon app un-installation**. During app un-installation, extensive testing was done to ensure that we captured an accurate behavior for Android. Care was taken while removing permission definitions, since only if there are no other apps defining the same permission, is that permission removed from the system. For this test case we constructed 3 test apps and performed worst case testing with respect to permission definitions and found Issue #2 described above. This is a grave issue since the documentation states that all normal permissions are always granted when their apps are installed on the device.

Explanation Using ACiA$_\alpha$ Model: From Table 5, we can see that the **DeleteApp** operation that models the app un-installation procedure is quite complex. Android allows apps to define custom permissions, so, after the un-installation of such apps, Android removes any custom permissions effectively defined by that app. However, in the event that another app with the same certificate defines the permissions to be removed, Android simply switches

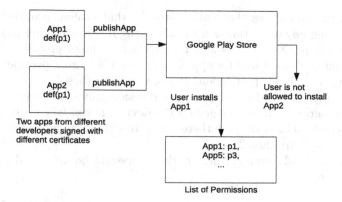

Fig. 6. Drawback of not enforcing custom permission names

the permission definition and keeps that permission from getting mistakenly deleted. Any and all updates to the permissions protecting app components, granted permissions or dangerous permissions requested by apps need to be postponed until after all such custom permission definitions effectively defined by the app being removed, have been dealt with; otherwise these permission definitions would be inconsistent with their expected behavior.

Rationale: This is because Android performs a wide array of book-keeping operations upon the un-installation of any apps, this is done to maintain consistency across the defined custom permissions and effective custom permissions that exist on the device, the permissions that are granted to apps and the dangerous permissions requested by apps to name a few.

5   Conclusion

We have built a model for ACiA and present it in brief, in this paper. Quite a few peculiar behaviors come to light as we delve deeper into Android, some of which we were able to discover and present in this work as well. Future work includes formal analysis to answer many interesting questions such as.

- Given an app and a system permission it does not posses, is there a way in which that app receives that permission? Which ways?
- Given an app and a system permission it does posses, is there a way in which that permission is revoked from this app? Which ways?
- Given an app and it's parameters, can this app be installed on an Android device? Which ways?
- Given an app and a content provider path, is there a way this app can receive a uri permission to that path? If yes, how many ways exist for the app to receive such a permission?

- • Can the app access that data stored by that content provider without obtaining any uri-permission to that path? If yes, which are those?
- – Given two apps, X and Y, where Y protects its content provider with a uri permission, is there a way for app X to access Y's content provider without obtaining the said uri permission? If yes, which are those?
- – Given a permission defined into a permission-group, is there a way its permission-group can be changed on the device? If yes, how many ways can this be achieved? Similarly, is there a way to change its protection level? If yes, how which are those?
- – Given an app and a component, can the component be associated with more than one app?

Acknowledgements. This work is partially supported by DoD ARO Grant W911NF-15-1-0518, NSF CREST Grant HRD-1736209 and NSF CAREER Grant CNS-1553696.

References

1. Android permission protection level "normal" are never re-granted! (2019). https://issuetracker.google.com/issues/129029397. Accessed 21 Mar 2019
2. Android Permissions—Android Open Source Project (2019). https://source.android.com/devices/tech/config. Accessed 17 June 2019
3. Issue about Android's permission to permission-group mapping (2019). https://issuetracker.google.com/issues/128888710. Accessed 21 Mar 2019
4. Request App Permissions—Android Developers (2019). https://developer.android.com/training/permissions/requesting/. Accessed 12 Mar 2019
5. Bagheri, H., Kang, E., Malek, S., Jackson, D.: Detection of design flaws in the android permission protocol through bounded verification. In: Bjørner, N., de Boer, F. (eds.) FM 2015. LNCS, vol. 9109, pp. 73–89. Springer, Cham (2015). https://doi.org/10.1007/978-3-319-19249-9_6
6. Bagheri, H., Kang, E., Malek, S., Jackson, D.: A formal approach for detection of security flaws in the android permission system. Formal Aspects Computi. **30**(5), 525–544 (2018)
7. Bagheri, H., Sadeghi, A., Garcia, J., Malek, S.: COVERT: compositional analysis of android inter-app permission leakage. IEEE Trans. Softw. Eng. **41**(9), 866–886 (2015)
8. Betarte, G., Campo, J., Cristiá, M., Gorostiaga, F., Luna, C., Sanz, C.: Towards formal model-based analysis and testing of android's security mechanisms. In: 2017 XLIII Latin American Computer Conference (CLEI), pp. 1–10. IEEE (2017)
9. Betarte, G., Campo, J., Luna, C., Romano, A.: Formal analysis of android's permission-based security model 1. Sci. Ann. Comput. Sci. **26**(1), 27–68 (2016)
10. Betarte, G., Campo, J.D., Luna, C., Romano, A.: Verifying android's permission model. In: Leucker, M., Rueda, C., Valencia, F.D. (eds.) ICTAC 2015. LNCS, vol. 9399, pp. 485–504. Springer, Cham (2015). https://doi.org/10.1007/978-3-319-25150-9_28
11. Enck, W., Ongtang, M., McDaniel, P.: Understanding android security. IEEE Secur. Priv. **7**(1), 50–57 (2009)

12. Fragkaki, E., Bauer, L., Jia, L., Swasey, D.: Modeling and enhancing android's permission system. In: Foresti, S., Yung, M., Martinelli, F. (eds.) ESORICS 2012. LNCS, vol. 7459, pp. 1–18. Springer, Heidelberg (2012). https://doi.org/10.1007/978-3-642-33167-1_1

13. Shin, W., Kiyomoto, S., Fukushima, K., Tanaka, T.: A formal model to analyze the permission authorization and enforcement in the android framework. In: Proceedings - SocialCom 2010: 2nd IEEE International Conference on Social Computing, PASSAT 2010: 2nd IEEE International Conference on Privacy, Security, Risk and Trust, pp. 944–951 (2010)

14. Tuncay, G.S., Demetriou, S., Ganju, K., Gunter, C.A.: Resolving the predicament of android custom permissions. In: Proceedings of the 2018 Network and Distributed System Security Symposium. Internet Society, Reston (2018)

Security Analysis of Unified Access Control Policies

Mahendra Pratap Singh[1], Shamik Sural[1(✉)], Vijayalakshmi Atluri[2], and Jaideep Vaidya[2]

[1] Department of CSE, Indian Institute of Technology Kharagpur, Kharagpur, India
mahoo15@gmail.com, shamik@cse.iitkgp.ac.in
[2] Department of MSIS, Rutgers University, Newark, USA
atluri@rutgers.edu, jsvaidya@business.rutgers.edu

Abstract. In the modern computing era, access to resources is often restricted through contextual information and the attributes of users, objects and various other entities. Attribute-Based Access Control (ABAC) can capture those requirements as a policy, but it is not yet adopted like Role Based Access Control (RBAC) due to lack of a comprehensive administrative model. In the last few years, several efforts have been made to combine ABAC with RBAC, but they are limited to specification and enforcement only. Recently, we have presented a unified framework along with a role based administrative model that enables specification, enforcement and maintenance of unified access control policies, such as ABAC, RBAC and Meta-Policy Based Access Control (MPBAC). This paper describes role-based administrative model components and then present a methodology which uses a fixed-point based approach for verifying the security properties (like safety and liveness) of those policies in the presence of the administrative model. We also analyse the impact of ABAC, RBAC, MPBAC and administrative model components on the time taken for security analysis. Experimental results demonstrate that the proposed approach is scalable as well as effective.

Keywords: Security analysis · Fixed-point analysis · Attribute Based Access Control · Role Based Access Control · Meta-Policy Based Access Control

1 Introduction

RBAC [4] has been widely accepted due to its simple policy administration, and still, it is in use. ABAC [3] has shown multiple dimensions (e.g., user attributes, object attributes, environment attributes) based access control that is yet to be adopted like RBAC. In ABAC and RBAC, authorisation to a user is granted through attribute-based policies and roles, respectively. Both ABAC and RBAC have some limitations. There is some research work [20] to overcome the limitations of these models but restricted to specification and enforcement only.

© Springer Nature Singapore Pte Ltd. 2020
S. K. Sahay et al. (Eds.): SKM 2019, CCIS 1186, pp. 126–146, 2020.
https://doi.org/10.1007/978-981-15-3817-9_8

Nowadays, organisations are evolving in terms of resources and their usage by different types of users of the same or other organisations. Therefore, there is a need for a flexible and scalable authorisation system that can specify, enforce and maintain multi-attribute policies for enabling access to resources to users.

Recently, an approach [1] is presented that enables specification, enforcement and maintenance of unified security policies which can be multi-dimensional multi-granular in nature. There is some work for the development of administrative models for ABAC and RBAC as well as their security analysis in the presence of its administrative models. Owing to the absence of an administrative model for unified security policies, no work is reported related to comprehensive security analysis of them.

The unique contributions of this paper are as follows:

- First, the components of role based administrative model are described.
- Then, a methodology is introduced for analysing unified access control policies in the presence of the administrative model.

There are various security properties which need to verify before deploying an access control system. In this paper, we consider safety and liveness properties which are stated below:

- *Safety:* Whether a user u can perform an operation ac on an object o in the environmental condition ec.
- *Liveness:* Whether there exists a policy which allows a user u to perform an operation ac.

To do the security analysis, we use μZ [21] which is part of Z3 [22] and is freely available.

The rest of the paper is structured as follows. Role based administrative model components are introduced in Sect. 2. Section 3 presents formal representation of ABAC, RBAC, MPBAC and administrative model components. In Sect. 4, we describe how various security properties for ABAC, RBAC and MPBAC can be analysed using fixed-point based approach μZ [21]. The experimental results are discussed in Sect. 5. Section 6 reviews the related literature while conclusion and future research directions are presented in Sect. 7.

2   Administrative Model for ABAC, RBAC and MPBAC

This section describes components of the role based administrative model presented in [1] for managing ABAC, RBAC and MPBAC. The administrative model is named as RBAMARM (Role Based Administrative Model for ABAC, RBAC and MPBAC).

2.1   Overview of Role Based Administrative Model for ABAC, RBAC and MPBAC (RBAMARM) Relations and Commands

The RBAMARM main components include a set AU of administrative users, a set AR of administrative roles, where each administrative role $ar \in AR$ can be assigned to an administrative user $au \in AU$.

In RBAMARM, each administrative relation is denoted as *(ar, Const, Argu)*, where *ar* represents an administrative role, *Const* denotes an optional boolean expression or range, and *Argu* represents an optional argument or a range. A command of the form *(Argu₁, Argu₂, Argu₃)* along with pre and post constraints is associated with each relation, where $Argu_1$, $Argu_2$ and $Argu_3$ denote an argument, an optional argument and an argument, respectively.

Table 1. Commands and administrative relations for RBAMARM

Admin Relation$_1$: *Can_assign_UAV_user (ar, Cond(uav₁), uav)*

Command$_1$: *assign_user_UAV (au, u, uav)*

Pre-constraints: *(au, ar) ∈ User_adminrole_assignment,*
                (u, uav) ∉ User_UAV_assignment, Cond(uav₁) == True

Post-constraints: *User_UAV_assignment = User_UAV_assignment ∪*
                {u, uav}

Admin Relation$_2$: *Can_delete_UAV_user (ar, Cond(uav₁), uav)*

Command$_2$: *delete_user_UAV (au, u, uav)*

Pre-constraints: *(au, ar) ∈ User_adminrole_assignment,*
                (u, uav) ∈ User_UAV_assignment, Cond(uav₁) == True

Post-constraints: *User_UAV_assignment = User_UAV_assignment -*
                {u, uav}

Admin Relation$_3$: *Can_assign_OAV_object (ar, Cond(oav₁), oav)*

Command$_3$: *assign_object_OAV (au, o, oav)*

Pre-constraints: *(au, ar) ∈ User_adminrole_assignment,*
                (o, oav) ∉ Object_OAV_assignment, Cond(oav₁) == True

Post-constraints: *Object_OAV_assignment = Object_OAV_assignment ∪*
                {o, oav}

Admin Relation$_4$: *Can_delete_OAV_object (ar, Cond(oav₁), oav)*

Command$_4$: *delete_object_OAV (au, o, oav)*

Pre-constraints: *(au, ar) ∈ User_adminrole_assignment,*
                (o, oav) ∈ Object_OAV_assignment, Cond(oav₁) == True

Post-constraints: *Object_OAV_assignment = Object_OAV_assignment -*
                {o, oav}

Admin Relation$_5$: *Can_assign_user (ar, Cond(r₁), r)*

Command$_5$: *assign_userrole (au, u, r)*

Pre-constraints: *(au, ar) ∈ User_adminrole_assignment,*
                (u, r) ∉ User_role_assignment, Cond(r₁) == True

Post-constraints: *User_role_assignment = User_role_assignment ∪ {u, r}*

(contniued)

Table 1. (*continued*)

Admin Relation$_6$:	*Can_revoke_user (ar, r)*
Command$_6$:	*revoke_userrole (au, u, r)*
Pre-constraints:	*(au, ar)* $\in$ *User_adminrole_assignment,*
	(u, r) $\in$ *User_role_assignment*
Post-constraints:	*User_role_assignment = User_role_assignment - {u, r}*
Admin Relation$_7$:	*Can_assign_permission (ar, r$_1$, r)*
Command$_7$:	*assign_permrole (au, pr (r$_1$), r)*
Pre-constraints:	*(au, ar)* $\in$ *User_adminrole_assignment,*
	(r, pr (r$_1$)) $\notin$ *Permission_role_assignment*
Post-constraints:	*Permission_role_assignment =*
	Permission_role_assignment $\cup$ *{r, pr (r$_1$)}*
Admin Relation$_8$:	*Can_revoke_permission (ar, r)*
Command$_8$:	*revoke_permrole (au, r, pr)*
Pre-constraints:	*(au, ar)* $\in$ *User_adminrole_assignment,*
	(r, pr) $\in$ *Permission_role_assignment*
Post-constraints:	*Permission_role_assignment =*
	Permission_role_assignment - {r, pr}
Admin Relation$_9$:	*Can_create_policy (ar)*
Command$_9$:	*create_policy(au, p)*
Pre-constraints:	*(au, ar)* $\in$ *User_adminrole_assignment, p* $\notin$ *Policy*
Post-constraints:	*Policy = Policy* $\cup$ *{p}*
Admin Relation$_{10}$:	*Can_delete_policy (ar, p)*
Command$_{10}$:	*delete_policy(au, p)*
Pre-constraints:	*(au, ar)* $\in$ *User_adminrole_assignment, p* $\in$ *Policy*
Post-constraints:	*Policy = Policy - {p}*
Admin Relation$_{11}$:	*Can_modify_policy (ar, p)*
Command$_{11}$:	*modify_policy(au, p)*
Pre-constraints:	*(au, ar)* $\in$ *User_adminrole_assignment, p* $\in$ *Policy*
Post-constraints:	*Policy = Policy* $\cup$ *{p}*

When an administrative user tries to execute a command, the system performs the following steps to check whether the administrative user can execute the command.

1. It takes the administrative user and the command as input and fetches the administrative roles associated with the administrative user through the relation *User_adminrole_assignment*.
2. Finally, it finds a policy through the relation with which the command is associated and in which administrative role is either a subset or same as of the administrative roles fetched in Step 1.

2.2   RBAMARM Relations and Commands

RBAMARM mainly includes three types of relations. The first type of relations manages the set of users, objects, rights, roles, permissions, user attributes, object attributes, and environmental attributes. The second type of relations is meant for managing user-role, role-permission and role-role components of RBAC. While the third type of relations manages user to user attribute value assignments, object to object attribute value assignments, environment conditions and policy-related components of ABAC.

Table 1 summarizes the second type and the third type few administrative relations along with their commands, pre constraints and post constraints. The relations shown in the table can influence the state of a system and restrict administrative users access to various components of ABAC, RBAC and MPBAC. As an example, consider the relation $can\_modify\_policy\ (ar, p)$ which is meant for modifying ABAC policy p components. If an administrative user au has the administrative role ar, then he can modify the ABAC policy p components.

3   Formal Representation of ABAC, RBAC, MPBAC and RBAMARM

This section presents the formal representation of ABAC, RBAC, MPBAC and RBAMARM relations presented in [1]. This representation can act as the basis to model ABAC, RBAC, MPBAC and RBAMARM using any first-order logic language. Through logical expression, we also show how RBAMARM relations impact various components of ABAC, RBAC and MPBAC.

A common set of notations is used to unify the ABAC, RBAC, MPBAC and RBAMARM policies. The relations *User* and *Object* represent the set U of users and set O of objects, respectively. The jth member of these sets is represented as u_j and o_j, respectively. The set AC of access rights is represented using the relation *Right*, and the jth access right of AC is denoted as ac_j.

3.1   Representation of ABAC Components as Relations

The set UA of user attributes, set OA of object attributes and set EA of environment attributes are represented using the relations *User_attribute*, *Object_attribute* and *Environment_attribute*, and the jth member of these sets is represented as ua_j, oa_j and ea_j, respectively. The relations *User_attribute_value* and *Object_attribute_value* represent the set UAV of user attribute values and set OAV of object attribute values, respectively. Let the functions *UAttributeValue(ua)* and *OAttributeValue(oa)* return the values of a user attribute and an object attribute, respectively. The relations *User_UAV_assignment*, *Object_OAV_assignment* and *Environment_EAV_assignment* denote user to user attribute value assignments, object to object attribute value assignments and environment to environment attribute value assignments, respectively.

The functions $UserAttributeValue(u_j)$, $ObjectAttributeValue(o_j)$ and $EnvAttributeValue(ec_j)$ return the set of attribute values assigned to the user u_j, object o_j and environment condition ec_j, respectively. The relation $Policy$ denotes the set of policies, and its jth policy is represented as p_j. In ABAC, a policy is composed of the values of attributes of user, object and environment, and an access right. The policy-user attribute value assignments, policy-object attribute value assignments, policy-environment condition assignments and policy-right assignments are represented using the relations $Rule\_UAV\_assignment$, $Rule\_OAV\_assignment$, $Rule\_EAV\_assignment$ and $Rule\_right\_assignment$, respectively. The notations p_j (uav), p_j (oav), p_j (ec) and p_j (ac) return the set of user attribute values, object attribute values, environment conditions, and the access right associated with the jth policy.

3.2   Representation of RBAC Components as Relations

The set R of roles and set PR of permissions are represented using the relation $Role$ and $Permission$, and r_j and pr_j represent the jth member of these sets, respectively. The set UR of user-role assignments and set RP of role-permission assignments are represented using the relations $User\_role\_assignment$ and $Permission\_role\_assignment$, respectively. The function $UserRole(u)$ returns the set of roles associated with a user u either through $User\_role\_assignment$ or $Role\_hierarchy$. Similarly, the function $RolePerm(r)$ returns the set of permissions associated with the role r either through $Permission\_role\_assignment$ or $Role\_hierarchy$.

The role hierarchy is represented using the relations $Role\_hierarchy$. The functions $SenRole(r)$ and $JunRole(r)$ return the set of roles senior and junior to r, respectively. The definition of permissions in the form of access rights on objects is represented using the relation $Permission\_object\_assignment$, and the function $PermObj(pr_j)$ returns the access right and object associated with the jth permission.

3.3   Representation of MPBAC Components as Relations

In MPBAC, meta-policies are specified using ABAC relations, RBAC relations and policy result combining approaches (PRCAs). Therefore, it uses the same notation for the ABAC and RBAC relations as described in Subsects. 3.1 and 3.2, respectively. The set of meta-policies is represented as MP, and its jth meta-policy is represented as mp_j. The set of PRCAs is represented as PA, and pa_j represents its jth approach. The function $PolicyApproach(mp_j)$ returns the policy result combining approach used in the jth meta-policy.

3.4   Representation of RBAMARM Components as Relations

The set AR of adminroles and set AP of adminpermissions are denoted using the relations $Adminrole$ and $Adminpermission$, respectively. The notations ar_j and ap_j represent the jth adminrole and adminpermission of these sets, respectively. The relations *User_adminrole_assignment* and *Adminpermission_adminrole_assignment* represent user to adminrole assignments and adminrole to adminpermission assignments, respectively. The partial ordering of adminroles in an organization is represented using the relation *Adminrole_hierarchy*, and the functions *SenAdminRole(ar)* and *JunAdminRole(ar)* return the set of adminroles senior and junior to ar, respectively.

Representation of Administrative Relations. Administrative relations shown in Table 1 are described as follows.

- *Can_assign_UAV_user (ar, Cond(uav₁), uav):* Administrative users can assign existing user attribute values to users if the following condition satisfies:

$$\exists\,(ar, Cond(uav_1), uav) \in Can\_assign\_UAV\_user\,|\,\exists\,au \in User\,|\,\exists\,(au, ar) \in$$
$$User\_adminrole\_assignment\,|\,Cond(uav_1) == True \tag{1}$$

The successful execution of the command *assign_user_UAV (au, u, uav)* associated with the relation *Can_assign_UAV_user*, meant for assigning user attribute value to user, causes assignment of a new value *uav* of a user attribute *ua* to a user *u* into the relation *User_UAV_assignment*. The new set of user attribute values associated with the user *u* is as follows:
$$User\_UAV\_assignment = User\_UAV\_assignment \cup \{u, uav\}$$

- *Can_delete_UAV_user (ar, Cond(uav₁), uav):* Administrative users can revoke user attribute values from users if the following condition satisfies:

$$\exists\,(ar, Cond(uav_1), uav) \in Can\_revoke\_UAV\_user\,|\,\exists\,au \in User\,|\,\exists(au, ar) \in$$
$$User\_adminrole\_assignment\,|\,Cond(uav_1) == True \tag{2}$$

The successful execution of the command *delete_user_UAV (au, u, uav)* associated with the relation *Can_delete_UAV_user* removes a value *uav* of a user attribute *ua* from a user *u*. The new set of user attribute values associated with the user *u* in the relation *User_UAV_assignment* is as follows:
$$User\_UAV\_assignment = User\_UAV\_assignment - \{u, uav\}$$

- *Can_assign_OAV_object (ar, Cond(oav₁), oav):* Administrative users can assign existing object attribute values to objects if the following condition satisfies:

$$\exists\,(ar, Cond(oav_1), oav) \in Can\_assign\_OAV\_object\,|\,\exists\,au \in User\,|\,\exists(au, ar)$$
$$\in User\_adminrole\_assignment\,|\,Cond(oav_1) == True \tag{3}$$

The successful execution of the command *assign_object_OAV (au, o, oav)* associated with the relation *Can_assign_OAV_object*, meant for assigning object attribute value to object, assigns a new value *oav* of an object attribute *oa* to an object *o* into the relation *Object_OAV_assignment*. The new set of Object attribute values associated with the object *o* is as follows:
$$Object\_OAV\_assignment = Object\_OAV\_assignment \cup \{o, oav\}$$

– *Can_delete_OAV_object (ar, Cond(oav₁), oav):* Administrative users can revoke object attribute values from objects if the following condition satisfies:

$$\exists\ (ar,\ Cond(oav_1),\ oav) \in Can\_revoke\_OAV\_object\ |\ \exists\ au \in User\ |\ \exists\ (au, ar)$$
$$\in User\_adminrole\_assignment\ |\ Cond(oav_1)\ ==\ True \qquad (4)$$

The successful execution of the command *delete_object_OAV (au, o, oav)* associated with the relation *Can_delete_OAV_object* removes a value *oav* of an object attribute *ua* from an object *o*. The new set of object attribute values associated with the object *o* in the relation *Object_OAV_assignment* is as follows:

Object_OAV_assignment = Object_OAV_assignment - $\{o, oav\}$

– *Can_assign_user (ar, Cond(r₁), r):* New user to role assignments can be inserted into the relation *User_role_assignment* if the following condition satisfies:

$$\exists\ (ar,\ Cond(r_1),\ r) \in Can\_assign\_user\ |\ \exists\ au \in User\ |\ \exists\ (au, ar)$$
$$\in User\_adminrole\_assignment\ |\ Cond(r_1) == True \qquad (5)$$

The successful execution of the command *assign_userrole (au, u, r)* associated with the relation *Can_assign_user*, meant for assigning a role to a user, causes assignment of a new role *r* to a user *u*. The new set of user role assignments in the relation *User_role_assignment* is as follows:

User_role_assignment = User_role_assignment $\cup\ \{u, r\}$

– *Can_revoke_user (ar, r):* Existing user to role assignments can be removed from the relation *User_role_assignment* if the following condition satisfies:

$$\exists\ (ar, r) \in Can\_revoke\_user\ |\ \exists\ au \in User\ |\ \exists\ (au, ar) \in User\_adminrole\_assignment$$
$$(6)$$

The successful execution of the command *revoke_userrole (au, u, r)* associated with the relation *Can_revoke_user* removes an existing role *r* from a user *u*. The new set of user role assignments in the relation *User_role_assignment* is as follows:

User_role_assignment = User_role_assignment - $\{u, r\}$

– *Can_assign_permission (ar, r₁, r):* New permission to role assignments can be inserted into the relation *Permission_role_assignment* if the following condition satisfies:

$$\exists\ (ar, r_1, r) \in Can\_assign\_permission\ |\ \exists\ au \in User\ |\ \exists\ (au, ar) \in User\_adminrole\_assignment$$
$$(7)$$

The successful execution of the command *assign_permrole (au, pr (r₁), r)* associated with the relation *Can_assign_permission*, meant for assigning a permission to a role, assigns a new permission *pr* of a role r_1 to a role *r*. The new set of permission role assignments in the relation *Permission_role_assignment* is as follows:

Permission_role_assignment = Permission_role_assignment $\cup\ \{r, pr\}$

- *Can_revoke_permission (ar, r):* Existing permission to role assignments can be removed from the relation *Permission_role_assignment* if the following condition satisfies:

$$\exists\ (ar,\ r)\ \in\ Can\_revoke\_permission\ |\ \exists\ au\ \in\ User\ |\ \exists\ (au,\ ar)\ \in\ User\_adminrole\_assignment \tag{8}$$

The successful evaluation of constraints and execution of the command *revoke_permrole (au, r, pr)* associated with the relation *Can_revoke_permission* cause removal of an existing permission *pr* from a role *r*. The new set of permission role assignments in the relation *Permission_role_assignment* is as follows:

$Permission\_role\_assignment = Permission\_role\_assignment$ - $\{r, pr\}$

- *Can_create_policy (ar):* Administrative users can create new policies if the following condition satisfies:

$$\exists\ ar\ \in\ Can\_create\_policy\ |\ \exists\ au\ \in\ User\ |\ \exists\ (au,\ ar)\ \in\ User\_adminrole\_assignment \tag{9}$$

The successful execution of the command *create_policy (au, p)* and evaluation of constraints (pre and post) associated with the relation *Can_create_policy* create a new policy *p* into the relation *Policy*. The new set of policies in the relation *Policy* is as follows:

$Policy = Policy \cup \{p\}$

- *Can_delete_policy (ar, p):* Administrative users can delete existing policies if the following condition satisfies:

$$\exists\ (ar,\ p)\ \in\ Can\_delete\_policy\ |\ \exists\ au\ \in\ User\ |\ \exists\ (au,\ ar)\ \in\ User\_adminrole\_assignment \tag{10}$$

The successful execution of the command *delete_policy (au, p)* and evaluation of constraints (pre and post) associated with the relation *Can_delete_policy* remove an existing policy *p* from the relation *Policy*. The new set of policies in the relation *Policy* is as follows:

$Policy = Policy$ - $\{p\}$

- *Can_modify_policy (ar, p):* Administrative users can modify existing policies if the following condition satisfies:

$$\exists\ (ar,\ p)\ \in\ Can\_modify\_policy\ |\ \exists\ au\ \in\ User\ |\ \exists\ (au,\ ar)\ \in\ User\_adminrole\_assignment \tag{11}$$

The successful execution of the command *modify_policy (au, p)* associated with the relation *Can_modify_policy*, meant for modifying a policy, modifies the components of the existing policy *p*. The new set of policies in the relation *Policy* is as follows:

$Policy = Policy \cup \{p\}$

3.5   Representation of Security Properties

The various security properties (such as safety and liveness) for ABAC, RBAC and MPBAC are defined as follows:

Safety Property

- The relation *user_access_a (u, o, ac, ec)* is used for representing the ABAC safety property. It returns true if the following condition satisfies:
  $\exists p_i \in Policy \,|\, p_i$ *(uav)* $\subseteq$ *UserAttributeValue (u)* $\wedge$ p_i *(oav)* $\subseteq$ *Object AttributeValue (o)* $\wedge$ p_i *(ac)* $==$ *ac* $\wedge$ p_i *(ec)* $\subseteq$ *(ec)*
- The relation *user_access (u, o, ac)* is used for representing the RBAC safety property. It returns true if the following condition satisfies:
  $\exists \{u, r\} \in$ *UserRole(u)* $\wedge$ $\exists \{r, pr\} \in$ *RolePerm(r)* $\wedge$ $\exists \{pr, o, ac\} \in$ *Permission_object_assignment*
- The relation *access (u, o, ac, ec)* is used for representing the MPBAC safety property. It returns true if the following condition satisfies according to a PRCA involved in a meta-policy:
  PRCA: Allow access if any sub-policy allows access
  user_access_a (u, o, ac, ec) $\vee$ *user_access (u, o, ac)*
  PRCA: Allow access if all sub-policies allow access
  user_access_a (u, o, ac, ec) $\wedge$ *user_access (u, o, ac)*

Liveness Property

- The relation *liv_ABAC (ac)* is used for defining the ABAC liveness property. It returns true if the following conditions satisfies:
  $\exists p_i \in Policy \,|\, p_i$ *(uav)* $\subseteq$ *UserAttributeValue (u)* $\wedge$ p_i *(ac)* $==$ *ac*
- The relation *liv_RBAC (ac)* is used for defining the RBAC liveness property. It returns true if the following conditions satisfies:
  $\exists \{pr, o, ac\} \in$ *Permission_object_assignment* $\wedge$ $\exists \{r, pr\} \in$ *Permission_role_assignment* $\wedge$ $\exists \{u, r\} \in$ *User_role_assignment*
- The relation *liv_MP (ac)* is used for defining the MPBAC liveness property. It returns true if the following condition satisfies according to a PRCA involved in a meta-policy:
  PRCA: Allow access if any sub-policy allows access
  liv_ABAC (ac) $\vee$ *liv_RBAC (ac)*
  PRCA: Allow access if all sub-policies allow access
  liv_ABAC (ac) $\wedge$ *liv_RBAC (ac)*

Thus, the issue of security analysis is to demonstrate that the above-mentioned safety and liveness properties are satisfied for ABAC, RBAC and MPBAC relations respectively described in Subsects. 3.1, 3.2 and 3.3 in the presence of RBAMARM relations described in Subsect. 3.4.

4   Analysis of Security Properties

This section demonstrates how μz can be used to perform the security analysis of ABAC, RBAC and MPBAC policies. μz is a fixed-point based analyser that takes these policies in *Datalog* form as input and verifies security properties (like safety and liveness) of them. We also show how the presence of administrative relations influences the security properties of those policies.

4.1   Modeling of Security Properties Using μZ

For performing security analysis, the components of ABAC, RBAC, MPBAC and RBAMARM are modeled using *Datalog* that serves as knowledge base. The model thus generated is passed as input to μZ verification tool Z3. When a security query is presented to the tool, it returns *sat* or *unsat*.

– *Modeling ABAC Safety Property:* To verify ABAC safety property, the following rules are defined through *Datalog*. The facts that an analyser can derive from the rules are described below.

Can_assign_UAV_user(ar, uav_1, uav_2): can_assg_uav(ar, uav_1, uav_2)
Can_assign_UAV_user(ar, uav_1, uav_2): can_assg_uav(ar, uav_1, uav_3), Can-_assign_UAV_user(ar, uav_3, uav_2)
Can_assign_OAV_object(ar, oav_1, oav_2): can_assg_oav(ar, oav_1, oav_2)
Can_assign_OAV_object(ar, oav_1, oav_2): can_assg_oav(ar, oav_1, oav_3), Can-_assign_OAV_object(ar, oav_3, oav_2)
user_access_a(u, o, ac, ec): assg_user_policy(u, p), assg_object_policy(o, p), p_right(p, ac), p_eav(p, ec)

The first and the second rules help analyser to find the set of *can_assg_uav* relations through which a user attribute value uav_2 can be assigned to a user who has a user attribute value uav_1. Similarly, the third and the fourth rules help analyser to find the set of *can_assg_oav* relations through which an object attribute value oav_2 can be assigned to an object who has an object attribute value oav_1. The last rule *user_access_a* returns *true* if there exists a policy which allows a user u to perform an access right ac on an object o in the presence of environment condition ec.

– *Modeling RBAC Safety Property:* To verify RBAC safety property, the following rules are defined through *Datalog*. The facts that an analyser can derive from the rules are described below.

Can_assign_user(ar, r_1, r_2): can_assg_u(ar, r_1, r_2)
Can_assign_user(ar, r_1, r_2): can_assg_u(ar, r_1, r_3), Can_assign_user(ar, r_3, r_2)
hier_assg_role(r_1, r_2): role_hier(r_1, r_2)
hier_assg_role(r_1, r_2): role_hier(r_1, r_3), hier_assg_role(r_3, r_2)
assg_user(u, r): user_role(u, r)
assg_user(u, r): user_role(u, r_2), hier_assg_role(r_2, r)
user_assgd(u, r): assg_user(u, r)
user_assgd(u, r): assg_user(u, r_2), Can_assign_user(ar, r_2, r)
user_assgd(u, r): assg_user(u, r_3), Can_assign_user(ar, r_3, r_2), hier_assg-role-(r_2, r)
Can_assign_permission(ar, r_1, r_2): can_assg_p(ar, r_1, r_2)
Can_assign_permission(ar, r_1, r_2):   can_assg_p(ar, r_1, r_3),   Can_assign_permis-sion(ar, r_3, r_2)
assg_perm(r, pr): role_perm(r, pr)
assg_perm(r, pr): hier_assg_role(r, r_1), role_perm(r_1, pr)
perm_assgd(r, pr): assg_perm(r, pr)

perm_assgd(r, pr): assg_perm(r_1, pr), Can_assign_permission(ar, r_1, r)
perm_assgd(r, pr):   assg_perm(r_2, pr),   Can_assign_permission(ar, r_2, r_1),
hier_assg_role(r, r_1)
user_perm(u, pr): user_assgd(u, r), perm_assgd(r, pr)
user_access(u, o, ac): object_perm(pr, o, ac), user_perm(u, pr)

The first and the second rules help analyser to find the set of *can_assg_u*
relations through which a role r_2 can be assigned to a user who has a role
r_1. The third and the fourth rules convey that a role r_1 gets a role r_2 either
directly or indirectly through *role_hier*. The fifth and sixth rules define that
a user *u* is associated with a role *r* if either there is a *(u,r)* in *user_role* or
if *u* gets role *r* through *role_hier*. The seventh and eighth rules convey that
a user *u* is associated with a role *r*, either through *user_role* or *role_hier*, or
it may get that due to presence of a *can_assg_u* fact. The ninth rule defines
that a user *u* gets a role *r*, either through *user_role* or through *role_hier*, due
to presence of a *can_assg_u* fact and inheritance of a role through *role_hier*.
The tenth and the eleventh rules help analyser to find the set of *can_assg_p*
relations through which a role r_1 permissions can be assigned to a user who
has a role r_2. The twelve and the thirteen rules define that a permission *pr*
is associated with a role *r* if either there is a *(r, pr)* in *role_perm* or if *r*
gets *pr* through *role_hier*. The fourteen and the fifteen rules convey that a
role *r* gets a permission *pr*, either through *role_perm* or *role_hier*, or it may
get that due to presence of a *can_assg_p* fact. The sixteen rule defines that
a role gets a permission *PR*, either through *role_perm* or *role_hier*, due to
presence of a *can_assg_p* fact and inheritance of a role through *role_hier*. The
seventeen rule states that a user *u* gets a permission *pr* through *user_assgd*
and *perm_assgd*. The last rule *user_access* returns *true* if there exists a permission *pr* which is available to a user *u* through a role *r*.

- *Modeling MPBAC Safety Property:* To verify MPBAC safety property, the
  above mentioned ABAC and RBAC safety analysis rules are referred that are
  defined through *Datalog*. The facts that an analyser can derive from those
  rules are described below.
  - *PRCA:* Allow access if all sub-policies allow access
    access(u, o, ac, ec): user_access_a(u, o, ac, ec), user_access(u, o, ac)
    The above rule returns true if the facts *user_access_a(u, o, ac, ec)* and
    user_access(u, o, ac) return true. In other words, the rule *access(u, o,
    ac, ec)* allows access if both ABAC and RBAC allow access.
  - *PRCA:* Allow access if any sub-policy allows access
    access(u, o, ac, ec): user_access_a(u, o, ac, ec)
    access(u, o, ac, ec): user_access(u, o, ac)
    The rule *access(u, o, ac, ec)* returns *true* if either the fact *user_access_a*
    or the fact *user_access* permits access. In other words, the rule *access(u,
    o, ac, ec)* allows access if either ABAC or RBAC allows access.

- *Modeling ABAC Liveness Property:* To verify ABAC liveness property, the
  following rules are defined using *Datalog*. The facts that an analyser can derive
  from the rules are described below.

Can_assign_UAV_user(ar, uav_1, uav_2): can_assg_uav(ar, uav_1, uav_2)
Can_assign_UAV_user(ar, uav_1, uav_2):   can_assg_uav(ar, uav_1, uav_3),   Can_assign_UAV_user(ar, uav_3, UAV_2)
assg_user_p(p): assg_user_policy(u, p)
liv_ABAC(ac): p_right(p, ac), assg_user_p(p)

The first and the second rules help analyser to find the set of *can_assg_uav* relations through which a user attribute value uav_2 can be assigned to a user who has a user attribute value uav_1. The third rule returns a policy p whose user attribute values are a subset or same as of user u attribute values. The last rule conveys that there is a policy p which allows a user u to perform an access right ac.

- *Modeling RBAC Liveness Property:* To verify RBAC liveness property, the following rules are defined using *Datalog*. The facts that an analyser can derive from the rules are described below.

assg_u(r): user_assgd(u, r)
user_p(pr): perm_assgd(r, pr), assg_u(r)
liv_RBAC(ac): object_perm(pr, o, ac), user_p(pr)

The first rule makes use of the fact *user_assgd* which refers seventh, eighth and ninth rules defined in the *Modeling RBAC Safety Property* and finds a user u associated with role r. Similarly, the second rule makes use of the fact *perm_assgd* which refers fourteen, fifteen and sixteen rules defined in the *Modeling RBAC Safety Property* and finds permission pr assigned to a role r that a user u gets through the role r. The last rule conveys that there is a permission pr which enables a user u to perform an access right ac through a role r.

- *Modeling MPBAC Liveness Property:* To verify MPBAC liveness property, the above mentioned ABAC and RBAC liveness rules are referred that are defined using *Datalog*. The facts that an analyser can derive from those rules are described below.

PRCA: Allow access if all sub-policies allow access
liv_MP(ac): liv_ABAC(ac), liv_RBAC(ac)

In the above rule, the facts *liv_ABAC* and *liv_RBAC* return *true* if there exists an attribute based policy and a role based policy defined using an access right ac.

PRCA: Allow access if any sub-policy allows access
liv_MP(ac): liv_ABAC(ac)
liv_MP(ac): liv_RBAC(ac)

In the above rules, the fact *liv_ABAC* or *liv_RBAC* returns *true* if there exists an attribute based policy or a role based policy defined using an access right ac.

Table 2. User to user attribute value assignment

User	Designation	Grade	Department
U_1	CSO	Manager	BB
U_2	RM	Deputy manager	TxB

Table 3. Object to object attribute value assignment

Object	Object type	Department
Tx_1	Transaction	TxB
O_1	Customer record	BB

4.2 Overview of Banking System Example

For security analysis, consider ABAC, RBAC and MPBAC in the banking system (BS) which is described in [1]. Initially, let there be four users $(U = \{U_1, U_2, U_3, U_4\})$, two objects $(O = \{Tx_1, O_1\})$, two roles $(R = \{CSO, RM\})$, two rights $AC = \{Read, Modify\}$, three user attributes $(UA=\{Grade = \{Manager, Deputy\ manager\}, Designation = \{CSO, RM\}, Department = \{BB, TxB\}\})$, two object attributes $(OA = \{Object\ type = \{Transaction, Customer\ record\}, Department = \{BB, TxB\}\})$ and two environment attributes $(EA = \{Working\ hours = \{09.00\ AM\text{-}04.00\ PM\}, Branch\ of\ posting = \{IIT\ KGP\}\})$ in the system. Tables 2 and 3 respectively capture user-user attribute value assignments and object-object attribute value assignments. Environment conditions are shown in Table 4.

The ABAC, RBAC and MPBAC policies correspond to the following BS requirements are shown in Tables 5, 6 and 7, respectively. It can be observed from the tables that ABAC and RBAC respectively can specify complete and partial requirements while MPBAC combines ABAC and RBAC policies, and can capture complete requirements.

- BS_1: It states that a user u, who is a *Manager* in the *Branch Banking (BB)* department, through the role *Customer service officer (CSO)*, can perform *Modify* operation on a customer record O_1 during working hours from the branch of posting.
- BS_2: It states that a user u, who is a *Deputy manager* in the *Forex and Treasury (TxB)* department, through the role *RM*, can perform *read* operation on a customer record O_1 during working hours from the branch of posting.

Let us assume that there are two admin roles $(AR = \{SSO, ASO_1\})$, and Table 8 shows user-admin role assignments. Two specific sets of administrative relations and commands are shown in Table 9 and their inclusion can take a system from a safe state to an unsafe state.

Table 4. Environment condition

Environment condition	Working hours	Branch of posting
EC1	09: 00 AM–04: 00 PM	IIT KGP

Table 5. ABAC policies for BS requirements

AP_1: $(AP_1\{uav\}=\{$CSO, Manager, BB$\}$, $AP_1\{oav\}=$
    $\{$Customer Record$\}$, $AP_1\{right\}=\{$Modify$\}$, $AP_1\{eav\}=\{$EC1$\})$
AP_2: $(AP_2\{uav\}=\{$RM, Deputy manager, TxB$\}$, $AP2\{oav\}=$
    $\{$Customer record$\}$, $AP_2\{right\}=\{$Read$\}$, $AP_2\{eav\}=\{$EC1$\})$

Table 6. RBAC policies for BS requirements

RB_1: (UR=$\{$U$_1$, CSO$\}$, RP=$\{$CSO, Pr$_1\}$, Pr=$\{$Pr$_1$, O$_1$, Modify$\})$
RB_2: (UR=$\{$U$_2$, RM$\}$, RP=$\{$RM, Pr$_2\}$, Pr=$\{$Pr$_2$, O$_1$, Read$\})$

4.3 Safety Analysis

To perform the safety analysis, we first define safe state for ABAC, RBAC and MPBAC as shown in Tables 5, 6 and 7, respectively. Then, we verify whether system remains in safe state in the presence and absence of administrative policies. As an example, the sets of administrative relations and commands shown in Table 9 are considered for discussing their impact on safety analysis.

For performing the safety analysis, safety queries in the following forms are raised to the analyser.

– $user\_access\_a$ $(U_2, O_1, Modify, EC_1)$: This query refers ABAC policies and asks analyser whether a user U_2 can $Modify$ a customer record O_1 during office hours from the branch of posting.
– $user\_access$ $(U_2, O_1, Modify)$: This query refers RBAC policies and asks analyser whether a user U_2 can $Modify$ a customer record O_1.
– $access$ $(U_2, O_1, Modify, EC_1)$: This query refers MPBAC policies and asks analyser whether a user U_2 can $Modify$ a customer record O_1 during office hours from the branch of posting.

If the analyser returns *unsat* for the above safety queries, then the system is in safe state only. In the absence of administrative relations and commands shown in Table 9, the analyser returns *unsat* for the queries mentioned above that means system safety is not violated. On the other side, in the presence of Set_1 administrative relations and commands shown in Table 9, the analyser returns *sat* that means system moves from a safe to an unsafe state. It may be noted that, in the absence of Set_1 administrative privileges, there is only one ABAC, RBAC, and MPBAC policy for $Modify$ operation that is represented as AP_1, RB_1, and MP_1, respectively. The user U_2 does not possess user attributes, role, and both

Table 7. MPBAC policies for BS requirements

MP_1:

$PRCA$: Allow access if all sub-policies allow access

SP_1: (SP_1uav={CSO, Manager, BB}, SP_1oav={Customer record},
  SP_1right={Modify}, SP_1eav={EC1})

SP_2: (UR={U_1, CSO}, RP={CSO, Pr_1}, Pr={Pr_1, O_1, Modify})

MP_2:

$PRCA$: Allow access if all sub-policies allow access

SP_1: (SP_1uav={RM, Deputy manager, TxB},
  SP_1oav={Customer record}, SP_1right={Read}, SP_1eav={EC1})

SP_2: (UR={U_2, RM}, RP={RM, Pr_2}, Pr={Pr_2, O_1, Read})

Table 8. User to administrative role assignment

User	Admin role
U_3	SSO
U_4	ASO_1

Table 9. Administrative relations and commands

Set_1:

Can_create_policy (SSO)

create_policy (U_3, {AP_3{uav}={RM, Deputy manager, TxB}, AP_3{oav}=
  {Customer record}, AP_3{right}={Modify}, AP_3{eav}={EC1}})

Can_assign_permission (SSO, CSO, RM)

assign_permrole (U_3, Pr_1 (CSO), RM)

Set_2:

Can_delete_policy (ASO_1, AP_2)

delete_policy (U_4, AP_2)

Can_revoke_permission (ASO_1, RM)

revoke_permrole (U_4, RM, Pr_2)

---

specified in the AP_1, RB_1, and MP_1, respectively. Hence, U_2 cannot perform *Modify* operation. However, in the presence of Set_1 administrative privileges, an administrative user U_3 who has an administrative role *SSO*, adds a new ABAC policy AP_3 and assigns *CSO* privileges to *RM* in the system that enables a user U_2 to perform *Modify* operation. It can thus be seen that the system moves from a safe state to an unsafe state. Therefore, it is necessary to analyse the impact of a security policy before inserting it into a system.

Table 10. Experimental results showing time (seconds) taken by μZ for safety analysis

Data set	Without administrative policy			With administrative policy		
	RBAC	ABAC	MPBAC	RBAC	ABAC	MPBAC
DS1	<.01	<.01	.01	.01	<.01	.02
DS2	.02	<.01	.03	.03	.02	.06
DS3	.04	.01	.05	.05	.03	.12
DS4	.20	.03	.28	.27	.29	.81
DS5	2.52	.58	7.63	8.08	6.86	16.43

4.4 Liveness Analysis

To analyse the liveness, queries in the following forms are posed to analyser.

– *liv_ABAC (Read):* This query utilizes ABAC policies and checks whether there exists a policy which enables at least one user to perform the *Read* operation.
– *liv_RBAC (Read):* This query utilizes RBAC policies and checks whether there exists a policy which enables at least one user to perform the *Read* operation.
– *liv_MPBAC (Read):* This query utilizes MPBAC policies and checks whether there exists a policy which enables at least one user to perform the *Read* operation.

If the analyser returns *sat* for the above liveness queries, then the system is live only. In the example *Banking System*, we posses ABAC, RBAC, and MPBAC liveness query respectively *liv_ABAC(Read)*, *liv_RBAC(Read)*, and *liv_RBAC(Read)*. Initially, there is one AP_2, RB_2, and MP_2 policy, the analyser returns *sat*. Next, in the presence of Set_2 administrative relations and commands shown in Table 9, the analyser returns *unsat* which means system is not *live* and any user cannot perform *Read* operation. This is due to the presence of *Can_delete_policy* and *Can_revoke_permission* administrative relations in administrative policy that enables an administrative user U_4 who has user attribute and role as ASO_1, to delete AP_2 policy and remove permission Pr_2 from the role RM, thus making the operation *Read* unreachable.

5 Experimental Results and Analysis

To analyse the impact of time on various components, we have used Z3 4.0 [22] on a Windows 10 operating system with 64 bit Intel i7 processor @ 3.60 GHz and 16 GB RAM.

The performance of the proposed methodology has been observed through synthetic Data Sets 1 to 5 of different size presented in [1]. These data sets capture ABAC, RBAC and MPBAC policies as data in tables, and also preserve the basic properties of ABAC (like a user can have multiple attributes,

Table 11. Experimental results showing time (seconds) taken by μZ for liveness analysis.

Data set	Without administrative policy			With administrative policy		
	RBAC	ABAC	MPBAC	RBAC	ABAC	MPBAC
DS1	<.01	<.01	<.01	<.01	<.01	.01
DS2	.02	.01	.02	.02	.02	.03
DS3	.03	.01	.03	.04	.04	.05
DS4	.13	.03	.17	.17	.06	.23
DS5	1.26	.39	2.80	3.11	.98	4.32

an attribute can one or more values, etc.) and RBAC (a user can have one or more roles, a role can inherit another role, a role can have one or more permissions, etc.). In Data Sets 1 to 5, the number of users, objects, roles, access rights, permissions, user-role assignments, and permission-role assignments are in the range of 100–500, 100–25000, 10–100, 5–10, 750–40000, 200–10000 and 150–40000, respectively. Similarly, the number of user attributes, user attribute values, user-user attribute value assignment, object attributes, object attribute values, object-object attribute value assignment, and policies are in the range of 5–250, 10–500, 200–50000, 5–250, 10–500, 200–50000, and 25–1250, respectively.

For Data Sets 1 to 5, RBAMARM contains two administrative roles. The number of can assign user, can revoke user, can assign permission, can revoke permission, can create policy, and can delete policy entries are in the range of 5–25 for Data Sets 1 to 5.

Tables 10 and 11 show time taken to analyse the five different size of ABAC, RBAC and MPBAC policies in the absence and presence of administrative policies. It can be observed from the tables that analysis time increases due to rise in data set size, and in the number of rules and facts in the presence of the RBAMARM. For Data set 5, the safety analysis of ABAC, RBAC and MPBAC policies takes <9 sec, <7 sec and <17 sec, respectively. The liveness analysis of ABAC, RBAC and MPBAC policies takes <4 sec, <1 sec and <5 sec, respectively. Thus, the proposed approach is effective and scalable.

6 Related Work

In the last few years, several efforts have been made to develop the administrative models [7,9,10,18] for RBAC [4] and its extensions [5,6]. A significant amount of contribution is also made towards the security analysis of RBAC [12] and its extensions [8,13,14,16,18] in the presence of administrative models.

An increasing amount of interest has also been seen towards the development of administrative models [11,17] for ABAC [3]. Along with that few approaches have been presented for analysing the security properties of ABAC [17,19] in the presence of administrative model. In the paper [19], Jha et al. have presented an attribute based administrative model and a methodology for analysing the security properties such as safety and liveness. As they have used attributes (other than regular user's attributes) for controlling administrative users access, we feel that the proposed approach may further complicate the administration of administrative users.

In a panel discussion, Ferraiolo et al. [15] emphasized the need of meta-model. In response to that Rajpoot et al. [20] have presented an approach and demonstrated that RBAC [4] components (such as role and permission) can be constrained by user attributes, object attributes and environment attributes. But their work is limited to specification and enforcement, and requires few modification in RBAC [4].

Recently, Singh et al. [1,2] have presented a framework along with a role based administrative model that not only keeps standard RBAC and ABAC unaltered but also enables specification, enforcement and maintenance of different types of access control policies.

7   Conclusion and Future Work

In this paper, we have described a role based administrative model, which is named as RBAMARM, components for managing unified security policies and then introduced a methodology for verifying the correctness of these policies using the RBAMARM. First, an overview of RBAMARM is presented. Next, a formal representation of ABAC, RBAC, MPBAC and RBAMARM is presented and the desired security properties (like safety and liveness) are also stated formally. Then, facts are generated using the rules by passing policies as input to them. Finally, the effect of various components on the time taken to analyse security properties is discussed in detail.

In this paper, we have considered a few components of RBAMARM. In future, a plan is to introduce comprehensive RBAMARM which can manage various other components, e.g., user, object, user attribute, etc.

Acknowledgments. Research reported in this publication was supported by the National Institutes of Health under award R01GM118574 and by the National Science Foundation under awards CNS-1564034, CNS-1624503, and CNS-1747728. The content is solely the responsibility of the authors and does not necessarily represent the official views of the agencies funding the research.

References

1. Singh, M.P., Sural, S., Vaidya, J., Atluri, V.: Managing attribute-based access control policies in a unified framework using data warehousing and in-memory database. Comput. Secur. **86**, 183–205 (2019)
2. Singh, M.P., Sural, S., Atluri, V., Vaidya, J., Yakub, U.: Managing multi-dimensional multi-granular security policies using data warehousing. In: Qiu, M., Xu, S., Yung, M., Zhang, H. (eds.) NSS 2015. LNCS, vol. 9408, pp. 221–235. Springer, Cham (2015). https://doi.org/10.1007/978-3-319-25645-0_15

3. Hu, V.C., et al.: Guide to Attribute Based Access Control (ABAC) Definition and Considerations. NIST Special Publication (2014)
4. Sandhu, R.S., Coyne, J.E., Feinstein, H.L., Youman, C.E.: Role based access control models. IEEE Comput. **29**, 38–47 (1996)
5. Aich, S., Mondal, S., Sural, S., Majumdar, A.K.: Role based access control with spatiotemporal context for mobile applications. In: Gavrilova, M.L., Tan, C.J.K., Moreno, E.D. (eds.) Transactions on Computational Science IV. LNCS, vol. 5430, pp. 177–199. Springer, Heidelberg (2009). https://doi.org/10.1007/978-3-642-01004-0_10
6. Bertino, E., Andrea, B.P., Ferrari, E.: TRBAC: a temporal role-based access control model. ACM Trans. Inf. Syst. Secur. **4**, 191–233 (2001)
7. Sandhu, R., Bhamidipati, V., Munawer, Q.: The ARBAC97 model for role-based administration of roles. ACM Trans. Inf. Syst. Secur. **2**, 105–135 (1999)
8. Mondal, S., Sural, S., Atluri, V.: Towards formal security analysis of GTRBAC using timed automata. In: Proceedings of the 14th ACM Symposium on Access Control Models and Technologies, pp. 33–42 (2009)
9. Sharma, M., Sural, S., Vaidya, J., Atluri, V.: AMTRAC: an administrative model for temporal role-based access control. Comput. Secur. **39**, 201–218 (2013)
10. Sharma, M., Sural, S., Atluri, V., Vaidya, J.: An administrative model for spatio-temporal role based access control. In: Bagchi, A., Ray, I. (eds.) ICISS 2013. LNCS, vol. 8303, pp. 375–389. Springer, Heidelberg (2013). https://doi.org/10.1007/978-3-642-45204-8_28
11. Jin, X., Krishnan, R., Sandhu, R.: Reachability analysis for role based administration of attributes. In: Proceedings of the 2013 ACM Workshop on Digital Identity Management, pp. 73–84 (2013)
12. Ninghui, N.L., Tripunitara, M.V.: Security analysis in role-based access control. ACM Trans. Inf. Syst. Secur. **9**, 391–420 (2006)
13. Mondal, S., Sural, S.: Security analysis of temporal-RBAC using timed automata. In: Proceedings of the 4th International Conference on Information Assurance and Security, pp. 37–40 (2008)
14. Jha, S., Sural, S., Vaidya, J., Atluri, V.: Security analysis of temporal RBAC under an administrative model. Comput. Secur. **46**, 154–172 (2014)
15. Ferraiolo, D., Atluri, V.: A meta model for access control: why is it needed and is it even possible to achieve? In: Proceedings of the 13th ACM Symposium on Access Control Models and Technologies, pp. 153–154 (2008)
16. Jha, S., Sural, S., Vaidya, J., Atluri, V.: Temporal RBAC security analysis using logic programming in the presence of administrative policies. In: Prakash, A., Shyamasundar, R. (eds.) ICISS 2014. LNCS, vol. 8880, pp. 129–148. Springer, Cham (2014). https://doi.org/10.1007/978-3-319-13841-1_8
17. Jha, S., Sural, S., Atluri, V., Vaidya, J.: An administrative model for collaborative management of ABAC systems and its security analysis. In: Proceedings of the 2016 IEEE 2nd International Conference on Collaboration and Internet Computing, pp. 64–73 (2016)
18. Uzun, E., Atluri, V., Sural, S., Madhusudan, P.: Analyzing temporal role-based access control models. In: Proceedings of the 12th ACM Symposium on Access Control Models and Technologies, pp. 177–186 (2012)
19. Jha, S., Sural, S., Vaidya, J., Atluri, V.: Security analysis of ABAC under an administrative model. IET Inf. Secur. **13**, 96–103 (2018)

20. Rajpoot, Q.M., Jensen, C.D., Krishnan, R.: Attributes enhanced role-based access control model. In: Fischer-Hübner, S., Lambrinoudakis, C., Lopez, J. (eds.) Trust-Bus 2015. LNCS, vol. 9264, pp. 3–17. Springer, Cham (2015). https://doi.org/10.1007/978-3-319-22906-5_1

21. Hoder, K., Bjørner, N., de Moura, L.: $\mu Z-$ an efficient engine for fixed points with constraints. In: Gopalakrishnan, G., Qadeer, S. (eds.) CAV 2011. LNCS, vol. 6806, pp. 457–462. Springer, Heidelberg (2011). https://doi.org/10.1007/978-3-642-22110-1_36

22. de Moura, L., Bjørner, N.: Z3: an efficient SMT solver. In: Ramakrishnan, C.R., Rehof, J. (eds.) TACAS 2008. LNCS, vol. 4963, pp. 337–340. Springer, Heidelberg (2008). https://doi.org/10.1007/978-3-540-78800-3_24

On the Feasibility of RBAC to ABAC Policy Mining: A Formal Analysis

Shuvra Chakraborty[1,2]($\boxtimes$), Ravi Sandhu[1,2], and Ram Krishnan[1,3]

[1] Institute for Cyber Security, University of Texas at San Antonio,
San Antonio, TX, USA
{shuvra.chakraborty,ravi.sandhu,ram.krishnan}@utsa.edu
[2] Department of Computer Science, University of Texas at San Antonio,
San Antonio, TX, USA
[3] Department of Electrical and Computer Engineering,
University of Texas at San Antonio, San Antonio, TX, USA

Abstract. Given a Role-Based Access Control (RBAC) system along with supporting attribute data, the process of automated migration to an Attribute-Based Access Control (ABAC) system is a particular instance of the ABAC policy-mining problem. In this paper, we formulate and investigate the feasibility problem of RBAC to ABAC policy mining. Specifically, the ABAC RuleSet Existence problem is introduced formally for the first time in RBAC context. In case of infeasibility, the notion of ABAC RuleSet Infeasibility Correction is formalized and a solution developed utilizing role-based attributes.

Keywords: Attribute-Based Access Control · ABAC policy mining · Feasibility · RBAC · Rule mining

1 Introduction

Following its inception in the mid-nineties, Role-Based Access Control (RBAC) [3,10] has achieved clear dominance over other contemporary access control models and remains prevalent. In recent years, the emerging interest in the Attribute-Based Access Control (ABAC) model as an evolution of RBAC motivates the practical problem of migrating to ABAC from existing access control models.

While there have been differing opinions about which one of RBAC or ABAC is more flexible, scalable, auditable, and provides better support for dynamic environments [12], the benefits of ABAC are increasingly evident. ABAC can be configured to do Discretionary Access Control (DAC), Mandatory Access Control (MAC) and RBAC [7]. It is suitable for large enterprises and notably overcomes some limitations of RBAC such as role explosion [5]. Consequently, ABAC has attracted interest across industry, government applications, and is the fastest-growing access control model today [4]. Therefore, converting an already deployed access control system to an ABAC system is an emerging research problem. Based on this context, ABAC policy mining [11,15] is the process of

S. K. Sahay et al. (Eds.): SKM 2019, CCIS 1186, pp. 147–163, 2020.
https://doi.org/10.1007/978-981-15-3817-9_9

automated migration to an equivalent ABAC policy when an existing access control model along with supporting data is given. Such automation reduces the manual effort needed for migration as well as time and possibilities of error [15].

ABAC policy mining problem was first mentioned by Xu and Stoller [15] where, given user-permission relation, consistent ABAC policy rules with generalized constraints are generated. In [1], the ABAC RuleSet Existence problem was introduced where the feasibility of consistent ABAC policy generation was investigated when an enumerated authorization system along with attribute data is given. In this paper, we study another instance of the general feasibility problem: migration to the ABAC system when an RBAC system and accompanying attribute data are provided. To the best of our knowledge, we have formalized this problem in RBAC context for the first time.

Our major contributions in this paper are as follows.

- We have introduced the idea of partition-based ABAC RuleSet Existence problem in the RBAC context for the first time.
- An approach for determining ABAC RuleSet Existence as well as a correction procedure (in the case of infeasibility) has been presented with examples. Role-based attributes are defined in this context to remove infeasibility.
- Some significant directions for future enhancement are identified.

The rest of the paper is organized as follows. Section 2 defines RBAC and ABAC terminologies to facilitate further discussions. Section 3 introduces ABAC RuleSet Existence and infeasibility correction problems along with associated definitions. In Sect. 4, an infeasibility solution approach utilizing role-based attributes is presented, along with associated proofs. Section 5 presents some future work directions. Finally, Sect. 6 gives a brief discussion of related work.

2   RBAC and ABAC Terminologies

This section represents the RBAC and ABAC related terminologies of the current work. Although the ABAC terminologies were defined in our previous paper [1], these are also included here for completeness. They are identified by explicit reference to corresponding definition in our work [1]. There are some other definitions from our previous work [1], which are included in the subsequent sections; they are customized in RBAC context and marked as adapted.

Every access control system should specify and enforce a function checkAccess (Def. 1, [1]) which is typically a logical formula. This function abstracts the evaluation of an access request from underlying implementation details of the system. Given a complete access control system, a user $u \in U$ is allowed to perform an operation $op \in OP$ on object $o \in O$ iff $checkAccess(u, o, op)$ is True where U, O and OP are the sets of users, objects and operations in the system, respectively.

The key component of RBAC system is role [3], an intermediary between user and permissions in the system. For example, all users assigned to a role "manager" may practice all permissions associated with that role. A complete RBAC system is defined as follows:

Table 1. RBAC system of Example 1

Roles	RPA	RUA	authPerm	authUser
r1	$\{(o1, op1)\}$	$\{u1\}$	$\{(o1, op1), (o3, op1)\}$	$\{u1\}$
r2	$\{(o2, op2)\}$	$\{u3\}$	$\{(o2, op2)\}$	$\{u3\}$
r3	$\{(o3, op1)\}$	$\{u4, u5\}$	$\{(o3, op1)\}$	$\{u1, u4, u5\}$
r4	$\{(o1, op1), (o3, op1)\}$	$\{u2\}$	$\{(o1, op1), (o3, op1)\}$	$\{u2\}$

Definition 1. *RBAC system*

An RBAC system $\langle U, O, OP, Roles, RPA, RUA, RH, checkAccess_{RBAC} \rangle$ is a tuple where,

1. *U, O, and OP are finite sets of users, objects, and operations, respectively.*
2. *$P = O \times OP$, is the set of all possible permissions in the system. A permission $p \in P$ is an object-operation pair where $ops(p)$ and $obj(p)$ denote the operation and object associated with p, respectively.*
3. *Roles is a finite set of role names.*
4. *The set of permissions directly assigned to a role $r \in Roles$ is given by $RPA(r)$ where, $RPA: Roles \rightarrow 2^P$. The set of users directly assigned to a role $r \in Roles$ is given by $RUA(r)$ where, $RUA: Roles \rightarrow 2^U$.*
5. *The role hierarchy relation is $RH \subseteq Roles \times Roles$ where RH must be acyclic. Here, $(r, r') \in RH$ denotes r is a senior role than r'.*
6. *Let reflexive transitive closure of RH be denoted by RH'. A role $r \in Roles$ acquires the set of permissions associated with all junior roles according to given hierarchy, and denoted by $authPerm(r) = \{p \in RPA(r')|(r, r') \in RH'\}$. A role $r \in Roles$ inherits all the users associated with seniors roles in hierarchy, and denoted by $authUser(r) = \{u \in RUA(r')|(r', r) \in RH'\}$.*
7. *$checkAccess_{RBAC}(u: U, o: O, op: OP) \equiv \exists r \in Roles.(u \in authUser(r) \wedge p \in authPerm(r) \wedge (o, op) = (obj(p), ops(p))$. In simple words, given a role $r \in Roles$, a user $u \in authUser(r)$ may practice all permissions $p \in authPerm(r)$.*

Example 1. The sets of users (U), objects (O), operations (OP) and roles (Roles) are $\{u1, u2, u3, u4, u5\}$, $\{o1, o2, o3\}$, $\{op1, op2\}$, and $\{r1, r2, r3, r4\}$, respectively. Given, $RH = \{(r1, r3)\}$, the user and permission assignment for each *role* $\in$ *Roles* is shown in Table 1. Here, user u1 can perform operation op1 on object o3 since $checkAccess_{RBAC}(u1, o3, op1)$ evaluates to True.

The key component of ABAC policy is attribute, which represents characteristics of entities in the system. In ABAC, attribute values of the requesting user as well as the requested object are used to determine whether a particular access request can be granted or denied. To define an ABAC system, ABAC policy is defined first as follows:

Definition 2. ABAC policy (Def. 3, [1])
An ABAC policy, POL_{ABAC} is a tuple $\langle OP,\ UA,\ OA,\ RangeSet,\ RuleSet \rangle$,

- OP is a finite set of operations.
- UA and OA are finite sets of user and object attribute function names, where for convenience, we assume $UA \cap OA = \emptyset$.
- $RangeSet = \{(att, value)|att \in (UA \cup OA) \wedge value \in Range(att)\}$ where, $Range(att)$ specifies a finite set of atomic values.
- $RuleSet$ is a set of rules where, for each operation op, $RuleSet$ contains a single rule, $Rule_{op}$. Formally, $RuleSet = \{Rule_{op}|op \in OP\}$.
- Each $Rule_{op}$ is specified using the grammar defined below.
  $Rule_{op} ::= Rule_{op} \vee Rule_{op} | (Atomicexp)$
  $Atomicexp ::= Atomicuexp \wedge Atomicoexp | Atomicuexp | Atomicoexp$
  $Atomicuexp ::= Atomicuexp \wedge Atomicuexp | uexp$
  $Atomicoexp ::= Atomicoexp \wedge Atomicoexp | oexp$
  $uexp \in \{ua(u) = value \,|\, ua \in UA \wedge value \in Range(ua)\}$
  $oexp \in \{oa(o) = value \,|\, oa \in OA \wedge value \in Range(oa)\}$
  For a specific operation $op \in OP$, $Rule_{op}$ is specified with user u and object o as formal parameters. The formal semantics of $Rule_{op}$, evaluated for an actual user a and object b is given in Definition 3.

For the ease of further reference, **partially defined ABAC policy** [1] is a tuple, denoted by $POL_{ABAC-RuleSet} \equiv \langle OP, UA, OA, RangeSet \rangle$.

Definition 3. ABAC system (Def. 4, [1])
An ABAC system is a tuple, given by, $\langle U,\ O,\ UAValue,\ OAValue,\ POL_{ABAC},\ checkAccess_{ABAC} \rangle$ where,

- U and O are finite sets of users and objects, respectively. Here, OP, UA, OA, $RangeSet$ and POL_{ABAC} are defined as in Definition 2.
- $UAValue = \{UAValue_{ua} \,|\, ua \in UA\}$ where, $UAValue_{ua} : U \rightarrow Range(ua)$ such that $UAValue_{ua}(u)$ returns the value of attribute ua for user u. For convenience, we understand $ua(u)$ to mean $UAValue_{ua}(u)$.
- $OAValue = \{OAValue_{oa} \,|\, oa \in OA\}$ where, $OAValue_{oa} : O \rightarrow Range(oa)$ such that $OAValue_{oa}(o)$ returns the value of attribute oa for object o. For convenience, we understand $oa(o)$ to mean $OAValue_{oa}(o)$.
- $checkAccess_{ABAC}(a{:}U,\ b{:}O,\ op{:}OP) \equiv Rule_{op}(a{:}U,\ b{:}O)$ where $Rule_{op}$ is as stated in Definition 2. Given any user $a \in U$ along with attribute value assignments $ua(a)$, where $ua \in UA$ and an object $b \in O$ along with attribute value assignment $oa(b)$, where $oa \in OA$, the expression $Rule_{op}(a, b)$ is evaluated by substituting the values $ua(a)$ for $ua(u)$ and $oa(b)$ for $oa(o)$ in the $Rule_{op}$ expression. User a is permitted to do operation op on object b if and only if $Rule_{op}(a, b)$ evaluates to True.

A **partially defined ABAC system** [1] is a tuple, $\langle U,\ O,\ UAValue,\ OAValue,\ POL_{ABAC-RuleSet} \rangle$ where U, O, UAValue, OAValue are defined above. It represents an incomplete ABAC system where everything except the ABAC rules is given.

Table 2. ABAC data for Example 2

(a) UAValue		(b) OAValue		(c) Range	
User	uat1	Object	oat1	uat1	$\{F, G\}$
u1	F	o1	F	oat1	$\{F, G\}$
u2	F	o2	F		
u3	F	o3	G		
u4	G				
u5	G				

Example 2. The set of users (U), objects (O), operations (OP), user attribute names UA and Object attribute names (OA) are $\{u1, u2, u3, u4, u5\}$, $\{o1, o2, o3\}$, $\{op1, op2\}$, $\{uat1\}$, and $\{oat1\}$, respectively. Table 2 shows the user attribute value assignment (UAValue), object attribute value assignment (OAValue), and ranges of the attributes. It can be easily noticed that both Examples 1 and 2 have the same sets of U, O and OP. RuleSet consists of two rules: $Rule_{op1}$ and $Rule_{op2}$, respectively. For instance, if $Rule_{op1} \equiv \langle uat1(u) = G \wedge oat1(o) = G \rangle$, then both u4 and u5 are allowed to perform operation op1 on object o3.

In previous discussions, only atomic-valued attributes [7] are considered while generating ABAC rules. A set-valued attribute [1] is a function which takes an entity (user and object, here) and returns a subset of its range. For instance, given Range(att) = $\{a, b\}$, function att may return only one of $\{\{a, b\}, \{a\}, \{b\}, \{\}\}$. Since a set-valued attribute can be converted to atomic attributes [1], the ABAC rule and evaluation approach discussed earlier in this study are sufficient to manage set-valued attributes by reduction to atomic-valued.

3 Problem Definitions

In this section, ABAC RuleSet Existence and ABAC RuleSet Infeasibility Correction problems are defined in RBAC context. In order to do that, the meaning of equivalency between two access control systems is required. Given two access control systems, stm1 and stm2, with an identical set of users (U), objects (O), and operations (OP), stm1 and stm2 are equivalent iff $\forall(u, o, op) \in U \times O \times OP$. $checkAccess_{stm1}(u, o, op) \iff checkAccess_{stm2}(u, o, op)$. Based on the foregoing, ABAC RuleSet Existence problem [1] is defined in RBAC context as follows:

Definition 4. *ABAC RuleSet Existence problem (adapted from Def. 6 of [1])*
Given, an RBAC system and a partially defined ABAC system where U, O and OP are identical to the given RBAC system, does there exist a RuleSet so that the resulting ABAC system is equivalent to the given RBAC system? Such a RuleSet, if it exists, is said to be a suitable RuleSet.

To demonstrate the significance of the problem, let's consider the RBAC Example 1 and ABAC Example 2: does there exist a RuleSet so that the resulting ABAC system is equivalent to the given RBAC system? Note that it is always possible to generate equivalent ABAC system when explicit IDs are introduced for both user and object [13]. We strongly believe that the inclusion of such IDs is antithetical to the spirit of ABAC. Hence, we rule out the use of such IDs. For example, in RBAC Example 1, user u1 can perform operation op1 on object o1 whereas user u3, a user with the same attribute value assignment as u1, is not allowed to do so. It is clearly evident that no suitable ABAC RuleSet can exist.

In [1], ABAC RuleSet Existence problem is analyzed when an authorization relation $AUTH \subseteq U \times O \times OP$ and accompanying attribute data are given as input. Given an RBAC system, it is trivial to find an equivalent $AUTH$ relation, such that $(u, o, op) \in AUTH \Leftrightarrow checkAccess_{RBAC}(u, o, op)$. For example, AUTH for the RBAC Example 1 is given as $\{(u1, o1, op1), (u1, o3, op1), (u2, o1, op1), (u2, o3, op1), (u3, o2, op2), (u4, o3, op1), (u5, o3, op1)\}$. Since RBAC system to AUTH conversion takes $O(|U| \times |O|)$ complexity, the partition-based solution from [1] can be reused in RBAC context by simply deriving the equivalent AUTH relation for the given RBAC system. The following relation R generates a partition on the set of all possible user-object pairs:

Definition 5. Binary relation R (Def. 7, [1])
Given a partially defined ABAC system tuple as $\langle U, O, UAValue, OAValue, POL_{ABAC-RuleSet}\rangle$, the binary relation R on set $UO = U \times O$ is defined as $R \equiv \{((u1, o1), (u2, o2)) \mid (\forall ua \in UA.ua(u1) = ua(u2)) \wedge (\forall oa \in OA.oa(o1) = oa(o2))\}$

It is apparent that the binary relation R is an equivalence relation and thereby induces a partition on UO. Let P be the partition on UO induced by R and denoted by, $P = \{P_1, P_2, ..., P_n\}$, where $1 \leq n \leq |UO|$. For convenience, each $P_i \in P$ is called as partition element (or shortly partition) and P is called partition set (Def. 8, [1]) for the rest of the paper. By definition of R, each $P_i \in P$ is identified by a unique collection of (attribute name, value) pairs, given by $PV(P_i)$ where,

$PV(P_i) \equiv (UV(u1) \cup OV(o1))$ for any $(u1, o1) \in P_i$, where
$UV(u:U) \equiv \{(ua, value) \mid ua \in UA \wedge value = ua(u)\}$
$OV(o:O) \equiv \{(oa, value) \mid oa \in OA \wedge value = oa(o)\}$
The idea of conflict-free partition is defined in RBAC context as follows:

Definition 6. Conflict-free partition (adapted from Def. 9 of [1])
Given $\langle U, O, OP, Roles, RPA, RUA, RH, checkAccess_{RBAC}\rangle$ as an RBAC system and partition set P where U, O and OP are identical, a $P_i \in P$ is conflict-free with respect to a specific $op \in OP$ iff the following statement is true:
$\forall(u, o) \in P_i.checkAccess_{RBAC}(u, o, op) = True \vee \forall(u, o) \in P_i.checkAccess_{RBAC}(u, o, op) = False$
P_i has conflict with respect to $op \in OP$ otherwise. Partition set P is conflict-free with respect to given RBAC system iff for each $op \in OP$, every $P_i \in P$ is conflict-free. P is called a conflict partition set, otherwise.

It is shown in [1] that given an AUTH relation and partially defined ABAC system, a suitable RuleSet exists iff partition set P is conflict-free. The overall asymptotic complexity of ABAC RuleSet Existence problem [1] is $O(|OP| \times (|U| \times |O|))$. The construction of AUTH relation by enumerating every possible user-object-operation tuple from an RBAC system takes $O(|U| \times |O|)$ time, thus overall asymptotic complexity of determining ABAC RuleSet Existence in RBAC context remains the same as [1], $O(|OP| \times (|U| \times |O|))$. By definition, suitable RuleSet (Theorem 1, [1]) consists of $|OP|$ rules, one for each $op \in OP$. Each conflict-free partition $P_i \in P$ is included in $Rule_{op}$ as a conjunctive clause where, $P_i \times \{op\} \subseteq AUTH$. For a specific $op \in OP$, $Rule_{op}$ (Theorem 1, [1]) construction steps are shown below:

$$Rule_{op} = \bigvee_{P_i \times \{op\} \subseteq AUTH} (uexp(PV(P_i)) \wedge oexp(PV(P_i)))$$

$$uexp(PV(P_i)) = \bigwedge_{(ua,value) \in PV(P_i)} (ua(u) = value)$$

$$oexp(PV(P_i)) = \bigwedge_{(oa,value) \in PV(P_i)} (oa(o) = value)$$

Example 3. Using the RBAC tuple in Example 1 and accompanying attribute data in Example 2, partition set P is { {(u1, o1), (u1, o2), (u2, o1), (u2, o2), (u3, o1), (u3, o2)}, {(u4, o1), (u4, o2), (u5, o1), (u5, o2)}, {(u1, o3), (u2, o3), (u3, o3)},{(u4, o3), (u5, o3)} } and PV values are { {(uat1,F), (oat1,F)}, {(uat1,G), (oat1,F)}, {(uat1,F), (oat1,G)}, {(uat1,G), (oat1,G)} }, respectively. An equivalent AUTH is given by $\{(u1, o1, op1), (u1, o3, op1), (u2, o1, op1), (u2, o3, op1), (u3, o2, op2), (u4, o3, op1), (u5, o3, op1)\}$. It is apparent that partition set P is conflicted in this example as shown in Fig. 1. Here, bold user-object pair w.r.t. an operation in a partition represents those user-object-operation tuple belong to AUTH while others do not.

Example 4. In order to show a conflict-free partition set, let's consider the data in Table 3 along with same U, O, OP, Roles and RH in RBAC system of Example 1. Here, the same attribute data as in Example 2 are used. Hence, generated partition set P and PV values are same as Example 3. In this example, an equivalent AUTH $= \{(u1, o1, op1), (u1, o2, op1), (u1, o3, op1), (u2, o1, op1), (u2, o2, op1), (u2, o3, op1), (u3, o1, op1), (u3, o2, op1), (u3, o3, op1), (u4, o3, op2), (u5, o3, op2)\}$. By definition of conflict-free partition set, P is conflict-free in this case and generated RuleSet is $\{Rule_{op1}, Rule_{op2}\}$. Here, $Rule_{op1} = \langle (uat1(u) = F \wedge oat1(o) = F) \vee (uat1(u) = F \wedge oat1(o) = G) \rangle$ and $Rule_{op2} = \langle (uat1(u) = G \wedge oat1(o) = G) \rangle$.

If partition set P is not conflict-free, no suitable RuleSet exists [1]. Hence, in order to make the equivalent ABAC system generation always possible, one possible approach is to ensure that P is always conflict-free. There can be many possible ways to achieve this, either exact or approximate. In this study, ABAC RuleSet Infeasibility Correction problem in RBAC context is defined as follows.

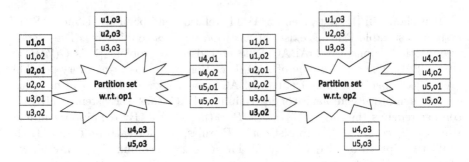

Fig. 1. Conflict partition set for Example 3

Table 3. RBAC system of Example 4

Roles	RPA	RUA	authPerm	authUser
r1	{(o1, op1)}	{u1, u2, u3}	{(o1, op1), (o2, op1)}	{u1, u2, u3}
r2	{(o3, op2)}	{u4, u5}	{(o3, op2)}	{u4, u5}
r3	{(o2, op1)}	{}	{(o2, op1)}	{u1, u2, u3}
r4	{(o3, op1)}	{u1, u2, u3}	{(o3, op1)}	{u1, u2, u3}

Definition 7. *ABAC RuleSet Infeasibility Correction problem* (adapted from Def. 10 of [1])
Given, RBAC system and partially defined ABAC system with unspecified Rule-Set where U, O, and OP are identical to the given RBAC system, and a conflicted partition set P, ABAC Ruleset Infeasibility Correction problem is adding new attributes to (1) only UA or only OA or, both UA, OA, and (2) assign appropriate values to the new attributes, so that suitable RuleSet generation is always possible.

In the next section, an exact solution algorithm is presented for ABAC RuleSet Infeasibility Correction problem with the help of role-based attributes.

4   ABAC RuleSet Infeasibility Correction Solution

It is already established that if partition set P is conflict-free an equivalent ABAC system generation is always possible, since each $P_i \in P$ is uniquely identified by attribute values. Given a conflict partition set P, new role-based attributes are added and values are assigned accordingly so that each conflict partition in P is split into conflict-free fragments uniquely identified by attribute values. Thereby, equivalent RuleSet can be generated. Here, each conflict partition is processed separately to prevent unnecessary split of conflict-free partitions.

According to the construction in [7], an RBAC system can be configured to equivalent ABAC system even if no user, subject and object attributes are provided. The role membership information of an RBAC system can be utilized

Table 4. Role-based attribute values for RBAC system in Example 1

Objects	$oroleAtt_{op1}$	$oroleAtt_{op2}$
o1	{r1, r4}	{}
o2	{}	{r2}
o3	{r1, r3, r4}	{}

Users	$uroleAtt$
u1	{r1, r3}
u2	{r4}
u3	{r2}
u4	{r3}
u5	{r3}

to generate appropriate attribute sets and value assignments. We adapt the construction in [7] to our user-object context as set-valued role membership attributes and omit the subject notion of [7].

Definition 8. *Role-based user attribute*
Given $\langle U, O, OP, Roles, RPA, RUA, RH, checkAccess_{RBAC} \rangle$ *as RBAC system tuple, role-based user attribute is a set-valued attribute,* $uroleAtt: U \rightarrow 2^{Roles}$. *For a user* $u \in U$, $uroleAtt(u) = \{r \in Roles | u \in authUser(r)\}$.

Definition 9. *Role-based object attribute*
Given $\langle U, O, OP, Roles, RPA, RUA, RH, checkAccess_{RBAC} \rangle$ *as RBAC system tuple, role-based object attribute for a* $op \in OP$ *is a set-valued attribute, denoted by* $oroleAtt_{op}: O \rightarrow 2^{Roles}$. *For an object* $o \in O$, $oroleAtt_{op}(o) = \{r \in Roles | p \in authPerm(r) \land (o, op) = (obj(p), ops(p))\}$.

Although $uroleAtt$ is set-valued by definition, it is treated specially in this study: same as an atomic attribute. In order to generate uexp, "value" is as given in the Definition 8 and to evaluate "uroleAtt(u) = value" in rule expression, "=" is considered as set equality operator. Similarly, each role-based object attribute w.r.t. a $op \in OP$ is treated specially as an atomic attribute. In order to generate oexp, "value" is as given in the Definition 9 and to evaluate "$oroleAtt_{op}(o) =$ value" in rule expression, "=" is considered as set equality operator.

Lemma 1. *Given an RBAC system, one user attribute as in Definition 8 and* $|OP|$ *object attributes as in Definition 9 (for each* $op \in OP$) *are sufficient to generate equivalent ABAC system.*

Proof:
Follows from the RBAC to ABAC configuration in [7]. Let the set of user attributes, UA = $uroleAtt$ and set of object attributes, OA = $\{oroleAtt_{op} | op \in OP\}$. The attribute value assignments of user and object attributes are as in Definitions 8 and 9, respectively. To generate an equivalent ABAC system, each $P_i \in P$ must be identified by unique PV values as well as partition set P should be conflict-free [1]. It is trivial to show that both conditions are true, thereby, equivalent ABAC system generation is always possible.

Table 5. Partition set in Example 5

Partition set
$\{(u1,o1)\}$
$\{(u1,o2)\}$
$\{(u1,o3)\}$
$\{(u2,o1)\}$
$\{(u2,o2)\}$
$\{(u2,o3)\}$
$\{(u3,o1)\}$
$\{(u3,o2)\}$
$\{(u3,o3)\}$
$\{(u4,o1), (u5,o1)\}$
$\{(u4,o2), (u5,o2)\}$
$\{(u4,o3), (u5,o3)\}$

Example 5. According to Lemma 1, the set of attributes and corresponding value assignment of RBAC system in Example 1 are shown in Table 4. Here, partition set P is shown in Table 5. For instance, PV($\{u1, o1\}$) is given by $\{(uat1, F),$ $(oat1, F), (uroleAtt, \{r1, r3\}), (oroleAtt_{op1}, \{r1, r4\}), (oroleAtt_{op2}, \{\})\}$. In this example, partition set P is conflict-free and for each $P_i \in P$, PV(P_i) is unique.

This unique property of role membership in RBAC system makes it independent of supporting attribute data. It is a significant difference as compared to given authorization relation in [1] where, a user and an object attributes are added to the attribute sets and unique random values are assigned to resolve infeasibility issue. The unique random value generation can be considered as an additional task whereas role membership attributes eliminate the need for such values and promotes self-sufficiency. Although Lemma 1 specifies the sufficiency of the role-based attributes to make an equivalent ABAC system generation, a more practical scenario is where supporting attribute data are provided. Therefore, the following definitions and proofs are presented to resolve ABAC Infeasibility Correction problem when supporting attribute data are provided; so that the resulting partition set becomes conflict-free where each partition element is uniquely identified by attribute values.

Definition 10. *Binary relation* $\mathbf{R_{Pi}}$ *on* $\mathbf{P_i} \in \mathbf{P}$ *([1])*
$R_{Pi} \equiv \{((u1, o1), (u2, o2)) | \forall o \in O.\forall op \in OP.((u1, o, op) \in AUTH \Leftrightarrow (u2, o, op) \in AUTH) \wedge \forall u \in U.\forall op \in OP.((u, o1, op) \in AUTH \Leftrightarrow (u, o2, op) \in AUTH)\}$

By inspection, R_{Pi} is an equivalence relation (Lemma 2, [1]). Let, R_{Pi} induces a partition on P_i, say $S_i = \{S_{i1}, S_{i2}, ..., S_{im}\}$, where $1 \leq m \leq |P_i|$. Each $S_{ik} \in S_i$ is called a partition element (or shortly partition) and S_i is called partition set. By definition, S_i further refines the partition P_i. Given a partition $P_i \in P$, let $uList_i$ and $oList_i$ denote the sets of users and objects present in P_i. By inspection of definition of R, $P_i = uList_i \times oList_i$. Let $uList_i$ be further partitioned as follows: any two users $u1, u2 \in ulist_i$ belong to same partition iff $\forall op \in OP.\forall o \in O.(u1, o, op) \in AUTH \iff (u2, o, op) \in AUTH$. Let this assumption split $uList_i$ into q partitions, denoted by $\{ul_{i1}, ..., ul_{iq}\}$. Similarly let $oList_i$ be partitioned as follows: any two objects $o1, o2 \in olist_i$ belong to same partition iff $\forall op \in OP.\forall u \in U.(u, o1, op) \in AUTH \iff (u, o2, op) \in AUTH$. Let this assumption split $oList_i$ into r partitions, denoted by $\{ol_{i1}, ..., ol_{ir}\}$.

Lemma 2. $S_i = \{ul_{i1}, ..., ul_{iq}\} \times \{ol_{i1}, ..., ol_{ir}\}$ and it is conflict-free.

Proof: Trivial [1].

Given a conflict partition $P_i \in P$, S_i has to be conflict-free and each $S_{ik} \in S_i$ should be identified uniquely by attribute values. The given set of attributes are not sufficient to serve this purpose unless there is some change in given attribute value assignments. The following definition adds the already defined role-based attributes to the given attribute set:

Definition 11. *Add new role-based user and object attributes*
Given ABAC RuleSet Infeasibility Correction instance, the following steps are proposed.

1. $UA_{new} = UA \cup uroleAtt$ and $OA_{new} = OA \cup \{oroleAtt_{op}|op \in OP\}$. *Hence, total $1 + |OP|$ attributes are added.*
   Note: Initially, all new attributes are assigned UND which specifies "Unknown" attribute value assignment.
2. *To ensure clarity, $PV_{new}(S_{ik} \in S_i)$ is introduced.*
   $PV_{new}(S_{ik}) \equiv (UV_{new}(u1) \cup OV_{new}(o1))$ *for any* $(u1, o1) \in S_{ik}$ *where*
   $UV_{new}(u{:}U) \equiv \{(ua, value)|ua \in UA_{new} \wedge value = ua(u)\}$
   $OV_{new}(o{:}O) \equiv \{(oa, value)|oa \in OA_{new} \wedge value = oa(o)\}$

Lemma 3. *Given a conflict partition $P_i \in P$ w.r.t. a $op \in OP$, $PV_{new}(S_{ik})$ is unique.*

Proof:
By inspection of definition of R, for each $P_i \in P$, $PV(P_i)$ is unique. By definition, S_i further refines the partition P_i. Hence, if it is proved that, given a conflict partition P_i w.r.t. a $op \in OP$, new user attribute can uniquely identify each element of $\{ul_{i1}, ..., ul_{iq}\}$ and similarly, $|OP|$ object attributes can do the same for $\{ol_{i1}, ..., ol_{ir}\}$, then $PV_{new}(S_{ik})$ is unique.

If $u1 \in ul_{im}$ and $u2 \in ul_{in}$ where $m \neq n$, let $uroleAtt(u1) = uroleAtt(u2)$. If $uroleAtt(u1) = uroleAtt(u2)$ then u1 and u2 cannot belong to two different partitions of $uList_i$ since it ensures uroleAtt(u1) and uroleAtt(u2) derives the exactly same set of permissions. Hence, $uroleAtt(u1) \neq uroleAtt(u2)$ proves. Thereby, each element of $\{ul_{i1}, ..., ul_{iq}\}$ is uniquely identified by uroleAtt value. However, given u3, u4 $\in ul_{im}$, it is possible that $uroleAtt(u3) \neq uroleAtt(u4)$,

---

Algorithm 1. confRefine

Require: Conflict partition P_i and corresponding ABAC Ruleset Infeasibility Correction instance

Ensure: Refined partition set S_i where each $PV_{new}(S_{ik} \in S_i)$ is unique

1: uL := $\{ul_{i1}, ..., ul_{iq}\}$
2: oL := $\{ol_{i1}, ..., ol_{ir}\}$
3: //If checked for Lemma 4
4: **if** $\exists u \in uList_i.uroleAtt(u) = UND$ **then**
5:     **while** $\exists partu \in uL$ **do**
6:         For all $u1 \in partu$, $uroleAtt(u1) := uroleAtt(u2)$ //where $u2 \in partu$ and $\forall u3 \in partu.\ |uroleAtt(u2)| \leq |uroleAtt(u3)|$
7:         $uL := uL \setminus partu$
8: //If checked for Lemma 4
9: **if** $\exists (o, op) \in oList_i \times OP.oroleAtt_{op}(o) = UND$ **then**
10:     **while** $\exists parto \in oL$ **do**
11:         **for** each $op \in OP$ **do**
12:            For all $o1 \in parto$, $oroleAtt_{op}(o1) := oroleAtt_{op}(o2)$ //where $o2 \in parto$ and $\forall o3 \in parto.|oroleAtt_{op}(o2)| \leq |oroleAtt_{op}(o3)|$
13:         $oL := oL \setminus parto$
14: **return** S_i //$\{ul_{i1}, ..., ul_{iq}\} \times \{ol_{i1}, ..., ol_{ir}\}$

---

although the resulting permissions are the same. By inspection, Algorithm 1 picks the minimum cardinality role set as role-based attribute value for every user in ul_{im}. Similarly, it can be proved that, If $o1 \in ol_{im}$ and $o2 \in ol_{in}$ where $m \neq n$, $\exists op \in Op.oroleAtt_{op}(o1) \neq oroleAtt_{op}(o2)$. Thereby, $PV_{new}(S_{ik})$ is unique.

Lemma 4. *Given $P_i = uList_i \times oList_i$ and $P_j = uList_j \times oList_j$, if $u1 \in uList_i$ and $u1 \in uList_j$, then $uList_i = uList_j$.*

Proof:
Follows from definition of R, it is trivial. Similarly, it can be proved that, if $o1 \in oList_i$ and $o1 \in oList_j$, then $oList_i = oList_j$.
Note: In Algorithm 1, Lemma 4 is used to prevent repeated role-based attribute value assignment of users and objects. Based on the foregoing, the following theorem states and proves the solution of ABAC RuleSet Infeasibility Correction problem.

Theorem 1. *Given an ABAC RuleSet Infeasibility Correction problem instance as in Def. 7, it is always possible to find a suitable RuleSet such that the resulting ABAC system is equivalent to given RBAC system (adapted from Theorem 2 of [1]).*

Proof:
Given an RBAC system, equivalent AUTH relation is generated first. Given a $op \in OP$, the $Rule_{op}$ construction procedure is described below. Here, partition set P construction entirely depend on the given attribute set only (no role-based attributes).

1. Each conflict-free partition $P_i \in P$ is included in $Rule_{op}$ as conjunctive clause where, $P_i \times \{op\} \subseteq AUTH$. For a $op \in OP$, such $Rule_{op}$ is defined in Sect. 3.
2. After applying Definition 11, each conflict partition $P_i \in P$ is further refined by Algorithm 1. By using Lemma 3, $\forall S_{ik} \in S_i$, $PV_{new}(S_{ik})$ is unique where each $S_{ik} \in S_i$ is conflict-free. A conjunctive clause is included in $Rule_{op}$ only if $S_{ik} \times \{op\} \subseteq AUTH$ where $S_{ik} \in S_i$. The following shows $Rule_{op}$ construction procedure for conflict partitions in P only:

$$Rule_{op} = \bigvee_{P_i \in CFP(P)} (uexp(PV_{new}(S_{ik})) \wedge oexp(PV_{new}(S_{ik})))$$

where CFP(P) consists of all conflict partitions in P with respect to $op \in OP$, $S_{ik} \in confRefine(P_i)$, and $S_{ik} \times \{op\} \subseteq AUTH$.

$$uexp(PV_{new}(S_{ik})) = \bigwedge_{(ua,value) \in PV_{new}(S_{ik})} (ua(u) = value)$$

$$oexp(PV_{new}(S_{ik})) = \bigwedge_{(oa,value) \in PV_{new}(S_{ik})} (oa(o) = value)$$

Here, $Rule_{op}$ is the disjunction of all the conjunctive clauses generated in step 1 and 2. By definition, RuleSet consists of total $|OP|$ rules, one for each $op \in OP$. Hence, a RuleSet can be constructed. To prove equivalency between the resulting ABAC system with constructed RuleSet and RBAC system, it is necessary and sufficient to show that, for a op in OP, $checkAccess_{RBAC}text(c, d, op) =$ True $\iff$ $Rule_{op}(c, d)$ where $c \in U$, $d \in O$ which implies $(c, d, op) \in AUTH \iff Rule_{op}(c, d)$.

The proof is divided into two parts: (i) only if and (ii) if. To prove (i): by inspection of partition and related definitions, $(c, d) \in U \times O$ belongs to only one partition in P. Let, $(c, d) \in P_i$ where $P_i \in P$. If P_i is conflict-free with respect to op then $\forall (u, o) \in P_i.(u, o, op) \in AUTH$ holds (step 1 in $Rule_{op}$ generation). If P_i is a conflict partition then step 2 is followed. Let, $(c,d) \in S_{ik}$ where $S_{ik} \in S_i$. Hence $\forall (u, o) \in S_{ik}.(u, o, op) \in AUTH$ holds. As a result, S_{ik} is included in $Rule_{op}$ as conjunctive clause (as per step 2 in $Rule_{op}$ construction procedure). Since $Rule_{op}$ consists of disjunction of all the conjunctive clauses generated in step 1 and 2, $Rule_{op}(c, d)$ evaluates to true and (i) is proved.

The part (ii) of the proof: by inspection of $Rule_{op}$ construction stated above, if $Rule_{op}(c, d)$ evaluates to true then there exists a conjunctive clause of $Rule_{op}$ which turned into true. By $Rule_{op}$ construction procedure, each such conjunctive clause in $Rule_{op}$ is presenting a particular partition where for all $(u, o) \in partition.(u, o, op) \in AUTH$. Thereby, the statement $(c, d, op) \in AUTH$ is true and (ii) is proved. Hence, the constructed RuleSet completes the ABAC system, and equivalent to given RBAC system (proved by construction).

Example 6. Given RBAC Example 1 and ABAC Example 2, partition set P is conflicted. The corresponding role attribute values are shown in Table 4. According to Theorem 1, $\{u1, u2, u3, u4, u5\}$ is split into $\{\{u1, u2\}, \{u3\}, \{u4, u5\}\}$. Similarly, $\{o1, o2, o3\}$ is split into $\{\{o1\}, \{o2\}, \{o3\}\}$. Table 6 shows the role-based attribute values after applying algorithm 1. Figure 2 shows the refined partition set where dotted rectangle represents the initial partition before correction. The resulting $Rule_{op1} = \langle\langle(\text{uat1}(u){=}F \land \text{oat1}(o){=} F \land uroleAtt(u) = \{r4\} \land oroleAtt_{op1}(o) = \{r1, r4\} \land oroleAtt_{op2}(o) = \{\})\lor(\text{uat1}(u){=}F \land \text{oat1}(o){=} G \land uroleAtt(u) = \{r4\} \land oroleAtt_{op1}(o) = \{r1, r3, r4\} \land oroleAtt_{op2}(o) = \{\})\lor(\text{uat1}(u){=}G \land \text{oat1}(o){=} G)\rangle$. Similarly, $Rule_{op2} = \langle(\text{uat1}(u) = F \land \text{oat1}(o){=} F \land uroleAtt(u) = \{r2\} \land oroleAtt_{op1}(o) = \{\} \land oroleAtt_{op2}(o) = \{r2\})\rangle$. In Fig. 2, the refined partition set is shown where each bold user-object pair belongs to the AUTH w.r.t. some $op \in OP$ while others are not.

Figure 3 shows the steps of ABAC Infeasibility Correction solution for Example 6. If partition set P is conflicted, one viable approach is to stop right there considering suspicious assignment, denoted by a "cross". Otherwise, the subsequent steps are followed to get an exact solution. One notable optimization at this point is: role-based attributes should be used only when they are needed. For example, if each user in the given user set is represented by a unique user attribute value assignment then there is no need to introduce a role-based user attribute, even if the partition set is conflicted. The same strategy can be applied for role-based object attribute: if each object is represented by unique attribute value assignment, role-based object attributes are unnecessary even if partition set is conflicted. If both of the cases do not hold, still role-based attributes can be removed while generating a conjunctive clause for a particular conflicted partition. For a conflict partition $P_i \in P$ where $P_i = uList_i \times oList_i$, if $|uList_i| = 1$ then role-based user attribute can be avoided while generating conjunctive clauses for P_i. Similarly, role-based object attribute can be ignored when $|oList_i| = 1$. For instance, Example 6 uses conjunctive clause $(\text{uat1}(u) = F \land \text{oat1}(o){=} G \land uroleAtt(u) = \{r4\} \land oroleAtt_{op1}(o) = \{r1, r3, r4\} \land oroleAtt_{op2}(o) = \{\})$ while generating rule for partition $\{\{u1, o3\}, \{u2, o3\}\}$. In this case, role-based object attributes can be omitted as unnecessary! Thus, the resulting conjunctive clause should be $(\text{uat1}(u){=}F \land \text{oat1}(o){=} G \land uroleAtt(u) = \{r4\})$.

According to the approach presented, the solution is found with 9 partitions only where 15 partitions were possible in the worst case (if user and object IDs are introduced).

One significant point is: the partition-based ABAC rule generation proposed in this study is free of unrepresented partition gproblem in [1]. The asymptotic complexity of ABAC RuleSet Infeasibility Correction in RBAC context is given by $O(|OP| \times (|U| \times |O|)^3)$, same as [1].

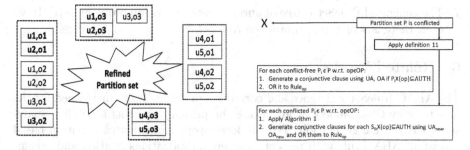

Fig. 2. Refined partition Set in Example 6   **Fig. 3.** Steps in Theorem 1

Table 6. Role-based attributes in Table 4 after applying Algorithm 1

Objects	$oroleAtt_{op1}$	$oroleAtt_{op2}$
o1	{r1, r4}	{}
o2	{}	{r2}
o3	{r1, r3, r4}	{}

Users	$uroleAtt$
u1	{r4}
u2	{r4}
u3	{r2}
u4	{r3}
u5	{r3}

5 Future Enhancements

According to the solutions provided in Sect. 4, it is obvious that each conflict partition with respect to an $op \in OP$ must be split (by inspection, at least two parts) unless there is any change in given attribute value assignment.

Now, question is, can we do better? We leave such questions to be addressed in future work. Some specific questions are listed below:

1. Can we find an approach so that it is always possible to split a conflict partition into two, even if more attributes are needed?
2. Can we propose different combinations of refinement approaches apart from current partition refinement so that asymptotic complexity can be improved?
3. Only positive rule generation has been considered here. The impact of using positive and negative rules together may or may not improve the current procedure.
4. By partition definition, each user object pair present in that partition is represented by the same attribute value combinations. What if there is an exception?
5. Although we had the independence of adding any number of extra attributes to resolve the infeasibility, further analysis is required to get the optimal outcome.
6. Algorithm 1 selects the minimal size of role set while choosing values for role-based attributes. It might not provide the optimal outcome; the system administrator and expert inputs could be considered for further optimization.

7. The generated RuleSet is free of unrepresented partition problem in [1]. However, there is scope to optimize the RuleSet.

6   Related Works

The ABAC RuleSet Existence and correction problem [1] are mentioned for the first time by Chakraborty et al., where the primary aim was feasibility analysis of ABAC rule generation. The proposed work [1] generates partition based consistent ABAC rule with respect to given authorizations relation and accompanying attribute data. Apart from that, this work [1] focuses on unrepresented partitions on ABAC policy mining context.

To mention about some other closely related works: ABAC policy mining problem [11,15] forms the background of feasibility analysis proposed in this paper. There have been a good number of works on ABAC policy mining, such as from Authorization [11,15], RBAC [13], log data [9,14], sparse log [2], etc. An evolutionary computation based solution towards ABAC policy mining is described in [8].

All the works noted so far deals with positive ABAC rules only. However, there is a ABAC policy mining approach [6] by Iyer and Masoumzadeh which deals with both positive and negative ABAC rules. In the proposed work [6], an existing rule mining algorithm called PRISM is used to generate consistent ABAC rules with respect to input log: it is assumed that a complete log is given as input or denied otherwise.

Acknowledgement. This work is partially supported by NSF CREST Grant HRD-1736209, CNS-1423481, CNS-1538418 and DoD ARL Grant W911NF-15-1-0518.

References

1. Chakraborty, S., Sandhu, R., Krishnan, R.: On the feasibility of attribute-based access control policy mining. In: IRI. IEEE (2019)
2. Cotrini, C., Weghorn, T., Basin, D.: Mining ABAC rules from sparse logs. In: EuroSP, pp. 31–46. IEEE (2018)
3. Ferraiolo, D., et al.: Proposed NIST standard for role-based access control. ACM TISSEC **4**(3), 224–274 (2001)
4. Hu, V.C., Kuhn, D.R., Ferraiolo, D.F.: Attribute-based access control. IEEE Comput. **2**, 85–88 (2015)
5. Hu, V., et al.: Guide to attribute based access control (ABAC) definition and considerations. NIST Spec. Publ. **800**, 162–800 (2014)
6. Iyer, P., Masoumzadeh, A.: Mining positive and negative attribute-based access control policy rules. In: SACMAT, pp. 161–172 (2018)
7. Jin, X., Krishnan, R., Sandhu, R.: A unified attribute-based access control model covering DAC, MAC and RBAC. DBSec **12**, 41–55 (2012)
8. Medvet, E., et al.: Evolutionary inference of attribute-based access control policies. In: Gaspar-Cunha, A., Henggeler Antunes, C., Coello, C. (eds.) EMO 2015. LNCS, vol. 9018, pp. 351–365. Springer, Heidelberg (2015). https://doi.org/10.1007/978-3-319-15934-8_24

9. Mocanu, D., Turkmen, F., Liotta, A.: Towards ABAC policy mining from logs with deep learning. In: IS 2015 (2015)
10. Sandhu, R.S., et al.: Role-based access control models. IEEE Comput. **2**, 38–47 (1996)
11. Talukdar, T., et al.: Efficient bottom-up mining of attribute based access control policies. In: IEEE CIC 2017, pp. 339–348 (2017)
12. Weil, T.R., Coyne, E.: ABAC and RBAC: scalable, flexible, and auditable access management. IT Prof. **15**(03), 14–16 (2013)
13. Xu, Z., Stoller, S.: Mining attribute-based access control policies from RBAC policies. In: CEWIT, pp. 1–6. IEEE (2013)
14. Xu, Z., Stoller, S.D.: Mining attribute-based access control policies from logs. In: Atluri, V., Pernul, G. (eds.) DBSec 2014. LNCS, vol. 8566, pp. 276–291. Springer, Heidelberg (2014). https://doi.org/10.1007/978-3-662-43936-4_18
15. Xu, Z., Stoller, S.: Mining attribute-based access control policies. IEEE TDSC **12**(5), 533–545 (2015)

Social Networks

An Investigation of Misinformation Harms Related to Social Media During Humanitarian Crises

Thi Tran[⊠], Rohit Valecha, Paul Rad, and H. Raghav Rao

Department of Information Systems and Cyber Security,
The University of Texas at San Antonio, San Antonio, USA
{thi.tran,rohit.valecha,peyman.najafirad,
hr.rao}@utsa.edu

Abstract. During humanitarian crises, people face dangers and need a large amount of information in a short period of time. Such need creates the base for misinformation such as rumors, fake news or hoaxes to spread within and outside the affected community. It could be unintended misinformation with unconfirmed details, or intentional disinformation created to trick people for benefits. It results in information harms that can generate serious short term or long-term consequences. Although some researchers have created misinformation detection systems and algorithms, examined the roles of involved parties, examined the way misinformation spreads and convinces people, very little attention has been paid to the types of misinformation harms. In the context of humanitarian crises, we propose a taxonomy of information harms and assess people's perception of risk regarding the harms. Such a taxonomy can act as the base for future research to quantitatively measure the harms in specific contexts. Furthermore, perceptions of related people were also investigated in four specifically chosen scenarios through two dimensions: Likelihood of occurrence and Level of impacts of the harms.

Keywords: Misinformation · Humanitarian crises · Disasters · Harms · Injuries · Taxonomy

1 Introduction

Humanitarian Crises are defined by Human Coalition (2018) as "an event or series of events that represents a critical threat to the health, safety, security, or wellbeing of a community or other large group of people, usually over a wide area". They can be categorized into natural disasters (hurricanes, tornadoes, floods, volcanoes, wildfires, tsunamis, earthquakes, etc.), man-made hazards (wars, gunshots, terrorism, big traffic accidents, pollutions, industrial accidents), and health emergencies (epidemics of infectious diseases or health issues due to large scale pollutions and poisoning).

In such humanitarian crises where a community faces large scale dangers or damages, people are hungry to seek information to save themselves or others. However, in a short period of time, official and legitimate sources of the governments or news organizations normally cannot offer enough confirmed/verified information, pushing the community to consume information mainly through fast acting social

S. K. Sahay et al. (Eds.): SKM 2019, CCIS 1186, pp. 167–181, 2020.
https://doi.org/10.1007/978-981-15-3817-9_10

media channels (Oh et al. 2013). Although social media can play a vital role in humanitarian crises with many active users uploading real time data about the crises (Holdeman 2018), it also presents risks. It is the source of widespread unintentional unconfirmed data or intentional scam information such as hoaxes, rumors, fake news, or even some types of cybercrimes like clickbait or phishing emails (Gupta et al. 2013; Holdeman 2018; Maddock et al. 2015; Rajdev 2015). Facebook, WhatsApp and Twitter have been identified as social media platforms that spread most misinformation in crises (Nealon 2017; Pang and Ng 2017). Such misinformation and its impacts can cause serious consequences for consumers and need to be thoroughly understood.

However, very few researchers have paid attention to analyzing the perception of risks for the harms from misinformation. Agrafiotis et al. (2018), Elliott (2019) and Ohlhausen (2017) focus on misinformation harms, but not including humanitarian crises. On the other hand, other researchers already addressed some types of harms in certain specific crises but not with in an overarching manner (Gupta et al. 2013; Holdeman 2018; Nealon 2017). This paper fills the gap by developing a framework for analyzing the constituents of harms and systematic taxonomy of harms from misinformation as applied to humanitarian crisis contexts. Such a taxonomy can also act as the base for other future research or application to solve issues of misinformation.

The paper is structured as follows: First we review the literature. Then we extract information and then we conduct surveys and analyze data to examine harms from misinformation during humanitarian crises. In the final section, we include a discussion and conclusion of the paper.

2 Literature Review

2.1 Background and Prior Research

Misinformation has been defined by many researchers to be incorrect information which can seem to be legitimate initially (Holdeman 2018). It can mislead, create worrisome or other types of harmful effects to the community (Pang and Ng 2017). Generally, the terms misinformation, disinformation, rumors or fake news have been used interchangeably in many contexts. However, some researchers have considered that misinformation is unintentionally incorrect due to the lack of official or confirmed information at a time while disinformation has the intention to mislead consumers for propaganda purpose (Pang and Ng 2017; Wardle and Derakhshan 2017). A few studies have pointed out that rumors or misinformation are beliefs or unverified information with no legitimate sources (Starbird et al. 2014) while some others have claimed that rumors can be both misinformation and disinformation (intentional propaganda efforts such as phishing or scammers' malicious information) (Holdeman 2018; Pang and Ng 2017). In general, Wardle and Derakhshan (2017) have named 7 types of misinformation or disinformation, including satire or parody, misleading content, imposter content, fabricated content, false connection, false context, and manipulated content. Maddock et al. (2015) suggest that misinformation is the byproduct of rumors.

Agrafiotis et al. (2018) have created a structural taxonomy of harms. They have defined five main categories of harms and their subcategories, including physical or digital harms, economic harms, psychology harms, reputational harms, and social or societal harms. The harms were considered based on the view of organizations. Similarly, Elliott (2019) has expounded on similar categories as well as short-term and long-term harms. In this paper we draw from these works and adapt it to humanitarian crises. We stress on the following definition: information harms or information injuries are the result of damages or risks of failures caused by misinformation (Bostrom 2011; Sandvik et al. 2017) that are meant to impact victims (Elliott 2019).

In the context of humanitarian crises, this paper focuses on information harms that effect a large community, directly or indirectly affected by disasters. The aim of this research is to broadly create (a) a systematic taxonomy of information harms applied to humanitarian crises, and specifically (b) an analysis on the perceptions of people about harms in such taxonomy.

2.2 Humanitarian Crises and Harms

When addressing misinformation harms in humanitarian crises, we consider some specific cases of each defined category of crises, including man-made, natural, and healthcare crises. Considering natural crises, Nealon (2017) has mentioned that a rumor during hurricane Harvey said, shelters would check hurricane victims for immigration status while a rumor during hurricane Irma stated that the government would give generators for victims, both of which were not true. The false information lead to unnecessary fears on the one hand and false expectations on the other, which severely affected evacuation decisions and support from authorities. Misinformation about Louisiana floods in 2006 from Facebook messages and posts confused FEMA (March 2016 floods) and the American Red Cross (Summer floods) with information overload (Holdeman 2018). Considering manmade crises, in the Boston Marathon Bombings in 2013, social media users incorrectly searched photos to help find the criminals and falsely accused innocent individuals, putting them at risk (Maddock et al. 2015, p. 230).

Sometimes an emergency is classified as a complex crisis since its causes are mixed between natural and man-made crises. An example of this type is the situation of California's Oroville Dam. Although the situation was related to heavy rainfalls, floods or even earthquakes (Chokshi and McPhate 2017; Rogers 2018), Oroville Dam's crises was also identified as the result of man-made activities, or specifically bad design by involved personnel (Alexander 2018; Rogers 2018). In 2017 there was an evacuation order as a result of incorrect information, with false pictures of huge floods, that got spread on social media. This later needed Facebook to use Live Videos to correct it (Holdeman 2018). This misinformation created unnecessary panic for the entire community.

In healthcare crises, the anti-vaccination situations related to crisis of public confidence in vaccination let the community become exposed to diseases such as measles-mumps-rubella, hepatitis B, and H1N1 (Peretti-Watel et al. 2014). In addition, in the crisis of Zika virus in 2016, harmful information overload caused problems for efforts to fight the dangerous infectious disease that resulted in people's health being at risk (Ghenai and Mejova 2017, p. 3).

To the best of our knowledge, this paper is the first to systematically consider harms and their types as well as impacts over a spectrum of crisis situations.

2.3 Identifying Some Types of Harms Associated with Certain Actual Crises

Drawing on examples extracted from the literature, we identify different types of humanitarian crises, types of misinformation, and certain types of associated harms in some specific crises, together with the sources of information from the literature (see Table 1). This table acts as the foundation for later considerations and chosen scenarios.

Table 1. Combined crises, misinformation and associated harms in example situations.

Crises of harms					
Type	Crises	Problems/ misinformation	Harms	Details	Source
Health care crises	Zika virus, 2016	Information overload in short period	Consume misinformation	Harmful information overload causes problems for efforts to face dangerous infectious disease and put people's health at risk	Ghenai et al. (2017)
	Anti-vaccination situations	Crisis of public confidence in vaccination	Expose to risks of diseases	The decline of vaccination coverage: MMR vaccine in Europe (2010), hepatitis B vaccine in France, and H1N1 vaccine in many countries (2009), 300% increase of measles (2019)	McNamara (2019), Miller (2019), Newton (2019)
Man made disasters	Boston Marathon Bombings, 2013	Using unmatched data for decision; spread of fake news	Personal safety and unnecessary panic	Falsely accused photos of innocent individuals; widespread fake news of shut down services and cancelled flights	Maddock et al. (2015), Madrigal (2013)
Natural disasters	Hurricane Harvey, 2017	False information	Delayed evacuation because of fear, causing dangers	Rumor on Twitter: officials ask for their immigration status	Nealon (2017)
	Hurricane Irma, 2017			Rumor: survivors would receive generators	Nealon (2017)
	Louisiana Floods, 2016	Information overload	Confused between legitimate and fake information	Misinformation from Facebook messages and posts confused FEMA (March 2016 floods) and The American Red Cross (Summer floods)	Holdeman (2018)
Complex crises	Oroville Dam Evacuation, 2017	Falsely assigned information into event	Worrisome and panic	Spreading the false pictures of huge flood covering the entire Sacramento County that needs Facebook Live Videos to correct it	Home-land Security Report (2018)

3 Initial Taxonomy of Harms in Humanitarian Crises Contexts

Drawing from taxonomies in other contexts and the literature on some typical information harms from specific crises, we define the categories of harms in humanitarian crises situations. We acknowledge that many types of harms overlap – for example, physical injury from discrimination due to wrongly accused crimes can be both long term and short term, or a single injury can be related to other types such as emotional, reputation, or financial harms. However, they are different dimensions of harms that can explain different angles of the situation. A further examination of the literature helps us to create a taxonomy of types of harms in Table 2.

When forming the taxonomy of misinformation harms, it is beneficial to systematically map the role of each harms into some types of dimensions. In this paper, we propose to use two dimensions: The Likelihood of Occurrence and the Levels of Impacts of specific harms. Likelihood of occurrence or the perceived possibility of happening and level of impacts or the perceived scale of influences are the two commonly used features to address risk assessment or measurement used by many authors in the literature (Berman 2018; Curtis and Carey 2012). Such information will help examine the urgency of a specific harms to be prioritized in responses.

From those main 8 categories of harms (physical, financial, psychological, reputational, social, security, privacy and confusion harms), we derived 15 different subtypes or subcategories of harms that will be thoroughly addressed later in the Methodology section of the paper, including: life, injury, income, business, emotion, trust, reputation, discrimination, connection, isolation, safety, access, privacy, decision and confusion harms.

Table 2. Categories of misinformation harms in humanitarian crises

Main types	Sub types	Adaptation to humanitarian crises	References
Direct harms	Direct emotional harms	Depression, stress, fear, loss of confidence or beliefs in others when becoming victims of misinformation	Sandvik et al. (2017)
	Direct physical harms	Harms on health, injuries, losses of lives or assets due to believing in the misinformation of the crises	Bostrom (2011)
Indirect harms	Information hazards	Unknown dangers of possible future harms, or effects through relationships with direct victims of crises	Bostrom (2011)
Physical harms	Bodily injury, lives, assets	Harm describing a physical negative effect on someone or something as victims of misinformation in crises: deaths, injuries, losses of assets, homelessness, etc	Agrafiotis et al. (2018, p. 7), Elliott (2019), Peretti-Watel et al. (2014), Speri (2014)

(continued)

Table 2. (*continued*)

Main types	Sub types	Adaptation to humanitarian crises	References
Financial/ economic harm	Loss/damage of business, jobs, valuable assets, etc.	Harm that relates to negative financial or economic consequences because of crisis misinformation: damaged houses, cars, business values, etc.	Agrafiotis et al. (2018, p. 7), Elliott (2019)
Psychological harm	Emotional harms, changed attitudes and beliefs	Harms on mental well-being from crises misinformation or rumors, such as: sadness, lack of trust, depression, stress	Agrafiotis et al. (2018, p. 7), Elliott (2019), Nealon (2017)
Reputational harm	Wrongly accused crime, discrimination	Wrongly accused crime or data breach caused by misinformation in crises can harm lives of many people in both short term and long term	Agrafiotis et al. (2018, p. 7), Elliott (2019), Maddock et al. (2015)
Social and Societal harm	Loss social connections, family members, etc.	Loss or damaged social relationships with family members or friends, or social separation because of damaged reputation caused by misinformation	Agrafiotis et al. (2018, p. 7)
Safety/security harms	Safety harms, identity thefts	Rumors can create unnecessary fear or lead to wrong choices that are much more dangerous in crises	Ohlhausen (2017), Sandvik et al. (2017)
	Identity thefts	Loss personal information leading to identity thefts due to the crises	FTC Informational Injury Workshop Report (2018)
	Biometric harms/medical identity thefts	Leaked biometric data in crises can lead to denied treatments or lead to wrong treatment, causing serious health consequences for a large affected community	FTC Informational Injury Workshop Report (2018), Sandvik et al. (2017)
Privacy harms	Physical intrusion	Loss of security at home or work in crises due to misinformation	Ohlhausen (2017)
	Sensitive data breach	Sensitive private data can fall into wrong hands in crises as policies and controls are not as strict as in other situations	FTC Informational Injury Workshop Report (2018)
Confusion		Confused information lead to not appropriate decisions	Holdeman (2018)
Short term		Physical harms, emotional harms, financial harms	Elliott (2019)
Long term		Reputational harms, financial harms	Elliott (2019)

4 Methodology

4.1 Defining the Approach

In order to examine misinformation harms, we decided to conduct a survey and we recruited participants by using Amazon Mechanical Turk (https://www.mturk.com/), which is a popular source that can be easily controlled and customized for specific needs. The main aim of the survey was to obtain judgements of people that have some level of expertise, deep knowledge or related experience, regarding the ways to handle crisis situations. The actual survey, which was officially approved by IRB (Institutional Review Board) of a southern University in the U.S., was designed on Qualtrics website (https://www.qualtrics.com/). When distributing the survey via Amazon Mechanical Turk (MTurk), participants were clearly explained the purpose of the research, and the type of information collected. They were also informed that there were no risks regarding identifiable or sensitive information.

Aiming for the quality of the responses, the survey focused on people with work experience related to humanitarian crisis response and recovery efforts. The survey was conducted in three rounds: The first round was a screening survey, in which targeted participants were filtered and chosen to join in later steps. Participants with relevant work experience included those in firefighter departments, police departments, Federal Emergency Management Agency (FEMA), the Red Cross, or hospitals and other healthcare organizations. We ensured the reliability of participants' claim that they had relevant work experience by asking them to list from 3 to 5 key steps they had performed to handle crisis situations. Based on the responses, we filtered qualified and not qualified respondents. In this round, we asked for 400 responses, all of whom were in the U.S., and then retained 273 responses (68.25%) based on the above criteria.

The second round was constructed to effectively assign the MTurk workers, to one of the defined scenarios of crises and misinformation. Workers were mainly asked whether they were familiar with one of the four described crises and related misinformation, and whether they had been involved in those situations (see Table 3). Familiarity of the scenarios were measured on a Likert scale from 1 to 5. These scenarios were chosen based on the literature of actual situations, including one natural (Hurricane Harvey 2017), one manmade (Boston Marathon Bombing 2013), one healthcare (Anti-vaccination) and one complex crises between natural and manmade crisis (Oroville Dam evacuation 2017). The criteria for choosing these scenarios were: (1) representing as many types of crises as possible, and (2) showing as many different types of misinformation as possible. In addition, popularity of the situation was also a criterion as we needed to make sure that many people were aware of such scenario. In other words, these scenarios were chosen to maximize diversity of details, and to maximize generalizability of the later results. Although we received 100% of 273 requested responses, some of them had to be removed due to some bad details such as answers of familiarity falling out of the accepted range (from 1 to 5), bringing the total qualified number down to 183 (or 67.03%).

Table 3. The 4 scenarios of humanitarian crises and involved misinformation

Scenario	Name	Type	Misinformation	Source
1	Anti-vaccination	Healthcare	Wrong overload and confusing information	Miller (2019), McNamara (2019), Newton (2019)
2	Boston Marathon Bombing, 2013	Man-made	Misinformation of shut down services	Maddock et al. (2015), Shih (2013), Madrigal (2013)
3	Hurricane Harvey, 2017	Natural	Wrong immigration checking information	Nealon (2017)
4	Oroville Dam evacuation, 2017	Complex	Mislead mapped pictures of floods	Homeland Security Report (2018)

In the third round, we sent specifically designed questionnaires to MTurk workers. Each questionnaire carried 2 scenarios, and the assigned worker was asked to give judgements about the 15 harms derived from the literature on two aspects: likelihood of occurrence or the perceived risk of happening, and the level of impacts or the perceived damages of the harms. The ratings ranged from 0 if the participants saw no chance of happening or no perceived impacts of a harm, to the highest level of 10. Out of 183 requested responses, we got 85 responses from qualified participants (46.45%).

SAS 9.4, Microsoft Excel and Tableau 10.2 were used to analyze, present and report the results of the three rounds. According to the nature and purpose of the study, we focused on obtaining the mean or average values of the variables.

4.2   Addressing Amazon Mechanical Turk Data Quality Concerns

For many years, debates are going on amongst scholars about the quality and validity of studies conducted on Amazon Mechanical Turk (in short as "MTurk"). Although raising concerns about appropriateness and overall quality of MTurk workers' responses, Cheung et al. (2017) has pointed out that MTurk responses passed various important validity tests. Importantly, most researchers agreed that MTurk workers and their responses are much more diverse than participants from other recruiting methods (Buhrmester et al. 2011; Casler et al. 2013; Heen et al. 2014; Majima et al. 2017; Sheehan 2018). We also applied various quality control measures as detailed below.

We filtered applicants in the very first round of the survey to only let people qualified as "Master". A Master in M-Turk terminology is someone with more than 90% previous approval rates to join. Further we used attention check questions (ACQ) to ensure that we got the best responses. Our records show high quality with regard to those ACQs.

Further on the M-Turk platform, we requested only for participants that had related Emergency Response and Recovery working experience or were victims of humanitarian crises to join the surveys, because they would have a better sense of the impact of misinformation in their settings. For quality check, we also asked eligible respondents to describe steps that had taken during emergency situations. We inspected each description manually to separate out the answers that were clearly good and those that were clearly irrelevant (two of the co-authors of this paper have had a lot of experience in the emergency response management domain). Most of the responses were of high quality. All these steps are crucial to guarantee high quality and appropriateness of the research design.

5 Data Analysis and Discussion

For the final 85 qualified respondents, each one addressed two scenarios in the same survey, yielding the number of records for all scenarios as 170 (i.e. 170 judgements for misinformation harms).

5.1 Examining Harms in Scenarios and Quadrants

This paper compares misinformation harms across two dimensions: likelihood of occurrence (in short termed as the "Likelihood") and levels of impacts (the "Impacts").

We considered that any value of Likelihood or Impact larger than 5 as large values. For the sake of visualization, we adjusted the values of both Likelihood and Impacts to better show the actual meaning of the ratings resulting in "adjusted likelihood" or "adjusted impacts".

Table 4. Ratings by all scenarios and quadrants with adjusted Likelihood and Impacts.

Harms	Scenario 1			Scenario 2			Scenario 3			Scenario 4			All scenarios		
	L	I	Q	L	I	Q	L	I	Q	L	I	Q	L	I	Q
Life	−0.77	**0.82**	2	**0.00**	**1.26**	4	**0.45**	**1.83**	4	−0.14	**0.62**	2	−0.15	**1.12**	2
Injury	−1.02	**0.70**	2	−0.03	**0.57**	2	−0.03	**1.28**	2	−1.57	**0.74**	2	−0.67	**0.81**	2
Income	−1.81	−0.50	1	−0.70	**0.33**	2	−0.45	**0.75**	2	−0.05	**0.41**	2	−0.82	**0.20**	2
Business	−1.46	−0.34	1	−0.65	−0.07	1	−0.79	**0.55**	2	−0.78	**0.10**	2	−0.95	**0.04**	2
Emotion	−1.13	**0.00**	2	**0.73**	**1.19**	4	**0.68**	**1.20**	4	−0.08	**0.79**	2	−0.01	**0.76**	2
Trust	−0.46	**0.35**	2	**0.35**	**0.64**	4	−0.16	**0.58**	2	**0.39**	**0.67**	4	**0.00**	**0.55**	4
Reputation	−1.02	**0.12**	2	−0.68	**0.00**	2	−0.95	**0.18**	2	−0.08	**0.10**	2	−0.71	**0.10**	2
Discrimination	−1.58	−0.58	1	−0.78	−0.21	1	**0.39**	**1.03**	4	−1.41	−0.85	1	−0.88	−0.18	1
Connection	−1.79	−0.34	1	−0.03	**0.24**	2	**0.16**	**0.10**	4	−0.35	**0.28**	2	−0.58	**0.05**	2
Isolation	−1.35	−0.28	1	−0.48	**0.31**	2	**0.16**	**0.80**	4	−0.92	**0.36**	2	−0.69	**0.26**	2
Safety	−1.58	−0.16	1	−0.05	**1.02**	2	−0.29	**1.50**	2	−0.81	**0.31**	2	−0.73	**0.63**	2
Access	−2.06	−0.50	1	−0.35	**0.64**	2	−0.29	**1.18**	2	−0.76	**0.08**	2	−0.93	**0.30**	2
Privacy	−1.92	−0.96	1	−0.80	**0.07**	2	−0.21	**0.80**	2	−0.92	−0.13	1	−1.02	−0.11	1
Decision	−0.54	**0.32**	2	**0.53**	**1.10**	4	**0.21**	**1.53**	4	−0.16	**0.85**	2	−0.02	**0.91**	2
Confusion	−1.10	−0.46	1	−0.28	**0.93**	2	**0.68**	**1.13**	4	**0.97**	**0.85**	4	−0.01	**0.55**	2

*Note: L: adjusted likelihood; I: adjusted impacts; Q: quadrants on the plot. High values are bolded.
Scenario 1: Anti-vaccination and misinformation overload; **Scenario 2:** Boston Marathon Bombing 2013 and rumors of cancelled services; **Scenario 3:** Hurricane Harvey 2017 and rumors about immigration check; **Scenario 4:** Oroville Dam evacuation 2017 and wrong accusation.

Accordingly, we plotted the combination values of each harm rated by the participants in graphs divided into four separate areas, or quadrants of risk (i.e. the product of likelihood and impact):

- Quadrant 1: Low likelihood, Low impact (Adjusted Likelihood < 0.0, Adjusted Impacts < 0.0)
- Quadrant 2: Low likelihood, high impact (Adjusted Likelihood < 0.0, Adjusted Impacts ≥ 0.0)
- Quadrant 3: High likelihood, low impact (Adjusted Likelihood ≥ 0.0, Adjusted Impacts < 0.0)
- Quadrant 4: High likelihood, high impact (Adjusted Likelihood ≥ 0.0, Adjusted Impacts ≥ 0.0)

Quadrant 1 has lowest risk; hence it is less critical to pay much attention when handling with the harms in this quadrant in a certain crisis. On the contrary, Quadrant 4 is the area of highest risk and needs highest priority to deal with. Even with low likelihood or risk of happening, Quadrant 2's harms have large damages that the response and recovery efforts should have some backup plans to call when needed. Though having low levels of impacts, harms in Quadrant 3 are more likely to appear and need constant readiness and resources to handle. Table 4 has the details of mean values of adjusted likelihood and adjusted impacts in each scenario as well as the quadrants those harms fall in.

The ratings vary between the scenarios. First, Scenario 3, the hurricane scenario, has high impacts and half of the likelihood is high, giving the impression that such scenario must be seriously focused on. Scenario 3 is also the one that has not only highest percentage of high impacts but also highest values of many impacts, reaching up to 1.83, and all of the harms fall into Quadrants 2 or 4. This can be due to the results that are associated with the impacts of the considered Hurricane, i.e., Harvey, or generally a natural crisis. It can also be the consequence of the concerned harms when people cannot not make the evacuation efforts as they fear the misinformation of immigration checks, which can cause dangerous outcomes.

Second, even though the total number of high impacts are slightly less in Scenario 2, the bombing scenario, compared to Scenario 4, dam evacuation scenario, (12 versus 13 high impact harms), the actual impact values are much higher. While the fourth scenario "Oroville Dam evacuation, 2017" (complex crisis) got impacts around 0.1 to 0.85, Scenario 2 "Boston Marathon Bombing 2013", has four harms with more than a score of 1. This indicates that the misinformation associated with Scenario 4 (wrong information leading to the unnecessary evacuation) does not have as serious impacts as the one in Scenario 2 to the affected community (broadly announced cancelled services, including air flights). Indeed, it could be because of the local level impacts of Scenario 4 compared to much broader influences in Scenario 2 where numerous people got unnecessarily worried about affected flight schedules.

Interestingly, many participants indicated that they were very familiar with the first Scenario, regarding vaccination and many of them were working in medical industry. Scenario 1 representing the healthcare crisis of antivaccination has the lowest records of both likelihood and impacts. The reason for this could be the effects of antivaccination are harder to be quantified or imagined, or even because partly in the pool of participants as participants, people still believe that antivaccination may not be a major issue, since most people get vaccinated anyway. Debates on this issue have been going on for a long time both in the popular media and in the scientific press.

For detailed consideration, we have combined the figures of Table 4 with the visualization in Fig. 1. We call each combination of Adjusted Likelihood and Adjusted Impacts as a Record, which is shown as a circle in Fig. 1.

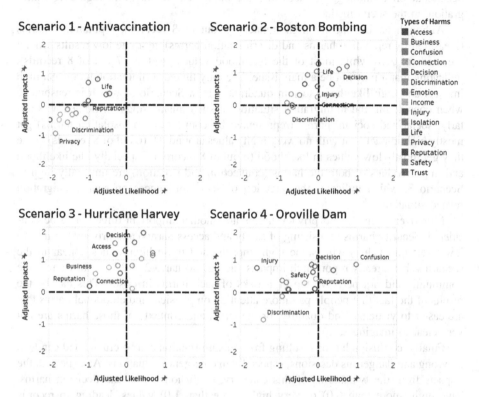

Fig. 1. Rated misinformation harms in different quadrants of likelihood and impacts.

We notice that the physical harms measured by life harms and injury harms get highest values of impacts in all four scenarios. However, mostly they get low to moderate likelihood except for Scenario 3 when life harms get into quadrant 4 with high likelihood. Injury harms remain in the second quadrant with low likelihood. We suspect that this is because cancelled service rumors do not significantly cause life or injury harms. Further participants may be influenced by the actual harms of the crises, i.e. the natural disaster Hurricane Harvey instead of the misinformation situation. Financial harms (measured by business harms and income harms) have low likelihood values, but 50% of the records indicate that they get high impacts in scenarios 2, 3 and 4, which falls into either quadrant 1 or 2 of the plots. This is reasonable as scenario 1 is hardly likely to be associated with perceived financial losses.

Besides materialistic related harms, psychological and mental related harms are also very important. Psychological harms, represented by emotion and trust harms, have higher impacts. In some cases, however, they have a low likelihood, leading to the positions within the first or second quadrants. While trust harms go from Quadrant 2 to

Quadrant 4 with high likelihood in Scenarios 2 and 4, due to the vast effects of misleading information regarding cancelled services and the evacuation order, emotion harms reache high likelihood in Scenario 2 and 3 as people nowadays are over dependent on technology services and the highly emotional news regarding immigration on the social media.

Although having mostly high impacts (5 out of 8 records), reputational harms (measured by reputation harms and discrimination harms) get quite low results around the score of zero while most of the likelihood values are low (7 out of 8 records), indicating that it may not be a main issue. The only time discrimination harms get high impacts and high likelihood to join quadrant 4 is in Scenario 3, which is reasonable when considering the immigration situation of such misinformation. Somehow similarly, social and societal harms (represented by connection and isolation harms) get mostly high impacts but with not very high values around 0.0 (6 out of 8 records) while they get mostly low values in likelihood (6 out of 8 records). Especially, the likelihood and impact values of both the harms (connection and isolation) are unusually high in Scenario 3, which indicates the attention of social influences on such immigration related situation.

Moreover, security and privacy harms are another important direction to be considered. Security harms (consisting of safety and access harms) and privacy harm have low likelihood values with some high impacts, and those high values appear in the scenarios that already report high impacts such as Scenario 2 and 3. It shows that the community did not perceive the high risks of such harms in crises. This can be the results of the fact that people pay more attention on physical and emotional harms that are easier to visualize and quantify, or the terms and contexts of those harms are not very clear to imagine.

Finally, confusion harms resulting from misinformation can be crucial and can lead to wrong and dangerous decisions, especially in emergency situations. As expected, the impacts from the two harms of this category, confusion harms and decision harms, have high (more than 0.0) or very high (more than 1.0) values, leading to records placed only in quadrants 2 or 4. Specifically, decision harms joins the first quadrant with high likelihood in Scenarios 2 and 3 as the effects are easier to be addressed, while the only time confusion harms move from quadrant 2 to the quadrant 4 is in Scenario 4. These results are somehow expected as the first scenario is quite hard to be addressed, the second and third scenarios are easier to think about, and the last scenario is more to the misleading information that affects the trust harms.

6   Conclusion

Humanitarian crises are situations in which people must face risks and confusions. The motivation to seek and spread helpful information as well as to find suitable solutions for the well-being of someone or the entire community is crucial. Social media can act much faster than official information sources, but it comes with the costs and risks of unconfirmed information and rumors that can create serious consequences. Many researchers have tried to tackle the situation by creating misinformation detection systems or algorithms, hypothesizing and testing the roles of behavioral characteristics of involved people, or finding the patterns of how misinformation can successfully spread and influence people. However, not much attention has been placed on categorizing the harms or impacts. This paper has summarized the findings of the literature to build a thorough taxonomy of misinformation harms in the context of humanitarian crises.

Moreover, by gathering judgements of people that have actual knowledge or experience related to the crises and the crisis response and recovery efforts, through various rounds of survey, this study systematically addressed the likelihood of occurrence, the level of impacts as well as the risk scores of 15 different harms derived from the literature. With the results from four chosen scenarios, covering four types of humanitarian crises (natural disasters, manmade crises, healthcare crises and complex emergencies) as well as different forms of misinformation (misinformation overload, misinformation about public services, misinformation related to discrimination and misinformation related to wrong accusation), the study investigated how harms can be viewed in different situations. These findings are expected to be beneficial not only for optimizing crisis response and recovery activities for prioritizing the use of resources, but also for future research studies to deepen and broaden such findings. The contributions of this research to both the practical side of benefiting the community or minimizing harms for victims and the academic size of forming a systematic background for humanitarian crises and emergency related researches are clearly significant.

Although we try to cover multiple diverse types of humanitarian crises and misinformation, this research does have some limitations. Due to the nature of online surveys, we could not ask participants to discuss their choices with others to reach mutual agreements or consensus on the values they chose. Finally, while we obtained misinformation harms from the literature, there can be many other possible harms in real life. Further qualitative or discovery research would be beneficial to define the best fit list of harms for later research consideration.

References

Agrafiotis, I., Nurse, J.R., Goldsmith, M., Creese, S., Upton, D.: A taxonomy of cyber-harms: defining the impacts of cyber-attacks and understanding how they propagate. J. Cybersecur. **4**, tyy006, 1–15 (2018)

Alexander, K.: What caused nearly 20,000 quakes at Oroville Dam? Scientists weigh in on mystery (2018). https://www.sfchronicle.com/news/article/What-caused-nearly-20-000-quakes-at-Oroville-Dam-13473254.php. Accessed 25 Aug 2019

Berman, M.: Risk assessments 101: the role of probability & impact in measuring risk (2018). https://ncontracts.com/articles/risk-assessments-101-the-role-of-probability-impact-in-measuring-risk/. Accessed 01 Sept 2019

Bostrom, N.: Information hazards: a typology of potential harms from knowledge. Rev. Contemporary Philosophy **10**, 44–79 (2011). http://search.proquest.com/docview/920893069/. Accessed 01 July 2019

Buhrmester, D.M., Kwang, N.T., Gosling, D.S.: Amazon's mechanical turk: a new source of inexpensive, yet high-quality, data? Perspect. Psychol. Sci. **6**(1), 3–5 (2011). https://doi.org/10.1177/1745691610393980

Casler, K., Bickel, L., Hackett, E.E.: Separate but equal? A comparison of participants and data gathered via Amazon's MTurk, social media, and face-to-face behavioral testing. Comput. Hum. Behav. **29**(6), 2156–2160 (2013)

Cheung, H.J., Burns, K.D., Sinclair, R., Sliter, M.: Amazon mechanical turk in organizational psychology: an evaluation and practical recommendations. J. Bus. Psychol. **32**(4), 347–361 (2017). https://doi.org/10.1007/s10869-016-9458-5

Chokshi, N., McPHate, M.: Flood risk near Oroville Dam causes thousands to evacuate in California (2017). https://www.nytimes.com/2017/02/12/us/california-oroville-dam-spillway-evacuate.html. Accessed 25 Aug 2019

Curtis, P., Carey, M.: Risk Assessment in Practice. Thought leadership in ERM. By Deloitte & Touche LLP, and COSO (Committee of Sponsoring Organizations of the Treadway Commission) (2012). https://www2.deloitte.com/content/dam/Deloitte/global/Documents/Governance-Risk-Compliance/dttl-grc-riskassessmentinpractice.pdf. Accessed 27 Aug 2019

Elliott, D.: Concept unwrapped – causing harms. Copyright © 2019 ethics unwrapped - McCombs School of Business – The University of Texas at Austin (2019). https://ethicsunwrapped.utexas.edu/video/causing-harm. Accessed 15 Feb 2019

FTC Informational Injury Workshop Report. FTC staff perspective (2018). https://www.ftc.gov/system/files/documents/reports/ftc-informational-injury-workshop-be-bcp-staff-perspective/inform'ational_injury_workshop_staff_report_-_oct_2018_0.pdf. Accessed 20 Apr 2019

Ghenai, A., Mejova, Y.: Catching zika fever: application of crowdsourcing and machine learning for tracking health misinformation on Twitter. arXiv.org (2017)

Gupta, A., Lamba, H., Kumaraguru, P., Joshi, A.: Faking Sandy: characterizing and identifying fake images on Twitter during Hurricane Sandy. In: Proceedings of the 22nd International Conference on World Wide Web (WWW 2013 Companion), pp. 729–736. ACM, New York (2013)

Heen, M.S., Lieberman, J.D., Miethe, T.D.: A comparison of different online sampling approaches for generating national samples. UNLV – Center Crime Justice Policy **1**, 1–8 (2014). Research In Brief. September 2014, CCJP 2014-01

Holdeman, E.: BLOG: disaster zone: how to counter fake news during a disaster. TCA Regional News, Chicago, 27 February 2018

Homeland Security Report. Countering false information on social media in disasters and emergencies. Department of Homeland Security – Science and Technology (2018). https://www.dhs.gov/sites/default/files/publications/SMWG_Countering-False-Info-Social-Media-Disasters-Emergencies_Mar2018-508.pdf. Accessed 20 Apr 2019

Human Coalition. What is a humanitarian emergency? (2018). https://www.humanitariancoalition.ca/info-portal/factsheets/what-is-a-humanitarian-crisis. Accessed 07 Dec 2018

Maddock, J., Starbird, K., Al-Hassani, H., Sandoval, D., Orand, M., Mason, R.: Characterizing online rumoring behavior using multi-dimensional signatures. In: Proceedings of the 18th ACM Conference on Computer Supported Cooperative Work & Social Computing, pp. 228–241. ACM (2015)

Madrigal, C.A.: #BostonBombing: the anatomy of a misinformation disaster (2013). https://www.theatlantic.com/technology/archive/2013/04/-bostonbombing-the-anatomy-of-a-misinformation-disaster/275155/. Accessed 14 June 2019

Majima, Y., Nishiyama, K., Nishihara, A., Hata, R.: Conducting online behavioral research using crowdsourcing services in Japan. Front. Psychol. **8** (2017) https://doi.org/10.3389/fpsyg.2017.00378

McNamara, A.: Facebook announces plan to combat anti-vaccine misinformation (2019). https://www.thedailybeast.com/facebook-announces-plan-to-combat-vaccine-misinformation. Accessed 14 June 2019

Miller, C.A.: Viral misinformation: rise of 'anti-vaxxer' movement requires news literacy inoculation. USA Today (2019). https://www.usatoday.com/story/opinion/2019/05/03/measles -spread-viral-anti-vaxxer-misinformation-internet-literacy-news-column/3650914002/. Acces sed 14 June 2019

Nealon: False tweets during Harvey, Irma under scrutiny by University at Buffalo Researchers. US Fed News Service, Including US State News, Washington, D.C, 29 September 2017. http://www.buffalo.edu/news/releases/2017/09/044.html. Accessed 15 Feb 2019

Newton, C.: Instagram will begin blocking hashtags that return anti-vaccination misinformation (2019). https://www.theverge.com/2019/5/9/18553821/instagram-anti-vax-vaccines-hashtag-blocking-misinformation-hoaxes. Accessed 14 June

Oh, O., Agrawal, M., Rao, H.: Community intelligence and social media services: a rumor theoretic analysis of tweets during social crises. MIS Q. **37**(2), 407–426 (2013)

Ohlhausen, M.K.: Informational injury in FTC privacy and data security cases, 19 September 2017. https://www.ftc.gov/system/files/documents/public_statements/1255113/privacy_speech_mk ohlhausen.pdf. Accessed 15 Feb 2019

Pang, N., Ng, J.: Misinformation in a riot: a two-step flow view. Online Inf. Rev. **41**(4), 438–453 (2017)

Peretti-Watel, P., Raude, J., Sagaon-Teyssier, L., Constant, A., Verger, P., Beck, F.: Attitudes toward vaccination and the H1N1 vaccine: poor people's unfounded fears or legitimate concerns of the elite? Soc. Sci. Med. **109**, 10–18 (2014)

Rajdev, M., Lee, K.: Fake and spam messages: detecting misinformation during natural disasters on social media. In: 2015 IEEE/WIC/ACM International Conference on Web Intelligence and Intelligent Agent Technology (WI-IAT), vol. 1, pp. 17–20. IEEE (2015)

Rogers, P.: Oroville Dam: Designer of failed spillway had almost no experience (2018). https:// www.mercurynews.com/2018/01/05/oroville-dam-new-report-details-what-caused-the-near-disaster-last-year/. Accessed 25 Aug 2019

Sandvik, K., Jacobsen, K., McDonald, S.: Do no harm: a taxonomy of the challenges of humanitarian experimentation, **99**(904), 319–344 (2017). https://doi.org/10.1017/S181638 311700042X

Sheehan, B.K.: Crowdsourcing research: data collection with Amazon's Mechanical Turk. Commun. Monogr. **85**(1), 140–156 (2018). https://doi.org/10.1080/03637751.2017.1342043

Shih, G.: Boston marathon bombings: how Twitter and Reddit got it wrong (2013). https://www. independent.co.uk/news/world/americas/boston-marathon-bombings-how-twitter-and-reddit-got-it-wrong-8581167.html. Accessed 14 June

Speri, A.: FEMA Is Trying To Get Back $5.8M in Hurricane Sandy Aid Money (2014). https:// news.vice.com/en_us/article/pa885v/fema-is-trying-to-get-back-58m-in-hurricane-sandy-aid-money. Accessed 15 Feb 2019

Starbird, K., Maddock, J., Orand, M., Achterman, P., Mason, R.M.: Rumors, false flags, and digital vigilantes: misinformation on Twitter after the 2013 Boston marathon bombing. In: iConference 2014 Proceedings, pp. 654–662 (2014). https://doi.org/10.9776/14308

Wardle, C., Derakhshan, H.: Information disorder: toward an interdisciplinary framework for research and policy making. Council of Europe report. DGI, September 2017

The Effect of Threat and Proximity
on Cyber-Rumor Sharing

Rohit Valecha[1]([✉]), Tejaswi Volety[1], K. Hazel Kwon[2],
and H. Raghav Rao[1]

[1] University of Texas at San Antonio, San Antonio, TX 78249, USA
{rohit.valecha,hr.rao}@utsa.edu,
teja.volety@gmail.com
[2] Arizona State University, Phoenix, AZ 85004, USA
khkwon@asu.edu

Abstract. Today's society faces a paramount challenge from cyber-rumors that become rapidly viral and transform into more harmful impacts in social networks. The problem of cyber-rumors is further exacerbated in the health crisis context. In the healthcare literature, it has been well established that threat situations facilitate citizens' behavior including cyber-rumor sharing. In this paper, we argue that in the healthcare context, both the threat attribute and cyber-rumor sharing are likely to be influenced by the proximity to health crisis. We argue that proximity is an important indicator of newsworthiness and shareworthiness in social media. In accordance, we investigate how the concept of proximity affects diffusion characteristics of cyber-rumor messages. We address the following research questions associated with cyber-rumor sharing in the context of Zika virus: How does proximity affect the threat appeal in a cyber-rumor message? How does proximity influence cyber-rumor sharing? The results indicate the negative effect of spatial and temporal distance on threat appeal, and the negative effect of spatial distance on cyber-rumor sharing. Such an investigation allows us to quickly identify the emergence of viral rumor messages and monitor the ongoing development of these messages in a timely manner.

Keywords: Rumor · Cyber-rumor sharing · Threat · Proximity

1 Introduction

Today's information and communication technologies (ICTs) faces a big challenge from cyber-rumors (Oh et al. 2013; Rao 2016). Cyber-rumors can become rapidly viral and transform into more harmful impacts in social networks (Webb et al. 2016). The problem of cyber-rumors in the health crisis context is further exacerbated due to the following reasons: The health sector cannot rely on public opinion to infer true information. In fact, much of the population is inadequately equipped to evaluate health-related information provided on the social media and healthcare communities. Reliable information from reputable sources such as medical journals, medical societies, WHO, CDC, etc. takes a significant time delay. These delays encourage health-related cyber-rumors. The more citizens accept health-related cyber-rumors, the greater

© Springer Nature Singapore Pte Ltd. 2020
S. K. Sahay et al. (Eds.): SKM 2019, CCIS 1186, pp. 182–193, 2020.
https://doi.org/10.1007/978-981-15-3817-9_11

is the misunderstanding between healthcare experts and civil society, which can weaken the effectiveness of health crisis response (Valecha et al. 2017). This is the reason why, The Atlantic stated, "of all the categories of [misinformation], health news is the worst."[1]

A key element for successful health-related cyber-rumor management is "to understand what makes citizens prone to engaging in [health-related] cyber-rumor sharing" (Kwon and Rao 2017; p. 307). In the healthcare literature (though not related to cyber-space), it has been well established that threat situations facilitate citizens' behavior (Folkman 2013; Rogers 1975; Witte 1992). Prior literature in the rumor context has investigated the effect of threat on cyber-rumor sharing (Kwon and Rao 2017). It has found that threat increases the willingness of cyber-rumor sharing. In this paper, we define threat appeal as a persuasive message that attempts to arouse fear through the threat of impending danger or harm. We argue that, in the healthcare context, both the threat appeal of a cyber-rumor message and cyber-rumor sharing are likely to be influenced by the proximity to health crisis. Proximity has been considered as an important indicator of newsworthiness (Nossek and Berkowitz 2006) and "shareworthiness" in social media (Trilling et al. 2017). We investigate how the concept of proximity affects diffusion characteristics of cyber-rumor messages.

Based on the discussion by Trope and Libermann (2010), we utilize social, temporal and spatial distances (also referred to as psychological distances) to elaborate the notion of proximity in a generalizable and operational way, and address the following research questions associated with cyber-rumor sharing in the context of Zika virus: How does psychological distance affect the threat appeal in a cyber-rumor message? How does psychological distance influence cyber-rumor sharing? In order to address these research questions, using Twitter data, we investigate the effect of social, temporal and spatial distances on cyber-rumor sharing. The results indicate that spatial and temporal distance have a negative effect on threat appeal, while spatial distance has a negative influence on cyber-rumor sharing.

Such an investigation will allow us to quickly identify the emergence of viral rumor messages and monitor the ongoing development of these messages in a timely manner. It will also allow practitioners and policymakers flag and correct highly threatening messages in the proximity of the event and location to reduce chaos and uncertainty related to the event. It will allow more efficient utilization of communication channels in order to help healthcare officials to reduce panic situations and promote reliable information sharing (Volety et al. 2018). This research is a step towards "bright ICTs" that counter the negative effects of technologies and help establish a safe and secure society (Lee 2015, 2016). The rest of the paper is organized as follows: First we discuss the literature on cyber-rumor sharing as well as shed light on the theoretical lens. Then we discuss the methodology consisting of data collection, unsupervised machine learning and quantitative analysis. After discussing the results in the subsequent section, we conclude with future work for completing this research.

---

[1] https://www.theatlantic.com/health/archive/2017/06/of-all-the-categories-of-fake-news-health-news-is-the-worst/531540/.

2 Theoretical Background

2.1 Crisis Situation, Threat Appeal and Cyber-Rumor Sharing

People have started relying heavily on social media for any news updates (Valecha et al. 2010). Owing to the outpour of social media information from various user groups coupled with its unstructured nature, there is a high probability of false information being spread or the information getting manipulated through various discussions (Oh et al. 2013). There are numerous studies that have investigated diffusion characteristics and other metadata related properties around a message and the network from which the message is initiated (Li et al. 2014; Suh et al. 2010). Studies have also compared diffusion for non-rumor, rumor, and rumor-correcting messages (Lee et al. 2015; Shin et al. 2012).

Rumors diffuse even more readily under the crisis context that invokes a sense of fear in public minds (Pezzo and Beckstead 2006). In the context of Zika virus, a possibility of newborn's brain defect without a known treatment induces a high level of anxiety and uncertainty, the two prerequisites of threat situation (Oh et al. 2013), especially among pregnant women. Under such a threat situation, individuals will engage in various social behaviors that help reduce fear, such as religious activities (Solomon et al. 1991). Cyber-rumor sharing is one way to collectively manage fear associated with the threat situation (Kwon and Rao 2017). That is, the threat situation serves as an important antecedent of cyber-rumor sharing; it increases the willingness of cyber-rumor sharing. Nonetheless, as Kwon and Rao (2017) pointed out, "studies that investigate the threat situational effect in the real-world context are very rare" (p. 309).

In the context of social media messages, a message can depict threat in a certain way to invoke a sense of fear. We conceptualize a message's threat appeal as a persuasive attempt to arouse fear through the threat of impending danger or harm. The effect of threat appeal has been attested in cyber-rumoring contexts. For example, Valecha et al. (2017) have shown that threat appeals induced from a rumor message can influence citizens' cyber-rumor sharing. Kwon and Rao's (2017) study has also shown that anxiety aroused by different rumor topics can explain largest variances for citizens' willingness for rumor sharing. While prior literature has focused on the effect of threat appeal on cyber-rumor sharing, however, very few studies have investigated how attributes of a message shape threat appeal within the cyber-rumor messages.

2.2 Psychological Distance and Cyber-Rumor Sharing

Prior studies have contended that tie strength with a message sender influences perceived trustworthiness of rumors, which then influences rumor acceptance and transmission (Oh et al. 2013). Network analysis in the context of rumor diffusion has shown that social network ties and community structures are associated with ways in which rumors are spread (Ye et al. 2018). For example, Cheng et al. (2013) state that closer the ties are the more the message gets spread because it makes the rumor appear to be trustworthy. Similarly, Shin et al. (2012) demonstrate that believers of political rumors formed a more ideologically cohesive, denser community in Twitter than those who refuted rumors.

Tie strength is a way to measure interpersonal affinity (Marsden and Campbell 1984). Trope and Libermann (2010) have defined interpersonal affinity as social distance. While rumors studies have attested to social distance effects on rumor diffusion, little research has paid attention to other factors that together define an individual's overall state of psychological distance. Specifically, psychological distance is a composite construct of three distance variables including social distance, spatial distance and temporal distances (Trope and Liberman 2010). In Twitter context, Kwon et al. (2017) have defined social distance as the measure of how close a user perceives another person—who may be either a message sender or mentioned in the message—as a part of one's social life; spatial distance as the geometric distance of a message receiver from the place where the event occurs; and temporal distance as the distance measured in terms of the time gap between the occurrence of an event and the exposure to message. These three distance variables affect one's psychological distance, which may influence the diffusion of rumor messages.

3 Research Model

As the literature review above suggests, a message invoking a sense of threat/anxiety could increase online public's likelihood of engaging in cyber-rumor sharing. While previous studies on cyber-rumors were done in the contexts of security, politics, and financial crisis (e.g., Kwon and Rao 2017; Oh et al. 2013; Shin et al. 2017), threat appeal could be especially important to explain cyber-rumor sharing in a public health context such as Zika virus because consequences nuanced by the threat appeal could pose immediate relevance to one's personal health risk (Liberman and Chaiken 1991). Based on this rationale, we first examine the effect of rumor message's threat appeal on cyber-rumor sharing.

H1: Cyber-rumor sharing will be positively influenced by threat appeal in a rumor message

Social, spatial and temporal distance are the sub-units (or dimensions) of psychological distance, which may affect one's susceptibility to cyber-rumor message and its diffusion. We argue that the effects of psychological distance on cyber-rumor sharing may be a two-stage process. First, users who feel psychologically close to the Zika Virus issue may feel a greater sense of anxiety. To reduce such anxiety, users may be prone to engaging in conversations directly related to the threat appeal itself. Conversely, users who perceive the issue as a distant event will be less likely to engage with threat appeals. Based on this logic, we post following hypothesis.

H2: Psychological distance, (a) social, (b) spatial, and (c) temporal, will be negatively associated with the presence of threat appeal in a rumor message

Second, psychological distance will affect not only the threat appeal in rumor messages but also the likelihood of it being shared. For example, if a person claimed to be a witness to an event, users in the same social circle or who share similar social identity with the witness would be prone to believing the claim and sharing with their own social circle. Also, a message created from a location closer to where the event occurred would increase its "shareworthiness" (Trilling et al. 2017). Similarly, during the time when an event is rampant, there is a higher probability of a cyber-rumor message being shared (Takayasu et al. 2015) as compared to later in time. This is referred to as the hot topic or trending topic effect that involves connection to time. Accordingly, we argue that, if a cyber-rumor message is closer in social, spatial and temporal distance, there is a high probability that the rumor gets shared.

H3: Cyber-rumor sharing will be inversely influenced by psychological distance, (a) social, (b) spatial, and (c) temporal

Studies have also shown that there are other factors that also have an impact on information sharing behavior in social media, such as hashtags and followers (Stieglitz and Dang-Xuan 2013). We include these variables as controls in the model (Fig. 1).

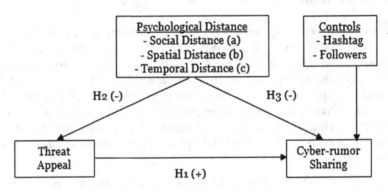

Fig. 1. Research model

4   Methodology

To address our research questions, we developed an approach that streamlines the (iterative) process of data acquisition, data cleansing, and data visualization.

4.1   Data Collection

In this paper, we collected data for Zika outbreak from Twitter about the epidemic by recording the date, content, user, retweet count, Follower count, URL of web content, location from September 2015 to May 2017. Twitter provides three APIs to enable researchers and developers to collect data, namely STREAMING, REST and SEARCH APIs. Satisfying user specified filtering criteria (based on keywords, location, language, etc.), STREAMING API is used to get tweets and their corresponding user's data in real time, REST API is used to get the data in select historical time period, and SEARCH API provides data on relevant searches on Twitter (Valecha et al. 2016). We collected 155,589 tweets by searching data for #zika, #zikavirus and other Zika related hashtags. The tweets were then cleaned, lemmatized and stemmed. This ensured that there are no special characters except line break tweets within the list of sentences. Then we collected known Zika Virus rumors from various sources.

Known rumors in the context of Zika virus were obtained from:
➢ https://www.nytimes.com/interactive/2016/02/18/health/what-causes-zika-virus-theories-rumors.html?mcubz=0
➢ https://www.elsevier.com/about/press-releases/research-and-journals/zika-conspiracy-theories-on-social-media-putting-vulnerable-people-at-risk
➢ https://undark.org/2016/06/01/zika-conspiracy-theories-twitter/
➢ http://www.snopes.com/americans-immune-zika-virus/

These known rumors were identified as follows:
a) Genetically modified mosquitoes are the real cause of the birth defects
b) Larvicide in drinking water causes microcephaly (Zika virus symptom)
c) Rumors have blamed both a "bad batch of rubella vaccine" and the intro-duction of a new pertussis vaccine in Brazil, or aluminum in that vaccine
d) Brazil has been undercounting Microcephaly (A symptom where baby's head is significantly smaller than expected, could be due to Zika)
e) Most pregnant women who have Zika have normal babies
f) Microcephaly is caused by the MMR vaccine and pharmaceutical compa-nies are blaming Zika virus in order to profit from selling Zika vaccines.
g) Americans are immune to the Zika virus

From this corpus of Twitter data, we extracted 45,500 unique English tweets related to known rumors in the Zika context. We encountered these rumors from December 2015 to February 2017. We utilized Jaccard matching for matching the tweets with known rumors.

4.2   Measurement

For the dependent variable, cyber rumor-sharing, we chose retweet count that denotes the number of times the rumor tweet has been shared. The control variables, hashtag and followers, were measured as the number of hashtags present in the rumor message, and the natural log of the number of followers of the Twitter user respectively. We chose to use natural log transformation for the follower variable because the followers for some users can be in magnitudes of 10^4 or more. Natural log transformation allows rescaling of the follower variable to be comparable with other variables.

For coding the threat appeal, we utilized content of the tweet. We resorted to unsupervised machine learning using Neural Networks. Our aim was to find the keywords used in similar context as threat within the rumor tweets. This was accomplished in 3 steps: (1) From the 45,500 extracted rumor tweet samples, we created a dataset. (2) We cleaned, lemmatized and stemmed the rumored tweets. (3) We trained a Word2Vec model to identify similar words in a text (where similarity is based on the distance between the keywords).

Word2Vec is a neural network-based algorithm (Goldberg and Levy 2014) that takes words as inputs by converting the words into word embedding. It is an unsupervised machine learning model that does not require any labels and can learn the weights of words as word vector representations incorporating most of the semantically rich information. These vectors can then be used to find similarities between words to get relations. In this study, GenSim Word2Vec model, a Python-based content analysis program, was employed for the analysis of text. Word2Vec model utilized skip-gram algorithm, which predictively learnt the word embedding or the numeric vector representation of words. The algorithm was trained with a window of 4, i.e. the context spans over to at max 4 words to the left and 4 words to the right of the target word, during training. Dimensionality of the feature vectors was set to 45,500, with negative sampling (noise words) was set to 10, to prevent over fitting and increase accuracy, of the learned vectors. The model was trained for 50 epochs.

This trained neural network model understood the context of each word in the dataset, which was then utilized to find specific words indicative of the threat, for example "vector, bacteriophage, virus, arbovirus." The output of the neural network was used as the input for quantitative content analysis.

For coding social distance, we borrowed from Snefjella and Kuperman (2015). They have identified words that are used in similar context as the words that quantify social distance – the degree of willingness to establish some kith with representatives of a social group. The classification identifies acquaintance as the individual's acceptance to a social group using words like "mother, baby, child, family, father, friend" to denote lower social distance, and words such as "neighbor, peer, colleague, mate, tourist, people" to denote higher social distance. For example, the tweet "… experience in brazil zika funding is tremendous victory for sfl grateful to work colleagues who care about our community as it battles the virus" was coded as higher social distance since it refers to the community. These words were used as the input for quantitative content analysis. For quantitative content analysis, the frequency of occurrence for each keyword was used as an indicator of the importance or emphasis, referred to as a "hit". We used the number of hits per rumor tweet and the total number of words contained in that rumor tweet to calculate "hit-density," which represents how densely the keywords are populated in the rumor tweet (Kim et al. 2005; Park et al. 2007). Finally, we dichotomize hit-density to denote the presence or absence of threat within the rumor tweet.

Temporal distance was measured as the natural log of the number of hours between the tweet posting date and the event's peak time, where the peak time quantifies the time of the most influential tweet in that event. Here we assume that tweet peaks denote an important event in that period.

Spatial distance was measured as the natural log of the geographical distance from Brazil – the locus of Zika-related scare. For this purpose, the combination of latitude and longitude of the tweet was used to calculate the distance from Brazil. For example, the tweet "the zika crisis's second wave some babies with zika infection develop microcephaly months after" was reported with location 42.631°, −71.147°. This was compared with location of Brazil 14.235°, 51.925° using Google Distance Matrix API[2] to calculate the distance of 4290 miles.

4.3 Descriptive Statistics

The Spearman rank correlation test (Table 1) indicates that all correlations are less than 0.6, indicating that no significant multi-collinearity problems exist (Kishore et al. 2004). Spearman's coefficient is appropriate for both continuous and discrete ordinal variables. Both Spearman's ρ and Kendall's τ can be formulated as special cases of a more general correlation coefficient. The sample size is large enough to suppress the potential Type I and Type II errors. The concern of Type II errors can be suppressed with a large sample size, and the immunity of Type I error can be ensured by the significance of p-value (Larson-Hall 2010).

Table 1. Correlation results

	1	2	3	4	5	6
1	1					
2	0.598***	1				
3	−0.299***	−0.347***	1			
4	0.045***	0.057***	−0.010*	1		
5	0.098***	−0.492***	0.590***	−0.007	1	
6	−0.042***	−0.159***	0.019***	−0.077***	0.059***	1

* $p < 0.05$; ** $p < 0.01$, *** $p < 0.001$
Legend: (1) Followers, (2) Hashtags, (3) Ln (Spatial Distance), (4) Ln (Temporal Distance), (5) Social Distance and (6) Threat Appeal

4.4 Analysis

In order to examine the hypotheses, we utilized path analysis. Path analysis is suitable for simultaneous equation models. PLS analysis was conducted on the dataset using MPlus tool. The endogenous variables in the model, retweet is a count variable while threat appeal is a binary variable. This leads to violation of normality in residuals. As a result, Ordinary Least Square (OLS) regression cannot estimate the appropriate statistics. Negative binomial regression has been suggested as a possible method to deal with count endogenous variables (Osgood 2000), and logistic regression has been suggested for dealing with binary endogenous variables. In line with this, we specified the cyber-rumor sharing as a count variable and threat appeal as a categorical variable in MPlus. This allows MPlus to model the effect of social, spatial and temporal distances, as well as threat appeal on cyber-rumor sharing (retweet) using negative binomial regression. In addition, based on the specification, MPlus models the effect of

---

[2] https://developers.google.com/maps/documentation/distance-matrix/intro.

social, spatial and temporal distances on threat appeal using logistic regression. Both logistic and negative binomial regression allow for log likelihood parameter estimation.

5   Results

The results of the analysis are summarized in Table 2. First of all, as hypothesized, spatial and temporal distances are negatively associated with threat appeal at $p < 0.01$ and $p < 0.001$ respectively. This implies that cyber-rumors that are spatially and temporally close to Zika crisis report higher level of threat appeal, supporting H2b and H2c. Contrary to our expectation, social distance is positively associated with threat appeal, opposite to H2a. Further, the results show that the negative effect of spatial distances is significant at $p < 0.001$, implying that closer the spatial distance from the Zika crisis epicenter, greater the likelihood of cyber-rumor sharing. H3b is supported. However, the effect of social and temporal distance on cyber-rumor sharing is positive, contrary to H3a and H3c. We also find opposite effect (i.e. negative) of threat appeal on cyber-rumor sharing. So H1 is not supported.

Table 2. Results of path analysis

	Coefficient	Std. Error	Odds	Support
Effect on threat appeal				
Social distance	0.275***	0.022	1.317	H2a not supported
Ln (spatial distance)	−0.036**	0.012	0.965	H2b supported
Ln (temporal distance)	−0.141***	0.009	0.898	H2c supported
Effect on retweet				
Hashtag	0.426***	0.004	1.531	
Followers	0.007***	0.001	1.007	
Social distance	0.003	0.054	1.003	H3a not supported
Ln (spatial distance)	−0.164***	0.021	0.849	H3b supported
Ln (temporal distance)	0.018	0.023	1.018	H3c not supported
Threat appeal	−0.308***	0.056	0.735	H1 not supported

* $p < 0.05$; ** $p < 0.01$, *** $p < 0.001$

6   Discussion and Conclusion

We examined the effect of social, spatial and temporal distances on threat appeal and sharing of a cyber-rumor message in the Zika Virus context. We analyzed Twitter data generated within the time span of September 2015 to May 2017. The results indicate that spatial and temporal distance is negatively associated with threat appeal. This needs contextual interpretation from the view of "proximity to threat" as follows: Cyber-rumor messages coming from close to Brazil and around important Zika-related events report higher levels of threat appeal associated with the pandemic. Another interesting finding is that spatial distance is negatively associated with the likelihood of cyber-rumor sharing. From the contextual viewpoint, this denotes that cyber-rumor messages coming from close to Brazil spread more.

One reason for the positive effect of social distance on threat appeal is that the group associated with the higher social distance can consist of a larger population (such as neighbors, tourists, etc.) than the group associated with lower social distance. It may provoke large-scale panic due to the collective stress reaction about immediately threatening circumstances to large populations (Oh et al. 2013). Furthermore, the positive effect of temporal distance on cyber-rumor sharing can be explained as the exposure effect – the amount of time the cyber-rumor message is exposed; if the message is exposed for a longer while, it can have more opportunity to accumulate more retweets.

In terms of practical implications, findings of this study can offer directions to practitioners and policy makers to promote mitigation of cyber-rumor messages in the aftermath of health crisis incidents (Valecha et al. 2017). For example, educational or awareness campaign may be employed to flag and correct highly threatening messages coming from close to the location of interest and around key events in order to reduce chaos and uncertainty related to the event. This preliminary study lays the foundation for future studies targeting at uncovering more complex issues.

As a theoretical contribution, we have demonstrated the effect of proximity on threat appeal and sharing behavior. Prior literature has established that threat situation serves as an important antecedent of cyber-rumor sharing (Kwon and Rao 2017). In this paper, we have shown support for our claim that in addition to threat situation, proximity also serves as an important antecedent of cyber-rumor sharing. Proximity is an underlying mechanism that forms the exposure to threat (Kwon et al. 2017), which in turn affects social media users' willingness to share cyber-rumor messages. In this way, proximity can also be considered as one way to collectively manage fear associated with the threat situation.

This study has some limitations. Some of the Twitter messages were in Spanish. We dropped them from the analysis, due to research team's lack of proficiency in Spanish. We coded social distance as a binary variable. A richer scale can be created using individual binary measures for each social circle, such as family, friends, colleagues, etc. Furthermore, the public's characteristics such as age, gender may also influence the relationship between proximity and cyber-rumor sharing[3]. However we do not have such data from Twitter APIs. In order to complete the research further, we plan to investigate if proximity moderates the effect of threat appeals on cyber-rumor sharing. Given the counterintuitive results regarding psychological distance, another potential next step might be to conduct a mediation test (psychological distances - threat appeal - rumor sharing). As a potential future work, we can consider time-varying effect of threat appeal and proximity on cyber-rumor sharing. To elaborate, threat appeal and proximity in the current period may influence cyber-rumor sharing in the next time period. Future studies could also examine generalizability of findings from this one specific event of emerging infectious disease, Zika, to the other events (See footnote 3).

---

[3] We would like to thank an anonymous reviewer for pointing this out.

Acknowledgements. This research has been funded in part by NSF under grants 1651475. Usual disclaimer applies. The authors would like to thank the reviewers whose comments have greatly improved the paper.

References

Cheng, J.J., Liu, Y., Shen, B., Yuan, W.G.: An epidemic model of rumor diffusion in online social networks. Eur. Phys. J. B **86**(1), 29 (2013)

Folkman, S.: Stress: Appraisal and Coping. Encyclopedia of Behavioral Medicine, pp. 1913–1915. Springer, New York (2013). https://doi.org/10.1007/978-1-4419-1005-9

Goldberg, Y., Levy, O.: Word2vec explained: deriving Mikolov et al.'s negative-sampling word-embedding method. arXiv preprint arXiv:1402.3722 (2014)

Kim, D.J., Song, Y.I., Braynov, S.B., Rao, H.R.: A multidimensional trust formation model in B-to-C e-commerce: a conceptual framework and content analyses of academia/practitioner perspectives. Decis. Support Syst. **40**(2), 143–165 (2005)

Kishore, R., Agrawal, M., Rao, H.R.: Determinants of sourcing during technology growth and maturity: an empirical study of e-commerce sourcing. JMIS **21**(3), 47–82 (2004)

Kwon, K.H., Chadha, M., Pellizzaro, K.: Proximity and terrorism news in social media: a construal-level theoretical approach to networked framing of terrorism in Twitter. Mass Commun. Soc. **20**(6), 869–894 (2017)

Kwon, K.H., Rao, H.R.: Cyber-rumor sharing under a homeland security threat in the context of government Internet surveillance: the case of South-North Korea conflict. Govt. Inf. Q. **34**, 307–316 (2017)

Larson-Hall, J.: Changing the Way We Do Statistics: Hypothesis Testing, Power, Effect Size, and Other Misunderstood Issues. A Guide to Doing Statistics Research Using SPSS. Routledge, New York (2010)

Lee, J., Agrawal, M., Rao, H.R.: Message diffusion through social network service: the case of rumor and non-rumor related tweets during Boston bombing 2013. Inf. Syst. Front. **17**(5), 997–1005 (2015)

Lee, J.K.: Research framework for AIS grand vision of the bright ICT initiative. MISQ **39**(2), iii–xii (2015)

Lee, J.K.: Invited commentary—reflections on ICT-enabled bright society research. Inf. Syst. Res. **27**(1), 1–5 (2016)

Li, J., Vishwanath, A., Rao, H.R.: Retweeting the Fukushima nuclear radiation disaster. Commun. ACM **57**(1), 78–85 (2014)

Liberman, A., Chaiken, S.: Value conflict and thought-induced attitude change. J. Exp. Soc. Psychol. **27**(3), 203–216 (1991)

Marsden, P.V., Campbell, K.E.: Measuring tie strength. Soc. Forces **63**(2), 482–501 (1984)

Nossek, H., Berkowitz, D.: Telling "our" story through news of terrorism: mythical newswork as journalistic practice in crisis. Journalism Stud. **7**(5), 691–707 (2006)

Oh, O., Agrawal, M., Rao, H.R.: Community intelligence and social media services: a rumor theoretic analysis of tweets during social crises. MIS Q. **37**(2), 407–426 (2013)

Osgood, D.W.: Poisson-based regression analysis of aggregate crime rates. J. Quant. Criminol. **16**(1), 21–43 (2000)

Park, I., Sharman, R., Rao, H.R., Upadhyaya, S.: Short term and total life impact analysis of email worms in computer systems. Decis. Support Syst. **43**(3), 827–841 (2007)

Pezzo, M.V., Beckstead, J.W.: A multilevel analysis of rumor transmission: effects of anxiety and belief in two field experiments. Basic Appl. Soc. Psychol. **28**(1), 91–100 (2006)

Rao, H.R.: Behavioral infosec research - towards global trust building. In: Keynote Presented at Workshop on The Bright Internet and Global Trust Building, ICIS 2016, Dublin, Ireland (2016)

Rogers, R.W.: A protection motivation theory of fear appeals and attitude change1. J. Psychol. **91**(1), 93–114 (1975)

Shin, J., Jian, L., Driscoll, K., Bar, F.: Political rumoring on Twitter during the 2012 U.S. presidential election: rumor diffusion and correction. New Med. Soc. **19**(8), 1214–1235 (2017)

Snefjella, B., Kuperman, V.: Concreteness and psychological distance in natural language use. Psychol. Sci. **26**(9), 1449–1460 (2015)

Solomon, S., Greenberg, J., Pyszczynski, T.: A terror management theory of social behavior: the psychological functions of self-esteem and cultural worldviews. Adv. Exp. Soc. Psychol. **24**, 93–159 (1991)

Stieglitz, S., Dang-Xuan, L.: Emotions and information diffusion in social media—sentiment of microblogs and sharing behavior. J. Manag. Inf. Syst. **29**(4), 217–248 (2013)

Suh, B., Hong, L., Pirolli, P., Chi, E.H.: Want to be retweeted? Large scale analytics on factors impacting retweet in Twitter network. In: 2010 IEEE Second International Conference on Social Computing (SOCIALCOM), pp. 177–184. IEEE, August 2010

Takayasu, M., Sato, K., Sano, Y., Yamada, K., Miura, W., Takayasu, H.: Rumor diffusion and convergence during the 3.11 earthquake: a Twitter case study. PLoS One **10**(4), e0121443 (2015)

Trilling, D., Tolochko, P., Burscher, B.: From newsworthiness to shareworthiness: how to predict news sharing based on article characteristics. J. Mass Commun. Q. **94**(1), 38–60 (2017)

Trope, Y., Liberman, N.: Construal-level theory of psychological distance. Psychol. Rev. **117**(2), 440 (2010)

Valecha, R., Bachura, E., Chen, R., Rao, H.R.: An exploration of public reaction to the OPM data breach notifications. In: Proceedings of Workshop on E-business (WEB) 2016, Dublin, Ireland (2016)

Valecha, R., Oh, O., Rao, H.R.: An exploration of collaboration over time in collective crisis response during the Haiti 2010 earthquake. In: Proceedings of International Conference on Information Systems (ICIS) 2013, Milan, Italy (2013)

Valecha, R., Volety, T., Vemprala, N., Kwon, H., Rao, H.R.: An Investigation of Cyber-rumor Sharing: The Case of Zika Virus. Workshop on Bright Internet & Global Trust Building, Seoul, Korea (2017)

Volety, T., Valecha, R., Vemprala, N., Kwon, H., Rao, H.R.: Cyber-rumor sharing: the case of Zika virus. In: American Conference on Information Systems, New Orleans, LA (2018)

Webb, H., et al.: Digital wildfires: propagation, verification, regulation, and responsible innovation. ACM TOIS **34**(3), 15 (2016)

Witte, K.: Putting the fear back into fear appeals: the extended parallel process model. Commun. Monogr. **59**(4), 329–349 (1992)

Ye, X., Li, S., Yang, X., Lee, J., Wu, L.: The fear of Ebola: a tale of two cities in China. Big Data Support of Urban Planning and Management. AGIS, pp. 113–132. Springer, Cham (2018). https://doi.org/10.1007/978-3-319-51929-6_7

Securing Trust in Online Social Networks

Vishnu S. Pendyala[(✉)]

San Jose State University, San Jose, CA 95192, USA
vishnu.pendyala@sjsu.edu

Abstract. Trust in Online Social Networks (OSN) is a contentious topic. On one hand, there is an increasing reliance on them for trustworthy information and on the other, wariness to believe anything on it. Although the providers of OSNs have tried multiple ways to boost the trustworthiness of the information posted on their websites and weed out millions of fake accounts, the problem is largely unsolved and poses a formidable challenge. This paper examines the problem is some detail, discusses existing solutions to the problem using Machine Learning and other techniques and concludes by discussing some more ideas on enhancing the trustworthiness of the OSNs.

Keywords: Online Social Networks · Machine Learning · Trust management·

1 Introduction

Of the 7.7 billion people in the world, it is expected that more than 3 billion will be using Online Social Networks (OSN) like Facebook and Twitter by the end of 2021. However, this is no indication of the trustworthiness of the OSNs. A year ago, Microblogging site, Twitter announced that it is purging millions of fake accounts and continuing its fight against bots. Around the same time, the CEO of Facebook, Mark Zuckerberg testified to the US Congress on fake news and other inappropriate use of the platform, acknowledging that the company did not do enough in these respects. The power and reach of the OSNs also led to a significant increase in the number of human and bot spammers, fake users, and malicious entities on the OSN websites. While some of them spread spam messages and fake news, the others try to steal personal information and misuse it. Cognitive hacking and fraud on OSNs have been rampantly impactful. All this raises serious questions about trust and the need for trust management in Social Networks.

This paper surveys various techniques that can be used to build trust in Online Social Networks, which include dealing with challenges such as the cold start problem described below, prediction of trust in the posted information, social spam detection, and fake profile identification. The paper concludes with some ideas for future directions in securing trust in the Online Social Networks.

2 Background

Veracity, or truthfulness of information, particularly that on the OSNs is a major problem today. Veracity is regarded as the fourth 'V' of Big Data after Volume, Variety, and Velocity, which characterize Big Data. Online Social Networks contribute

© Springer Nature Singapore Pte Ltd. 2020
S. K. Sahay et al. (Eds.): SKM 2019, CCIS 1186, pp. 194–201, 2020.
https://doi.org/10.1007/978-981-15-3817-9_12

a substantial part of today's Big Data and are particularly impacted by the problem of veracity. A more comprehensive discussion on the various approaches to securing trust in Online Social Networks in particular and Big Data in general is given in [1].

Breach of trust in Social Networks manifests in many ways. Fake profiles and privacy concerns are just two aspects of trustworthiness of OSNs. Fake profiles are created to stealthily get access to genuine users' private information. They are also used to promote personal agenda with a malicious intent. Trust management therefore also extends to the content that is being shared on the Social Networks. In the past few years, Online Social Networks have also started serving as a medium for latest news and updates. This power of the OSNs as a powerful news disseminator led to the increasing number of fake news and updates and spam in general. There have been instances where malicious information posted on microblogging websites caused companies to lose significant market capitalization. Pump and dump schemes, where miscreants pump up the stock price by spreading rumors on Social Media and then dump their stock at that hyped price, making huge profits. Once the truth dawns on the shareholders, the stock price falls, causing huge losses to many shareholders.

Then there is the case of Colombian hacker, Andrés Sepúlveda, who rigged the presidential elections in many Latin American countries by using bots to post misleading information on the microblogging websites to resort to cognitive hacking and swaying people's opinions. The magnitude of the problem can be understood by the fact that even the presidential elections of countries are at stake because of the malicious use of the Social Networks. Decisions, such as choosing the President of a country are based on the trust in the information that the electorate has access to. The 500 million tweets that are posted on Twitter alone in a day, on an average, account for substantial reliance on it as a source of public discourse. Trust in information plays a tremendous role in most decision making.

There are a few challenges in securing trust in OSNs. The first is a cold start problem. Trust in Social Networks, like in real life, is built from experience with the entity using a feedback process. When the interaction with an entity results in a breach of trust, the value of the trust in that entity decreases and when the interaction is positive, the value increases. But when there is no experience interacting with the entity or when the behavior of the entity is not fully known, we hit a "cold start" problem. The other challenge is akin to Computer viruses and trojans trying to outpace the anti-virus systems. Spamming, stealing users' private information, creating fake accounts and other anti-social activities get increasingly smart and behaviors change rapidly making it difficult for the anti-spamming systems to keep up. Machine Learning relies on features and the growing number of malicious behaviors implies dealing with a rapidly increasing feature space, when used for anti-spamming.

3 Approaches to Securing Trust in OSN

3.1 Web of Trust

A simple mechanism to enhance trustworthiness of social relations is to provide a data structure called "Web of Trust." The website, epinions.com provides such a data structure to its users. Epinions is essentially a reviewing system for products purchased. Users can register for free and review a wide variety of products. Obviously, trust is very important for this website. The system of trust has two components: "Web of Trust" and "Block List". Each user has her own "Web of Trust" and "Block List," which are populated by the user based on the experience with a different user. If another user, B's reviews are consistently unbiased, accurate and valuable to a user A, user A adds user B to her "Web of Trust". On the other hand, if user B's reviews are consistently useless or offensive to user A, user A can add user B to her Block List. The impact of a user A's Web of Trust is not just limited to that user, but impacts the users who trust this user A. More details about the PageRank like "Web of Trust" algorithm can be found in [2] authored by Richardson et al. They proposed a means for calculating the trust value for each user in a semantic web. The same concept could be extended to the Online Social Networks as well.

3.2   Collaborative Filtering

Social Networks are all about human judgments. Collaborative Filtering is an excellent tool for predicting a user's preferences based on other users' judgments. The book [1] describes how this tool can be used to quantify trust in a given claim. A user A's belief in a claim can be predicted based on the beliefs of other users with whom user A is positively correlated. This is similar to the real-world scenario. If a number of users who think like user A believe Global Warming is real, it is likely that user A is also likely to believe it is real. Correlations between users is mathematically computed and so is the percentage of belief in the claim, based on other users' percentages of belief. This is also called as user-based Collaborative Filtering.

3.3   Handling the Cold Start Problem

Both the Web of Trust and the Collaborative Filtering techniques can run into cold start problem, when there is not much information about the users or the claims to start with. The cold start problem in user-based Collaborative Filtering can be resolved by using claim-based Collaborative Filtering, as described in [1]. Instead of computing the correlation between users, based on their beliefs, we compute the correlation between claims, based on how much users believe in them. The correlation so computed is purely syntactic and has no relation to the semantics of the claim. Solutions from Machine Learning can also be drawn for the cold start problem, particularly in the Web of Trust framework, as [3] demonstrates.

Nuñez-Gonzalez et al. in [3] use the epinions and Wikipedia datasets to demonstrate how user reputation features can be extracted from third party evidences, when the users do not have any prior interaction. They transform the cold start problem into a classification problem and use a number of Machine Learning algorithms to predict a trust value between two users when there is no prior interaction and compare the results. Trust is often mutual and is proven not to be a transitive relation, but the authors argue that reputation features extracted from Social Networks can be used to solve the cold start problem. Their model obtains two different types of reputation feature vectors. One is raw reputation feature vectors obtained directly from data and the second is probabilistic feature vectors. Probabilistic feature vectors are computed statistically from the data set. The classification algorithms using raw reputation feature vectors suffer from data imbalance, whereas the ones using probabilistic feature vectors produced more accurate results.

3.4   Trust Prediction and Modeling

In order to build a trust management system, it is important to build metrics that compute the trust quotient or credibility score or trustworthiness score that would help the users of these Online Social Networks whether to trust the other person, the information they post, whether to trust a particular news or article that has been shared across the Social Network platform. A lot of research has been going on in this domain and it is becoming one of the most sought-after challenge.

Information posted on OSN has features. [10] discusses how these features can be leveraged in Machine Learning algorithms to predict the trustworthiness of the posts. Taking the microblogging website, Twitter as an example, the paper lists out a number of features that can be used to classify the posts as trustworthy or not. It summarizes the approaches that can be taken to establish the truthfulness of information and presents ideas from formal methods and knowledge representation to deal with the problem. According to [8], formal methods have substantial potential to enhance the trustworthiness of information.

Bodner et al. in [11], proposed a user trust modeling approach along with increasing the veracity of the event detection. Their work confirmed that the metadata associated with a user's profile can determine whether the user's posts can be trusted. The metadata is transformed into feature vectors. The authors use the feature vectors so generated with 11 different classifiers to generate a "trust metric," based on which the user's posts are filtered out or further analyzed.

3.5   Spam Detection Techniques

Trust modeling discussed in the previous section may not always be needed for detecting malicious actions such as spam on OSNs. Spam detection in Social Networks has been extensively studied and researched in the recent times. In order to build trust management in Online Social Networks, spam detection is a key step. Zhu et al. in [4] used three different kinds of datapoints about users to classify a given user as a spammer or not. The three datasets they use are (a) activities of the user on the OSN, (b) user's relationships with other users on the OSN, and (c) annotated data classifying a small set of users as spammers or not. They use a technique called "Supervised Matrix Factorization with Social Regularization (SMFSR)" to induce latent features and then use the features in the Support Vector Machine (SVM) algorithm to improve the classification of the users into spammers and non-spammers. They show how SMFSR performs better than when just SVM is used and when SVM is used in conjunction with just Matrix Factorization and other combinations.

Zheng et al. [5] also proposed an SVM based spammer detection algorithm by using 18 features extracted from users' social behavior on the OSN and message contents. This is a simple method to categorize users, giving a good solid foundation towards building trust management, since identifying the spammers could help in developing methods to prevent them from accessing personal information of others and also to deactivate those users who are regarded as spammers. However, in order for this method to be highly successful, one important requirement is to have a classifier model with high precision and recall, so that the chances of misclassification would get significantly minimized, as even a slightly erroneous model could lead to losing potential non-spam user.

Markines et al. in [6] proposed the need to investigate the motivations of social spam to understand the various ways in which the spamming could be done in Online Social Networks to come up with the most efficient solution. This model is deemed to give a much better solution compared to the previous one as it includes layers that consider several factors to be included in their model. Their model includes finding tags and tag combinations that are unlikely to appear in legitimate posts. The model also includes finding out whether a spam resource is associated with high frequency tags which is an indication of spam activity. This is because the spammers gain by associating the spam resources with high frequency tags irrespective of whether they are related or not.

Other aspects of the above model include finding the web pages associated with social spam that have a document structure that is identical to that of an original page. The likelihood of whether a page is spam or not is calculated based on the similarity. Plagiarism is also checked to find out whether the spammers have copied the original contents of a page and automatically generated a spammed version of it. More often, the spammers create pages for the sole purpose of serving as an advertisement. There is also a need to find out whether a user profile is created for the sole purpose of spamming. Some of the fake profiles are created for the temporary purpose of stealing information from other users. Once the miscreants steal enough data, they delete these accounts, leaving broken links. The authors of [6] address the identification of such profiles as well. When all these features are incorporated, we can build a model with high precision and recall, that can better detect the spam in Online Social Networks.

3.6   Identification of Fake Profiles

A problem related to spam detection is to identify fake profiles. An increase in social spam resulted in a corresponding increase in the number of fake profiles. Although these could also be linked with spammers, some of the fake profile users, not only stole the personal information of others, but also indulged in several unethical, anti-social activities. Hence, identification of fake profiles becomes an important challenge. According to Forbes, Facebook has shut down nearly 1.2 billion fake accounts at the end of 2017. There has been a lot of research going on to detect fake profiles. Identification of fake profiles, therefore, is an important step towards building trust management in Online Social networks.

Fire et al. gave insights into how Facebook identified fake user profiles in [7]. Their architecture comprises of three different parts. The first being a "friend analyzer application". This application scans through a given user A's friend-list and uses machine learning models to give a credibility score. The results are sorted in the order of the likelihood and higher the likelihood, more likely that friend is a fake profile. In order to calculate this, the number of mutual friends between the user and the corresponding profile, the number of pictures in which they are tagged together are all taken as features. Once the results are displayed, the application provides the users the provision to restrict access to those users to their personal information. This option also enables the users to restrict access to those with whom they are unwilling to share their personal information. The second part is a Firefox add-on that provides the users with a one-step privacy check. The add-on, once installed in a user's browser, analyzes the applications installed in the user's Facebook profile and alerts the user about the ones that can compromise user's privacy. It also leverages the "friend analyzer application" to suggest friends that should probably be blocked.

Xiao et al. in [8], proposed a method to cluster the accounts into fake and real. Their approach included the machine learning algorithms that take the cluster level features as input and cluster the accounts into fake and real accounts. Their approach has been designed for Online Social Networks that have many daily user registrations and they use the features available at the time of account registration and shortly after that for their model. Profile featurizer is an important step in their approach where they extract features from the user accounts and broadly put them under three categories such as Basic distribution features comprising mainly of statistical measures, Pattern features, and Frequency features. Pattern features comprise of a few categories of patterns that the fake users to sign-up for their accounts. A "pattern encoding algorithm" maps a given text describing the pattern into a set of categories. The frequency of each feature value in the account data is computed and included in the frequency feature set. Using these features from the users' account data, the algorithm categorizes the accounts as fake or real.

3.7 Statistical Techniques

As pointed out earlier, OSNs have been used extensively to sway people's beliefs and opinions. Cognitive hacking has been rampant particularly in the microblogging domain. Sentiment analysis of the posts on these microblogging websites can reveal interesting patterns that can be used to detect malice and cognitive hacking. Authors of [9] describe how statistical techniques like modified CUSUM and Kalman Filter can help detect injected attacks on microblogging websites perpetrated by miscreants like Andres Sepulveda using bots and other means. CUSUM is an interesting change detection algorithm that analyzes a series of observations, in this case, the sentiment scores of microblogs to identify abnormalities. The authors simulate a number of scenarios of injected attacks and show the effectiveness of CUSUM in detecting the attacks. Kalman filter is used widely in a range of applications from battery state-of-charge estimation in electric vehicles to satellite navigation systems and seismology. For the purpose of injected attack detection, the authors of [9] use the Discrete Kalman Filter to analyze the sentiment scores of microblogs to identify abnormal fluctuations. They use the same set of scenarios as for the CUSUM algorithm and analyze the performances of both algorithms.

4   Future Directions

Section 2 listed a number of techniques, mostly from Machine Learning to address the problem of trustworthiness of Online Social Networks. However, it misses out on an important technology that is often associated with trust – Blockchain. Although Blockchain is increasingly being touted as the "future of trust," it is yet to be seen if it can be leveraged to secure trust in OSNs. There is some initial groundwork in that direction, such as in [12]. However, given the costs involved in implementing block-chain, it may not be practical to leverage blockchain in its current form for securing trust in OSNs. When it happens, blockchain-based Online Social Networks could usher-in the next generation of Social Media and the Web itself. Blockchain is certainly an area to watch out in the OSN space and the Web in general.

The next area that may hold promise is Formal Methods and Logic in particular. A recent paper [13] presents learning First-Order-Logic rules from Twitter posts to help infer truthfulness of the information posted. Given that automated theorem proving is entirely syntactic, proving claims as true or false may become a matter of syntax manipulations, provided that the knowledge is represented in forms suited for auto-mated theorem proving by syntactic operations. It may be possible that information on the Online Social Networks, if represented in appropriate forms of logic can even prevent false information from getting posted. Any new post that contradicts existing corpus of knowledge on the OSN can possibly be rejected. Contradiction or confor-mance can be established by reasoning and deduction mechanisms, such as those provided by languages like Prolog.

A third area that may show promise is Quantum Computing. With the computing power that it provides, which can make current cryptography algorithms obsolete, there are chances for faster mechanisms to detect fraud and malicious activity on OSNs. Quantum Computing may unleash a wide spectrum of new algorithms that can change the very concept of Online Social Networking and trust in it. Quantum Computing can probably help speed-up ensembles of the techniques highlighted in this paper and make it possible to achieve high accuracy rates of predicting spam and malicious activity. However, there is not much evidence that any work has started in this direction yet.

5   Conclusion

Securing trust in Online Social Networks is a formidable challenge, as it stands today. Plenty of research has been forthcoming over the years, but the problem remains largely unsolved. We do not even have the providers of OSNs such as Twitter quan-tifying their belief in the user posts, let alone completely prevent fake news from propagating. This paper surveyed a few techniques that have been effectively used to address the problem of trustworthiness in OSNs and speculated three specific areas that show promise for future. Using ensembles of the techniques listed in this paper can potentially enhance the accuracy of trust quantification. It is also hoped that this paper will motivate researchers to open-up the three areas listed in the future directions section, for application to OSNs.

Acknowledgement. The author acknowledges the help from his student, Ajith N. in doing some initial work for this paper.

References

1. Pendyala, V.: Veracity of Big Data: Machine Learning and Other Approaches to Verifying Truthfulness, 1st edn. Apress, USA (2018)
2. Richardson, M., Agrawal, R., Domingos, P.: Trust management for the semantic web. In: Fensel, D., Sycara, K., Mylopoulos, J. (eds.) ISWC 2003. LNCS, vol. 2870, pp. 351–368. Springer, Heidelberg (2003). https://doi.org/10.1007/978-3-540-39718-2_23
3. Nuñez-Gonzalez, D., Graña, M., Apolloni, B.: Reputation features for trust prediction in social networks. Neurocomputing **166**, 1–7 (2014)
4. Zhu, Y., Wang, X., Zhong, E., Liu, N., Li, H., Yang, Q.: Discovering spammers in social networks. In: Association for the Advancement of Artificial Intelligence Conference (2012)
5. Zheng, X., Zeng, Z., Chen, Z., Yu, Y., Rong, C.: Detecting spammers in social networks. Neurocomputing **159**, 27–34 (2015)
6. Markines, B., Cattuto, C., Menczer, F.: Social spam detection. ACM 978-1-60558-438-6 (2009)
7. Fire, M., Kagan, D., Elyashar, A., Elovici, Y.: Friend or foe? Fake profile identification in online social networks. arXiv:1303.3751v1 (2013)
8. Xiao, C., Freeman, D., Hwa, T.: Detecting clusters of fake accounts in online social networks. ACM (2015). ISBN 978-1-4503-3826-4/15/10
9. Pendyala, V.S., Liu, Y., Figueira, S.M.: A framework for detecting injected influence attacks on microblog websites using change detection techniques. Dev. Eng. **3**, 218–233 (2018)
10. Pendyala, V.S., Figueira, S.: Towards a truthful world wide web from a humanitarian perspective. In: 2015 IEEE Global Humanitarian Technology Conference (GHTC), October 8, pp. 137–143. IEEE (2015)
11. Bodnar, T., Tucker, C., Hopkinson, K., Bilen, S.: Increasing the veracity of event detection on online social networks through user trust modeling. In: Proceedings of the 2014 IEEE International Conference on Big Data, Washington D.C. (2014)
12. Chakravorty, A., Chunming R.: Ushare: user controlled social media based on blockchain. In: Proceedings of the 11th International Conference on Ubiquitous Information Management and Communication, p. 99. ACM (2017)
13. Senapati, M., Laurent, N., Praveen, R.: A method for scalable first-order rule learning on Twitter data. In: Proceedings of the 2019 IEEE 35th International Conference on Data Engineering Workshops (ICDEW), pp. 274–277. IEEE (2019)

Author Index

Printed in the United States
By Bookmasters